JONATHAN FRANZEN

FARTHER AWAY

FOURTH ESTATE • *London*

Fourth Estate
An imprint of HarperCollins*Publishers*
77–85 Fulham Palace Road
Hammersmith, London W6 8JB

This Fourth Estate paperback edition published 2013
1

First published in Great Britain by Fourth Estate in 2012
First published in the United States by Farrar, Straus and Giroux in 2012

A catalogue record for this book is
available from the British Library

ISBN 978-0-00-745953-7

Some of the contents of this book originally appeared, in slightly or
significantly different form, in the *New Yorker*, the *New York Times*, *Technology
Review*, *Guardian*, and various books, including *State by State: A Panoramic
Portrait of America* (Matt Weiland and Sean Wilsey, eds.).

Designed by Rodrigo Corral and Abby Kagan

Printed and bound in Great Britain by
Clays Ltd, St Ives plc

MIX
Paper from
responsible sources
FSC
www.fsc.org
FSC C007454

FSC™ is a non-profit international organisation established to promote
the responsible management of the world's forests. Products carrying the
FSC label are independently certified to assure consumers that they come
from forests that are managed to meet the social, economic and
ecological needs of present and future generations,
and other controlled sources.

Find out more about HarperCollins and the environment at
www.harpercollins.co.uk/green

From the reviews of *Farther Away*:

'These essays are exemplary instances of reader-friendly criticism in that they can be studied profitably even by people unfamiliar with the works in question ... One way or another, the essays in *Farther Away* are attempts to enlarge the place where literature and the responsiveness to it, can be preserved.'

GEOFF DYER, *Observer*

'The world of literature, besieged as he believes it is, needs authors who care. And Franzen *really* cares. His attitude might be aggressively highbrow, but his underlying concerns are simple and humane: family, age, grief, love.'

TIM WALKER, *Independent*

'As with the best of essayists, Mr Franzen uses personal thoughts or anecdotes as a springboard to explore wider themes ... A multifaceted and revealing collection, *Farther Away* actually brings the reader closer to the author.'   *Economist*

'In a book that is never less than superbly intelligent ... Franzen's wit and loving kindness comes as abrupt surprises as if a glossy, paunchy bishop has suddenly started to play hopscotch.'

RICHARD DAVENPORT-HINES, *Spectator*

BY THE SAME AUTHOR

NOVELS
Freedom
The Corrections
Strong Motion
The Twenty-Seventh City

NON-FICTION
The Discomfort Zone
How to Be Alone

TRANSLATION
Spring Awakening (by Frank Wedekind)

To Tom Hjelm, for the lessons in writing,
and to Göran Ekström, for the lessons in travel

CONTENTS

-------▶

FARTHER AWAY

PAIN WON'T KILL YOU

[commencement address, Kenyon College, May 2011]

- - - - - - ▶

Good morning, Class of 2011. Good morning, relatives and faculty. It's a great honor and pleasure to be here today.

I'm going to go ahead and assume that you all knew what you were getting into when you chose a literary writer to deliver this address. I'm going to do what literary writers do, which is to talk about themselves, in the hope that my experience has some resonance with your own. I'd like to work my way around to the subject of love and its relation to my life and to the strange technocapitalist world that you guys are inheriting.

A couple of weeks ago, I replaced my three-year-old Black-Berry Pearl with a much more powerful BlackBerry Bold, with a five-megapixel camera and 3G capability. Needless to say, I was impressed with how far the technology had advanced in three years. Even when I didn't have anybody to call or text or e-mail, I wanted to keep fondling my new Bold and experiencing the marvelous clarity of its screen, the silky action of its tiny track pad, the shocking speed of its responses, the beguiling elegance of its graphics. I was, in short, infatuated with my new device. I'd been similarly infatuated with my old device, of course; but over the years the bloom had faded from our relationship. I'd developed trust issues with my Pearl, accountability issues, compatibility issues, and even, toward the end, some doubts about my Pearl's very sanity, until I'd finally had to admit to myself that I'd outgrown the relationship.

Do I need to point out that—absent some wild, anthropomorphizing projection in which my old BlackBerry felt sad about the waning of my love for it—our relationship was entirely one-sided? Let me point it out anyway. Let me further point out how ubiquitously the word *sexy* is used to describe late-model gadgets; and how the extremely cool things that we can do now with these gadgets—like impelling them to action by speaking incantations, or doing that spreading-the-fingers iPhone thing that makes images get bigger—would have looked, to people a hundred years ago, like a magician's incantations, a magician's hand gestures; and how, when we want to describe an erotic relationship that's working perfectly, we speak, indeed, of *magic*. Let me toss out the idea that, according to the logic of techno-consumerism, in which markets discover and respond to what consumers most want, our technology has become extremely adept at creating products that correspond to our fantasy ideal of an erotic relationship, in which the beloved object asks for nothing and gives everything, instantly, and makes us feel all-powerful, and doesn't throw terrible scenes when it's replaced by an even sexier object and is consigned to a drawer: that (to speak more generally) the ultimate goal of technology, the *telos* of *techne*, is to replace a natural world that's indifferent to our wishes—a world of hurricanes and hardships and breakable hearts; a world of *resistance*—with a world so responsive to our wishes as to be, effectively, a mere extension of the self. Let me suggest, finally, that the world of technoconsumerism is therefore troubled by real love, and that it has no choice but to trouble love in turn.

Its first line of defense is to commodify its enemy. You can all supply your own favorite, most nauseating examples of the commodification of love. Mine include the wedding industry, TV ads that feature cute young children or the giving of automobiles as Christmas presents, and the particularly grotesque equation of diamond jewelry with everlasting devotion. The message, in each case, is that if you love somebody you should buy stuff.

A related phenomenon is the ongoing transformation, courtesy of Facebook, of the verb *to like* from a state of mind to an action that you perform with your computer mouse: from a feeling to an assertion of consumer choice. And liking, in general, is commercial culture's substitute for loving. The striking thing about all consumer products—and none more so than electronic devices and applications—is that they're designed to be immensely likable. This is, in fact, the *definition* of a consumer product, in contrast to the product that is simply itself and whose makers aren't fixated on your liking it. I'm thinking here of jet engines, laboratory equipment, serious art and literature.

But if you consider this in human terms, and you imagine a person defined by a desperation to be liked, what do you see? You see a person without integrity, without a center. In more pathological cases, you see a narcissist—a person who can't tolerate the tarnishing of his or her self-image that not being liked represents, and who therefore either withdraws from human contact or goes to extreme, integrity-sacrificing lengths to be likable.

If you dedicate your existence to being likable, however, and if you adopt whatever cool persona is necessary to make it happen, it suggests that you've despaired of being loved for who you really are. And if you succeed in manipulating other people into liking you, it will be hard not to feel, at some level, contempt for those people, because they've fallen for your shtick. Those people exist to make you feel good about yourself, but how good can your feeling be when it's provided by people you don't respect? You may find yourself becoming depressed, or alcoholic, or, if you're Donald Trump, running for president (and then quitting).

Consumer-technology products, of course, would never do anything this unattractive, because they're not people. They are, however, great allies and enablers of narcissism. Alongside their built-in eagerness to be liked is a built-in eagerness to reflect well on us. Our lives look a lot more interesting when they're filtered through the sexy Facebook interface. We star in our own movies, we photograph ourselves incessantly, we click the mouse and a machine confirms our sense of mastery. And, since our technology is really just an extension of ourselves, we don't have to have contempt for its manipulability, the way we might with actual people. It's all one big endless loop. We like the mirror and the mirror likes us. To friend a person is merely to include the person in our private hall of flattering mirrors.

I may be overstating the case, a little bit. Very probably, you're sick to death of hearing social media dissed by cranky fifty-one-year-olds. My aim here is mainly to set up a contrast between the narcissistic tendencies of technology and the problem of actual love. My friend Alice Sebold likes to talk about "getting down in the pit and loving somebody." She has in mind the dirt that love inevitably splatters on the mirror of our self-regard. The simple fact of the matter is that trying to be perfectly likable is incompatible with loving relationships. Sooner or later, for example, you're going to find yourself in a hideous, screaming fight, and you'll hear coming out of your mouth things that you yourself don't like at all, things that shatter your self-image as a fair, kind, cool, attractive, in-control, funny, *likable* person. Something realer than likability has come out in you, and suddenly you're having an actual life. Suddenly there's a real choice to be made, not a fake consumer choice between a BlackBerry and an iPhone, but a question: Do I love this person? And, for the other person: Does this person love me? There is no such thing as a person whose real self you like every particle of. This is why a world of liking is ultimately a lie. But there *is* such a thing as a person whose real self you love every particle of. And this is why love is such an existential threat to the technoconsumerist order: it exposes the lie.

One of the heartening things about the plague of cell phones in my Manhattan neighborhood is that, among all the texting zombies and the party-planning yakkers on the sidewalks, I sometimes get to walk alongside somebody who's having an honest-to-God fight with a person they love. I'm sure they'd prefer not to be having the fight on a public sidewalk, but here it's happening to them anyway, and they're behaving in a very, very uncool way. Shouting, accusing, pleading, abusing. This is the kind of thing that gives me hope for the world.

Which is not to say that love is only about fighting, or that radically self-involved people aren't capable of accusing and abusing. What love is really about is a bottomless empathy, born out of the heart's revelation that another person is every bit as real as you are. And this is why love, as I understand it, is always specific. Trying to love all of humanity may be a worthy endeavor, but, in a funny way, it keeps the focus on the self, on the self's own moral or spiritual well-being. Whereas, to love a specific person, and to identify with their struggles and joys as if they were your own, you have to surrender some of your self.

When I was a senior in college, I took the first seminar the college had ever offered in literary theory, and I fell in love with the most brilliant student in that seminar. Both of us liked how instantly powerful literary theory made us feel—it's similar to modern consumer technology in this regard—and we flattered ourselves on how much more sophisticated we were than the kids who were still doing those tedious old close-textual readings. For various theoretical reasons, we also thought it would be cool to get married. My mother, who had spent twenty years making me into a person who craved full-commitment love, now turned around and advocated that I spend my twenties, as she put it, "footloose and fancy-free." Naturally, since I thought she was wrong about everything, I assumed she was wrong about this. I had to find out the hard way what a messy business commitment is.

The first thing we jettisoned was theory. As my soon-to-be wife once memorably remarked, after an unhappy scene in bed, "You can't deconstruct and undress at the same time." We spent a year on different continents and pretty quickly discovered that, although it was fun to fill the pages of our letters to each other with theoretical riffs, it wasn't so fun to read these pages. But what really killed theory for me—and began to cure me, more generally, of my obsession with how I appeared to other people— was my love of fiction. There may be a superficial similarity between revising a piece of fiction and revising your Web page or your Facebook profile; but a page of prose doesn't have those slick graphics to help bolster your self-image. If you're moved to try to return the gift that other people's fiction represents for you, you eventually can't ignore what's fraudulent or secondhand in your own pages. These pages are a mirror, too, and if you really love fiction you'll find that the only pages worth keeping are the ones that reflect you as you really are.

The risk here, of course, is rejection. We can all handle being disliked now and then, because there's such an infinitely big pool of potential likers. But to expose your whole self, not just the likable surface, and to have it rejected, can be catastrophically painful. The prospect of pain generally, the pain of loss, of breakup, of death, is what makes it so tempting to avoid love and stay safely in the world of liking. My wife and I, having married too young, eventually surrendered so much of ourselves and caused each other so much pain that we each had reason to regret ever having taken the plunge.

And yet I can't quite make myself regret it. For one thing, our struggle to honor our commitment actively came to constitute who we were as people; we weren't helium molecules, floating inertly through life; we bonded and we changed. For another thing—and this may be my main message to you all today—pain hurts, but it doesn't kill. When you consider the alternative—an anesthetized dream of self-sufficiency, abetted by technology—pain emerges as the natural product and natural indicator of being alive in a resistant world. To go through a life painlessly is not to have lived. Even just to say to yourself, "Oh, I'll get to that love and pain stuff later, maybe in my thirties," is to consign yourself to ten years of merely taking up space on the planet and burning up its resources. Of being (and I mean this in the most damning sense of the word) a consumer.

What I said earlier, about how engagement with something you love compels you to face up to who you really are, may apply particularly to fiction writing, but it's true of just about any work you undertake in love. I'd like to conclude here by talking about another love of mine.

When I was in college, and for many years after, I liked the natural world. Didn't love it, but definitely liked it. It can be very pretty, nature. And since I'd been fired up by critical theory, and was looking for things to find wrong with the world and reasons to hate the people who ran it, I naturally gravitated to environmentalism, because there were certainly plenty of things wrong with the environment. And the more I looked at what was wrong—an exploding world population, exploding levels of resource consumption, rising global temperatures, the trashing of the oceans, the logging of our last old-growth forests—the angrier and more people-hating I became. Finally, around the time my marriage was breaking up and I was deciding that pain was one thing but spending the rest of my life feeling ever angrier and more unhappy was quite another, I made a conscious decision to stop worrying about the environment. There was nothing meaningful that I personally could do to save the planet, and I wanted to get on with devoting myself to the things I loved. I still tried to keep my carbon footprint small, but that was as far as I could go without falling back into rage and despair.

But then a funny thing happened to me. It's a long story, but basically I fell in love with birds. I did this not without significant resistance, because it's very uncool to be a birdwatcher, because anything that betrays real passion is by definition uncool. But little by little, in spite of myself, I developed this passion, and although one half of a passion is obsession, the other half is love. And so, yes, I kept a meticulous list of the birds I'd seen, and, yes, I went to inordinate lengths to see new species. But, no less important, whenever I looked at a bird, any bird, even a pigeon or a sparrow, I could feel my heart overflow with love. And love, as I've been trying to say today, is where our troubles begin.

Because now, not merely liking nature but loving a specific and vital part of it, I had no choice but to start worrying about the environment again. The news on that front was no better than when I'd decided to quit worrying about it—was considerably worse, in fact—but now those threatened forests and wetlands and oceans weren't just pretty scenes for me to enjoy. They were the home of animals I loved. And here's where a curious paradox emerged. My anger and pain and despair about the planet were only increased by my concern for wild birds, and yet, as I began to get involved in bird conservation and learned more about the many threats that birds face, it became, strangely, easier, not harder, to live with my anger and despair and pain.

How does this happen? I think, for one thing, my love of birds became a portal to an important, less self-centered part of myself that I'd never even known existed. Instead of continuing to drift forward through my life as a global citizen, liking and disliking and withholding my commitment for some later date, I was forced to confront a self that I had to either straight-up accept or flat-out reject. Which is what love will do to a person. Because the fundamental fact about all of us is that we're alive for a while but will die before long. This fact is the real root cause of all our anger and pain and despair. And you can either run from this fact or, by way of love, you can embrace it.

Like I said, the bird thing was very unexpected to me. For most of my life, I hadn't given much thought to animals. And maybe I was unlucky to find my way to birds so relatively late in life, or maybe I was lucky to find my way to them at all. But once you're hit with a love like that, however late or early, it changes your relation to the world. In my case, for example, I'd abandoned doing journalism after a few early experiments, because the world of facts didn't excite me the way the world of fiction did. But after my avian conversion experience had taught me to run toward my pain and anger and despair, rather than away from them, I started taking on a new kind of journalistic assignment. Whatever I most hated, at a particular moment, became the thing I wanted to write about. I went to Washington in the summer of 2003, when the Bush administration was doing things to the country that enraged me. I went to China a few years later, because I was being kept awake at night by my anger about the havoc the Chinese are wreaking on the environment. I went to the Mediterranean to interview the hunters and poachers who were slaughtering migratory songbirds. In each case, when meeting the enemy, I found people whom I really liked—in some cases outright loved. Hilarious, generous, brilliant gay Republican staffers. Fearless, miraculous young Chinese nature lovers. A gun-crazy Italian legislator who had very soft eyes and who quoted the animal-rights advocate Peter Singer to me. In each case, the blanket antipathy that had come so easily to me wasn't so easy anymore.

When you stay in your room and rage or sneer or shrug your shoulders, as I did for many years, the world and its problems are impossibly daunting. But when you go out and put yourself in real relation to real people, or even just real animals, there's a very real danger that you might end up loving some of them. And who knows what might happen to you then?

Thank you.

FARTHER AWAY

-------▶

In the South Pacific Ocean, five hundred miles off the coast of central Chile, is a forbiddingly vertical volcanic island, seven miles long and four miles wide, that is populated by millions of seabirds and thousands of fur seals but is devoid of people, except in the warmer months, when a handful of fishermen come out to catch lobsters. To reach the island, which is officially called Alejandro Selkirk, you fly from Santiago in an eight-seater that makes twice-weekly flights to an island a hundred miles to the east. Then you have to travel in a small open boat from the airstrip to the archipelago's only village, wait around for a ride on one of the launches that occasionally make the twelve-hour outward voyage, and then, often, wait further, sometimes for days, for weather conducive to landing on the rocky shore. In the sixties, Chilean tourism officials renamed the island for Alexander Selkirk, the Scottish seaman whose tale of solitary living in the archipelago was probably the basis for Daniel Defoe's novel *Robinson Crusoe*, but the locals still use its original name, Masafuera: Farther Away.

By the end of last fall, I was in some need of being farther away. I'd been promoting a novel nonstop for four months, advancing through my schedule without volition, feeling more and more like the graphical lozenge on a media player's progress bar. Substantial swaths of my personal history were going dead from within, from my talking about them too often. And every morning the same revving doses of nicotine and caffeine; every evening the same assault on my e-mail queue; every night the same drinking for the same brain-dulling pop of pleasure. At a certain point, having read about Masafuera, I began to imagine running away and being alone there, like Selkirk, in the interior of the island, where nobody lives even seasonally.

I also thought it might be good, while I was there, to reread the book generally considered to be the first English novel. *Robinson Crusoe* was the great early document of radical individualism, the story of an ordinary person's practical and psychic survival in profound isolation. The novelistic enterprise associated with individualism—the search for meaning in realistic narrative—went on to become the culture's dominant literary mode for the next three centuries. Crusoe's voice can be heard in the voice of Jane Eyre, the Underground Man, the Invisible Man, and Sartre's Roquentin. All these stories had once excited me, and there persisted, in the very word *novel*, with its promise of *novelty*, a memory of more youthful experiences so engrossing that I could sit quietly for hours and never think of boredom. Ian Watt, in his classic *The Rise of the Novel*, correlated the eighteenth-century burgeoning of novelistic production with the growing demand for at-home entertainment by women who'd been liberated from traditional household tasks and had too much time on their hands. In a very direct way, according to Watt, the English novel had risen from the ashes of boredom. And boredom was what I was suffering from. The more you pursue distractions, the less effective any particular distraction is, and so I'd had to up various dosages, until, before I knew it, I was checking my e-mail every ten minutes, and my plugs of tobacco were getting ever larger, and my two drinks a night had worsened to four, and I'd achieved such deep mastery of computer solitaire that my goal was no longer to win a game but to win two or more games in a row—a kind of meta-solitaire whose fascination consisted not in playing the cards but in surfing the streaks of wins and losses. My longest winning streak so far was eight.

I made arrangements to hitch a ride to Masafuera on a small boat chartered by some adventurous botanists. Then I indulged in a little orgy of consumerism at REI, where the Crusovian romance abides in the aisles of ultralightweight survival gear and, especially perhaps, in certain emblems of civilization-in-wilderness, like the stainless-steel martini glass with a detachable stem. Besides a new backpack, tent, and knife, I outfitted myself with certain late-model specialty items, such as a plastic plate with a silicone rim that flipped up to form a bowl, ascorbic-acid tablets to neutralize the taste of water sterilized with iodine, a microfiber towel that stowed in a marvelously small pouch, organic vegan freeze-dried chili, and an indestructible spork. I also assembled large stores of nuts, tuna, and protein bars, because I'd been told that if the weather turned bad I could be stranded on Masafuera indefinitely.

On the eve of my departure for Santiago, I visited my friend Karen, the widow of the writer David Foster Wallace. As I was getting ready to leave her house, she asked me, out of the blue, whether I might like to take along some of David's cremation ashes and scatter them on Masafuera. I said I would, and she found an antique wooden matchbox, a tiny book with a sliding drawer, and put some ashes in it, saying that she liked the thought of part of David coming to rest on a remote and uninhabited island. It was only later, after I'd driven away from her house, that I realized that she'd given me the ashes as much for my sake as for hers or David's. She knew, because I had told her, that my current state of flight from myself had begun soon after David's death, two years earlier. At the time, I'd made a decision not to deal with the hideous suicide of someone I'd loved so much but instead to take refuge in anger and work. Now that the work was done, though, it was harder to ignore the circumstance that, arguably, in one interpretation of his suicide, David had died of boredom and in despair about his future novels. The desperate edge to my own recent boredom: might this be related to my having broken a promise to myself? The promise that, after I'd finished my book project, I would allow myself to feel more than fleeting grief and enduring anger at David's death?

And so, on the last morning of January, I arrived in heavy fog at a spot on Masafuera called La Cuchara (The Spoon), three thousand feet above sea level. I had a notebook, binoculars, a paperback copy of *Robinson Crusoe*, the little book containing David's remains, a backpack filled with camping gear, a grotesquely inadequate map of the island, and no alcohol, tobacco, or computer. Apart from the fact that, instead of hiking up on my own, I'd followed a young park ranger and a mule that was carrying my backpack, and that I'd also brought along, at various people's insistence, a two-way radio, a ten-year-old GPS unit, a satellite phone, and several spare batteries, I was entirely isolated and alone.

My first experience of *Robinson Crusoe* was having it read to me by my father. Along with *Les Misérables*, it was the only novel that meant anything to him. From the pleasure he took in reading it to me, it's clear that he identified as deeply with Crusoe as he did with Jean Valjean (which, in his self-taught way, he pronounced "Gene Val Gene"). Like Crusoe, my father felt isolated from other people, was resolutely moderate in his habits, believed in the superiority of Western civilization to the "savagery" of other cultures, saw the natural world as something to be subdued and exploited, and was an inveterate do-it-yourselfer. Self-disciplined survival on a desert island surrounded by cannibals was the perfect romance for him. He was born in a rough town built by his pioneer father and uncles, and he'd grown up working in road-building camps in the boreal swampland. In our basement in St. Louis, he kept an orderly workshop in which he sharpened his tools, repaired his clothes (he was a good seamster), and improvised, out of wood and metal and leather, sturdy solutions to home-maintenance problems. He took my friends and me camping several times a year, organizing our campsite by himself while I ran in the woods with my friends, and making himself a bed out of rough old blankets beside our fiberfill sleeping bags. I think, to some extent, I was an excuse for him to go camping.

My brother Tom, no less a do-it-yourselfer than my father, became a serious backpacker after he went away to college. Because I was trying to emulate Tom in all things, I listened to his stories of ten-day solo treks in Colorado and Wyoming and yearned to be a backpacker myself. My first opportunity came in the summer I turned sixteen, when I persuaded my parents to let me take a summer-school course called "Camping in the West." My friend Weidman and I joined a busload of teenagers and counselors for two weeks of "study" in the Rockies. I had Tom's obsolescent red Gerry backpack and (for taking notes on my somewhat randomly chosen area of study, lichens) a notebook identical to the one that Tom carried.

On the second day of a trek into the Sawtooth Wilderness, in Idaho, we were all invited to spend twenty-four hours by ourselves. My counselor took me off to a sparse grove of ponderosa pine and left me alone there, and very soon, although the day was bright and unthreatening, I was cowering in my tent. Apparently, all it took for me to become aware of the emptiness of life and the horror of existence was to be deprived of human company for a few hours. I learned, the next day, that Weidman, though eight months older than me, had been so lonely that he hiked back to within sight of the base camp. What enabled me to stick it out—and to feel, moreover, that I could have stayed alone for longer than a day—was writing:

THURSDAY JULY 3
This evening I begin a notebook. If anyone reads this, I trust they will forgive my overuse of "I." I can't stop it. I'm writing this.

As I came back to my fire after dinner this afternoon there was a moment when I felt my aluminum cup a friend, sitting on a rock, considering me. . . .

I had a certain fly (at least I think it was the same one) buzz around my head for a goodly long while this afternoon. After a time I stopped thinking of it as an annoying, nasty insect & subconsciously came to think it an enemy that I was really quite fond of and that we were just playing with each other.

Also this afternoon (this was my main activity) I sat out on a point of rock trying to set to words of a sonnet the different purposes of my life that I saw at different times (3—as in points of view). Of course I now see that I can't even do this in prose form so it was really futile. However, as I did this, I became convinced that life was a waste of time, or something like that. I was so sad and screwed up at the time that every thought was of despair. But then I looked at some lichens & wrote a bit about them & calmed down and figured out that my sorrow was due not to a loss of purpose but to the fact that I didn't know who I was or why I was and that I didn't show my love to my parents. I was coming close with my third point, but my next thought was a little off. I figured that the reason for the above was that time (life) is too short. This is, of course, true, but my sorrow wasn't caused by this. All of a sudden it hit me: I missed my family.

Once I'd diagnosed my homesickness, I was able to address it by writing letters. For the rest of the trip, I wrote in my journal every day and found myself moving away from Weidman and gravitating toward my female fellow-campers; I'd never been so successful socially. What had been missing was some halfway secure sense of my own identity, a sense achieved in solitude by putting first-person words on a page.

I was keen, for years afterward, to do more backpacking, but never quite keen enough to make it happen. The self I was discovering through writing turned out not to be identical to Tom's after all. I did hold on to his old Gerry backpack, although it was not a useful general-purpose piece of luggage, and I kept alive my dreams of wilderness by buying cheap nonessential camping gear, such as a jumbo bottle of Dr. Bronner's peppermint soap, which Tom periodically praised the virtues of. When I took a bus back to college for my senior year, I put the Dr. Bronner's in the backpack, and the bottle burst in transit, soaking my clothes and books. When I tried to rinse out the backpack in a dormitory shower, its fabric disintegrated in my hands.

Masafuera, as the boat approached it, was not inviting. My only map of the island was a letter-size printout of a Google Earth image, and I saw right away that I'd optimistically misinterpreted the contour lines on it. What had looked like steep hills were cliffs, and what had looked like gentle slopes were steep hills. A dozen or so lobsterman shacks were huddled at the bottom of a tremendous gorge, to either side of which the island's green shoulders rose thirty-five hundred feet into a cap of broodingly churning cloud. The ocean, which had seemed reasonably calm on the trip out, was beating in big swells against a gap in the rocks below the shacks. To get ashore, the botanists and I jumped down into a lobster boat, which motored to within a hundred yards of shore. There the boatmen hauled up the motor, and we took hold of a rope stretching out to a buoy and pulled ourselves farther in. As we neared the rocks, the boat lurched chaotically from side to side, water flooding into the stern, while the boatmen struggled to attach us to a cable that would drag us in. Onshore were breathtaking quantities of flies—the place's nickname is Fly Island. Competing boom boxes pumped North and South American music through the open doors of several shacks, pushing back against the oppressive immensity of the gorge and the coldly heaving sea. Adding to the stricken atmospherics was a grove of large, dead trees, aged to the color of bone, behind the shacks.

My companions for the trek to the interior were the young park ranger, Danilo, and a poker-faced mule. Considering the steepness of the island, I couldn't even pretend to be disappointed not to carry my own pack. Danilo had a rifle strapped across his back, in the hope of killing one of the nonnative goats that had survived a Dutch environmental foundation's recent effort to eradicate them. Under gray morning clouds that soon turned to fog, we hiked up interminable switchbacks and through a ravine lush with maqui, an introduced plant species that is used to repair lobster traps. There were discouraging quantities of old mule droppings on the trail, but the only moving things we saw were birds: a little gray-flanked cinclodes and several Juan Fernández hawks, two of Masafuera's five terrestrial bird species. The island is also the only known breeding site for two interesting petrels and one of the world's rarest songbirds, the Masa-fuera rayadito, which I was hoping to see. In fact, by the time I'd left for Chile, seeing new bird species was the only activity that I could absolutely count on not to bore me. The rayadito's population, most of which lives in a small high-altitude area on the island called Los Inocentes, is now thought to number as few as five hundred. Very few people have ever seen one.

Sooner than I'd expected, Danilo and I arrived at La Cuchara and saw, in the fog, the outlines of a small *refugio*, or ranger's hut. We'd climbed to three thousand feet in just over two hours. I'd heard that there was a *refugio* at La Cuchara, but I'd imagined a primitive shack and hadn't foreseen what a problem it would pose for me. Its roof was steep and tethered to the ground by cables, and inside it were a propane stove, two bunk beds with foam mattresses, an unappetizing but serviceable sleeping bag, and a cabinet stocked with dry pasta and canned foods; apparently, I could have brought along nothing but some iodine tablets and still survived here. The *refugio*'s presence made my already somewhat artificial project of solitary self-sufficiency seem even more artificial, and I resolved to pretend that it didn't exist.

Danilo took my pack off the mule and led me down a foggy path to a stream with enough water trickling in it to form a little pool. I asked him if it was possible to walk from here to Los Inocentes. He gestured uphill and said, "Yes, it's three hours, along the *cordones*." I thought of asking if we could go there right now, so that I could camp nearer to the rayaditos, but Danilo seemed eager to get back to the coast. He departed with the mule and his gun, and I bent myself to my Crusovian tasks.

The first of these was to gather and purify some drinking water. Carrying a filtration pump and a canvas waterskin, I followed what I thought was the path to the pool, which I knew wasn't more than two hundred feet from the *refugio*, and I immediately got lost in the fog. When I finally located the pool, after trying several paths, the tube on my pump cracked. I'd bought the pump twenty years earlier, thinking it would come in handy if I was ever alone in the wilderness, and its plastic had since gone brittle. I filled up the skin with somewhat turbid water and, despite my resolution, entered the *refugio* and poured the water into a large cooking pot, along with some iodine tablets. This simple task had somehow taken me an hour.

Since I was in the *refugio* anyway, I changed out of my clothes, which had been soaked by the climb through dew and fog, and tried to dry the inside of my boots with the surfeit of toilet paper I'd brought. I discovered that the GPS unit, the one gadget that I didn't have spare batteries for, had been switched on and draining power all day, which triggered an anxiety that I assuaged by wiping all the mud and water off the *refugio*'s floor with further wads of toilet paper. Finally, I ventured out onto a rocky promontory and scouted for a campsite beyond the *refugio*'s penumbra of mule droppings. A hawk dived right over my head; a cinclodes called pertly from a boulder. After much walking and weighing of pros and cons, I settled on a hollow that afforded some protection from the wind and no view of the *refugio*, and there I picnicked on cheese and salami.

I'd been alone for four hours. I put up my tent, lashing the frame to boulders and weighing down the stakes with the heaviest rocks I could carry, and made some coffee on my little butane stove. Returning to the *refugio*, I worked on my footwear-drying project, pausing every few minutes to open windows and shoo out the flies that kept finding their way inside. I seemed to be no more able to wean myself from the *refugio*'s conveniences than from the modern distractions that I was supposedly here to flee. I fetched another skin of water and used the big pot and the propane stove to heat some bathwater, and it was simply *much more pleasant*, after my bath, to go back inside and dry off with the microfiber towel and get dressed than to do this in the dirt and the fog. Since I was already so compromised, I went ahead and carried one of the foam mattresses down the promontory and put it in my tent. "But that's it," I said to myself, aloud. "That's the end of it."

Except for the hum of flies and the occasional call of a cinclodes, the silence at my campsite was absolute. Sometimes the fog lifted a little and I could see rocky hillsides and wet, fern-filled valleys before the ceiling lowered again. I took out my notebook and jotted down what I'd done in the past seven hours: got water, had lunch, put up tent, took bath. But when I thought about writing confessionally, in an "I" voice, I found that I was too self-conscious. Apparently, in the past thirty-five years, I'd become so accustomed to narrativizing myself, to experiencing my life as a story, that I could now use journals only for problem solving and self-investigation. Even at fifteen, in Idaho, I hadn't written from within my despair but only after I was safely over it, and now, all the more so, the stories that mattered to me were the ones told—selected, clarified—in retrospect.

My plan for the next day was to try to see a rayadito. Simply knowing that the bird was on the island made the island interesting to me. When I go looking for new bird species, I'm searching for a mostly lost authenticity, for the remnants of a world now largely overrun by human beings but still beautifully indifferent to us; to glimpse a rare bird somehow persisting in its life of breeding and feeding is an enduringly transcendent delight. The next morning, I decided, I would get up at dawn and devote, if necessary, the entire day to finding my way to Los Inocentes and getting back. Cheered by the prospect of this not unchallenging quest, I made myself a bowl of chili, and then, although the daylight hadn't faded yet, I zipped myself inside my tent. On the very comfortable mattress, in a sleeping bag I'd owned since high school, and with a headlamp on my forehead, I settled down to read *Robinson Crusoe*. For the first time all day, I felt happy.

One of *Robinson Crusoe*'s biggest early fans was Jean-Jacques Rousseau, who, in *Émile*, proposed that it be the primary text for the education of children. Rousseau, in the fine tradition of French bowdlerization, didn't have in mind the entire text, just the long central section, in which Robinson relates his survival for a quarter century on a desert island. Few readers would dispute that this is the novel's most compelling section, next to which the adventures of Robinson before and after (being enslaved by a Turkish pirate, fending off the attacks of giant wolves) seem lusterless and rote. Part of the survival story's appeal is the specificity of Robinson's recounting of it: the "three . . . hats, one cap, and two shoes that were not fellows" that are all that remain of his drowned shipmates, the catalogue of useful gear that he salvages from the wrecked ship, the intricacies of stalking the feral goats that populate the island, the nuts and bolts of reinventing the homely arts of making furniture, boats, pottery, and bread. But what really animates these adventureless adventures, and makes them surprisingly suspenseful, is their accessibility to the imagination of the ordinary reader. I have no idea what I would do if I were enslaved by a Turk or menaced by wolves; I might very well be too scared to do what Robinson does. But to read about his practical solutions to the problems of hunger and exposure and illness and solitude is to be invited into the narrative, to imagine what *I* would do if I were similarly stranded, and to measure my own stamina and resourcefulness and industry against his. (I'm sure my father was doing this, too.) Until the larger world impinges on the island's isolation, in the form of marauding cannibals, there's just the two of us, Robinson and his reader, and it's very cozy. In a more action-packed narrative, the pages detailing Robinson's everyday tasks and emotions would be what the critic Franco Moretti wryly calls "filler." But, as Moretti notes, the dramatic expansion of this kind of "filler" was precisely Defoe's great innovation; such stories of the quotidian became a fixture of realist fiction, in Austen and Flaubert as in Updike and Carver.

Framing and to some extent interpenetrating Defoe's "filler" are elements of the other major forms of prose narrative that preceded it: ancient Hellenistic novels, which included tales of shipwrecks and enslavement; Catholic and Protestant spiritual autobiographies; medieval and Renaissance romances; and Spanish picaresques. Defoe's novel follows also in the tradition of narratives libelously based, or purporting to be based, on the lives of actual public personages; in Crusoe's case, the model was Alexander Selkirk. It has even been argued that Defoe intended the novel as a piece of utopianist propaganda, extolling the religious freedoms and economic opportunities of England's New World colonies. The heterogeny of *Robinson Crusoe* illuminates the difficulty, maybe even the absurdity, of talking about the "rise of the novel" and of identifying Defoe's work as the first individual of the species. *Don Quixote*, after all, was published more than a century earlier and is clearly a novel. And why not call the romances novels, too, since they were widely published and read in the seventeenth century and since, indeed, most European languages make no distinction between *romance* and *novel*? Early English novelists did often specifically stress that their own work was not "mere romance"; but, then, so had many of the romance writers themselves. And yet, by the early nineteenth century, when leading specimens of the form were first collected in authoritative sets by Walter Scott and others, the English not only had a very clear idea of what they meant by "novels" but were exporting large numbers of them, in translation, to other countries. A genre now definitely existed where none had before. So what exactly is a novel, and why did the genre appear when it did?

The most persuasive account remains the political-economic one that Ian Watt advanced fifty years ago. The birthplace of the novel, in its modern form, happens also to have been Europe's most economically dominant and sophisticated nation, and Watt's analysis of this coincidence is blunt but powerful, tying together the glorification of the enterprising individual, the expansion of a literate bourgeoisie eager to read about itself, the rise in social mobility (inviting writers to exploit its anxieties), the specialization of labor (creating a society of interesting *differences*), the disintegration of the old social order into a collection of individual isolates, and, of course, among the newly comfortable middle class, the dramatic increase in leisure for reading. At the same time, England was rapidly becoming more secular. Protestant theology had laid the foundations of the new economy by reimagining the social order as a collection of self-reliant individuals with a direct relationship with God; but by 1700, as the British economy thrived, it was becoming less clear that individuals needed God at all. It's true that, as any impatient child reader can tell you, many pages of *Robinson Crusoe* are devoted to its hero's spiritual journey. Robinson finds God on the island, and he turns to Him repeatedly in moments of crisis, praying for deliverance and ecstatically thanking Him for providing the means of it. And yet, as soon as each crisis has passed, he reverts to his practical self and forgets about God; by the end of the book, he seems to have been saved more by his own industry and ingenuity than by Providence. To read the story of Robinson's vacillations and forgetfulness is to see the genre of spiritual autobiography unraveling into realist fiction.

The most interesting aspect of the novel's origin may be the evolution of English culture's answers to the question of verisimilitude: Should a strange story be accepted as true *because* it is strange, or should its strangeness be taken as proof that it is false? The anxieties of this question are still with us (witness the scandal of James Frey's "memoir"), and they were certainly in play in 1719, when Defoe published the first and best-known volume of *Robinson Crusoe*. The author's real name appeared nowhere in it. The book was identified, instead, as *The Life and Strange Surprizing Adventures of Robinson Crusoe . . . Written by Himself*, and many of its first readers took the story to be nonfiction. Enough other readers doubted its authenticity, however, that Defoe felt obliged to defend its truthfulness when he published the third and last of the volumes, the following year. Contrasting his story with romances, in which "the story is feign'd," he insisted that his story, "though allegorical, is also historical," and he affirmed that "there is a man alive, and well known too, the actions of whose life are the just subject of these volumes." Given what we know of Defoe's real life—like Crusoe, he got into trouble by pursuing risky business schemes, such as raising civet cats for perfume, and he had intimate knowledge of isolation from the debtors' prison in which bankruptcy twice landed him—and given also his assertion, elsewhere in the volume, that "life in general is, or ought to be, but one universal act of solitude," it seems fair to conclude that the "well known" man is Defoe himself. (There is, strikingly, that "oe" at the end of both names.) We now understand a novel to be a mapping of a writer's experience onto a waking dream, and a crucial turn toward this understanding can be seen in Defoe's tentative assertion of a less than strictly historical kind of truth—the novelist's "truth."

The critic Catherine Gallagher, in her essay "The Rise of Fictionality," takes up a curious paradox related to this kind of truth: the eighteenth century was not only the moment when fiction writers, beginning (sort of) with Defoe, abandoned the pretense that their narratives weren't fictional; it was also the moment when they began taking pains to make their narratives seem *not* fictional—when verisimilitude became paramount. Gallagher's resolution of the paradox hinges on yet another aspect of modernity, the necessity of taking risks. When business came to depend on investment, you had to weigh various possible future outcomes; when marriages ceased to be arranged, you had to speculate on the merits of potential mates. And the novel, as it was developed in the eighteenth century, provided its readers with a field of play that was at once speculative and risk-free. While advertising its fictionality, it gave you protagonists who were typical enough to be experienced as possible versions of yourself and yet specific enough to remain, simultaneously, *not you*. The great literary invention of the eighteenth century was, thus, not simply a genre but an attitude *toward* that genre. Our state of mind when we pick up a novel today—our knowledge that it's a work of the imagination; our willing suspension of disbelief in it—is in fact one half of the novel's essence.

A number of recent scholarly studies have undermined the old notion that the epic is a central feature of all cultures, including oral cultures. Fiction, whether fairy tale or fable, seems mainly to have been a thing for children. In premodern cultures, stories were read for information or edification or titillation, and the more serious literary forms, poetry and drama, required a certain degree of technical mastery. The novel, however, was within reach of anyone with pen and paper, and the kind of pleasure it afforded was uniquely modern. Experiencing a made-up story purely for pleasure became an activity in which adults, too, could now indulge freely (if sometimes guiltily). This historical shift toward reading for pleasure was so profound that we can hardly even see it anymore. Indeed, as the novel has proliferated subgenerically into movies and TV shows and late-model video games—most of them advertising their fictionality, all of them offering characters at once typical and specific—it's hardly an exaggeration to say that what distinguishes our culture from all previous cultures is its saturation in entertainment. The novel, as a duality of thing and attitude-toward-thing, has so thoroughly transformed our attitude that the thing itself is at risk of no longer being needed.

On Masafuera's sister island—originally named Masatierra, or Closer to Land, and now called Robinson Crusoe—I had seen the damage wrought by a trio of mainland plant species, maqui and murtilla and blackberry, which have monotonously overrun entire hills and drainages. Particularly evil-looking was the blackberry, which can overwhelm even tall native trees and which spreads in part by shooting out runners that look like thorny fiber-optic cables. Two native plant species have already gone extinct, and unless a massive restoration project is undertaken many more will follow. Walking on Robinson, looking for delicate endemic ferns at the blackberry's margins, I began to see the novel as an organism that had mutated, on the island of England, into a virulent invasive that then spread from country to country until it conquered the planet.

Henry Fielding, in *Joseph Andrews*, referred to his characters as "species"—as something more than individual, less than universal. But, as the novel has transformed the cultural environment, species of humanity have given way to a universal crowd of individuals whose most salient characteristic is their being identically entertained. This was the monocultural specter that David had envisioned and set out to resist in his epic *Infinite Jest*. And the mode of his resistance in that novel—annotation, digression, nonlinearity, hyperlinkage—anticipated the even more virulent and even more radically individualistic invader that is now displacing the novel and its offspring. The blackberry on Robinson Crusoe Island was like the conquering novel, yes, but it seemed to me no less like the Internet, that BlackBerry-borne invasive, which, instead of mapping the self onto a narrative, maps the self onto the world. Instead of *the* news, *my* news. Instead of a single football game, the splintering of fifteen different games into personalized fantasy-league statistics. Instead of *The Godfather*, "My Cat's Funny Trick." The individual run amok, Everyman a Charlie Sheen. With *Robinson Crusoe*, the self had become an island; and now, it seemed, the island was becoming the world.

I was awakened in the night by the beating of the sides of my tent against my sleeping bag; a big wind had blown up. I deployed my earplugs, but I could still hear the beating and, later, a loud whapping. When day finally came, I found my tent partly disassembled, a pole segment dangling from its fly. The wind had dispersed the clouds below me, opening up a view of the ocean, startlingly close, with dawn breaking redly above its leaden water. Mustering the particular efficiency I can bring to the pursuit of a rare bird, I ate a quick breakfast, packed my knapsack with the radio and the satellite phone and enough food for two days, and, at the last minute, because the wind was so strong, collapsed my tent and weighted down its corners with large stones, so that it wouldn't blow away while I was gone. Time was short—mornings on Masafuera tend to be clearer than afternoons—but I made myself stop at the *refugio* and mark its coordinates on the GPS unit before hurrying on uphill.

The Masafuera rayadito is a larger, duller-plumaged cousin of the thorn-tailed rayadito, a striking little bird that I'd seen in several forests in mainland Chile before coming to the islands. How such a small species landed five hundred miles offshore in sufficient numbers to reproduce (and, subsequently, evolve) will never be known. The Masafueran species requires undisturbed native fern forest, and its population, never large, appears to be declining, perhaps because when it nests on the ground it is prone to predation by invasive rats and cats. (Ridding Masafuera of rodents would entail capturing and safeguarding the island's entire hawk population and then using helicopters to blanket its rugged terrain with poisoned bait, at a total cost of maybe five million dollars.) I'd been told that the rayadito isn't hard to see in proper habitat; the difficulty is in getting to the habitat.

The heights of the island were still in cloud, but I was hoping that the wind would soon clear it out. As well as I could tell from my map, I needed to ascend to about thirty-six hundred feet in order to skirt two deep canyons that blocked the way south to Los Inocentes. I was cheered by the fact that the hike's net altitude gain would be zero, but, almost as soon as I'd left the *refugio* behind me, the clouds closed in again. Visibility dropped to a few hundred feet, and I began to stop every ten minutes to electronically mark my location, like Hansel leaving crumbs in the woods. For a while, I held to a trail marked with mule droppings, but the ground soon became too stony and scarred with goat tracks for me to be sure I was still on it.

At thirty-six hundred feet, I turned south and bushwhacked through dense, dripping ferns and found my way blocked by a drainage that ought to have been below me by now. I studied the map, but its Google Earth shadings hadn't become any less vague since the last time I'd studied it. I tried to work my way laterally around the sides of the canyon, but the fern cover concealed slippery rocks and deep holes, and the slope, as far as I could tell in the fog, seemed to be getting more vertical, and so I turned around and struggled back up to the ridge, orienting myself by GPS. An hour into my quest, I was thoroughly soaked and barely a thousand feet from where I'd started.

Checking the map, which was getting very wet, I recalled the unfamiliar word that Danilo had used. *Cordones*: it must mean ridges! I was supposed to follow the ridges! I charged uphill again, stopping only to scatter electronic bread crumbs, until I came to a solar-powered radio antenna, presumably a local summit. The wind, now stronger, was blowing cloud over the back side of the island, which I knew to consist of cliffs plunging three thousand feet down to the seal colony. I couldn't see them, but the mere thought of their proximity gave me vertigo; I'm very afraid of cliffs.

Fortunately, the *cordón* leading south from the antenna was fairly level and not too hard to pick my way along, even with high winds and near-zero visibility. I made good progress for half an hour, feeling elated to have deduced, from scant information, the right way to Los Inocentes. Eventually, however, the ridge began to branch, presenting me with choices between higher and lower routes. The map indicated pretty clearly that I should be at thirty-two hundred feet, not thirty-eight hundred. But when I followed the lower ridges, trying to reduce my elevation, I reached sickeningly precipitous dead ends. I returned to the high ridge, which had the added advantage of heading directly south toward Los Inocentes, and I felt gratified when it finally began to descend.

By now, the weather was really bad, the mist turning to rain and blowing horizontally, the wind gusting above forty miles an hour. As I picked my way down the ridge, it began to narrow alarmingly, until I found the way blocked by a small pinnacle. I could sort of make out that the ridge continued to descend on the far side of it, albeit very steeply. But how to get around it? If I scrambled around its leeward side, I risked being grabbed by a gust of wind and blown off. On the windward side, there was, for all I knew, a sheer three-thousand-foot drop; but at least, on this side, the wind would be pushing me against the rock, rather than pulling me off.

In my rain-filled boots, I edged out along the windward side, double-checking every foothold and handhold before relying on it. As I crept forward and was able to see a little farther, the ridge beyond the pinnacle began to look like another dead end, with nothing but dark space ahead and on either side of it. Although I was very determined to see the rayadito, there came a moment when I became afraid to take another step, and I was suddenly able to see myself: spread-eagled against a slippery rockface, in blinding rain and ferocious wind, with no assurance that I was going in the right direction. A sentence so clear that it seemed almost spoken popped into my head: *What you're doing is extremely dangerous.* And I thought of my dead friend.

David wrote about weather as well as anyone who ever put words on paper, and he loved his dogs more purely than he loved anything or anyone else, but nature itself didn't interest him, and he was utterly indifferent to birds. Once, when we were driving near Stinson Beach, in California, I'd stopped to give him a telescope view of a long-billed curlew, a species whose magnificence is to my mind self-evident and revelatory. He looked through the scope for two seconds before turning away with patent boredom. "Yeah," he said with his particular tone of hollow politeness, "it's pretty." In the summer before he died, sitting with him on his patio while he smoked cigarettes, I couldn't keep my eyes off the hummingbirds around his house and was saddened that he could, and while he was taking his heavily medicated afternoon naps I was learning the birds of Ecuador for an upcoming trip, and I understood the difference between his unmanageable misery and my manageable discontents to be that I could escape myself in the joy of birds and he could not.

He was sick, yes, and in a sense the story of my friendship with him is simply that I loved a person who was mentally ill. The depressed person then killed himself, in a way calculated to inflict maximum pain on those he loved most, and we who loved him were left feeling angry and betrayed. Betrayed not merely by the failure of our investment of love but by the way in which his suicide took him away from us and made the person into a very public legend. People who had never read his fiction, or had never even heard of him, read his Kenyon College commencement address in *The Wall Street Journal* and mourned the loss of a great and gentle soul. A literary establishment that had never so much as short-listed one of his books for a national prize now united to declare him a lost national treasure. Of course, he *was* a national treasure, and, being a writer, he didn't "belong" to his readers any less than to me. But if you happened to know that his actual character was more complex and dubious than he was getting credit for, and if you also knew that he was more lovable—funnier, sillier, needier, more poignantly at war with his demons, more lost, more childishly transparent in his lies and inconsistencies—than the benignant and morally clairvoyant artist/saint that had been made of him, it was still hard not to feel wounded by the part of him that had chosen the adulation of strangers over the love of the people closest to him.

The people who knew David least well are most likely to speak of him in saintly terms. What makes this especially strange is the near-perfect absence, in his fiction, of ordinary love. Close loving relationships, which for most of us are a foundational source of meaning, have no standing in the Wallace fictional universe. What we get, instead, are characters keeping their heartless compulsions secret from those who love them; characters scheming to *appear* loving or to prove to themselves that what feels like love is really just disguised self-interest; or, at most, characters directing an abstract or spiritual love toward somebody profoundly repellent—the cranial-fluid-dripping wife in *Infinite Jest*, the psychopath in the last of the interviews with hideous men. David's fiction is populated with dissemblers and manipulators and emotional isolates, and yet the people who had only glancing or formal contact with him took his rather laborious hyperconsiderateness and moral wisdom at face value.

The curious thing about David's fiction, though, is how recognized and comforted, how *loved*, his most devoted readers feel when reading it. To the extent that each of us is stranded on his or her own existential island—and I think it's approximately correct to say that his most susceptible readers are ones familiar with the socially and spiritually isolating effects of addiction or compulsion or depression—we gratefully seized on each new dispatch from that farthest-away island which was David. At the level of content, he gave us the worst of himself: he laid out, with an intensity of self-scrutiny worthy of comparison to Kafka and Kierkegaard and Dostoyevsky, the extremes of his own narcissism, misogyny, compulsiveness, self-deception, dehumanizing moralism and theologizing, doubt in the possibility of love, and entrapment in footnotes-within-footnotes self-consciousness.

At the level of form and intention, however, this very cataloguing of despair about his own authentic goodness is received by the reader as a gift of authentic goodness: we feel the love in the fact of his art, and we love him for it.

David and I had a friendship of compare and contrast and (in a brotherly way) compete. A few years before he died, he signed my hardcover copies of his two most recent books. On the title page of one of them I found the traced outline of his hand; on the title page of the other was an outline of an erection so huge that it ran off the page, annotated with a little arrow and the remark "scale 100%." I once heard him enthusiastically describe, in the presence of a girl he was dating, someone else's girlfriend as his "paragon of womanhood." David's girl did a wonderfully slow double take and said, *What?* Whereupon David, whose vocabulary was as large as anybody's in the Western Hemisphere, took a deep breath and, letting it out, said, "I'm suddenly realizing that I've never actually known what the word *paragon* means."

He was lovable the way a child is lovable, and he was capable of returning love with a childlike purity. If love is nevertheless excluded from his work, it's because he never quite felt that he deserved to receive it. He was a lifelong prisoner on the island of himself. What looked like gentle contours from a distance were in fact sheer cliffs. Sometimes only a little of him was crazy, sometimes nearly all of him, but, as an adult, he was never entirely not crazy. What he'd seen of his id while trying to escape his island prison by way of drugs and alcohol, only to find himself even more imprisoned by addiction, seems never to have ceased to be corrosive of his belief in his lovability. Even after he got clean, even decades after his late-adolescent suicide attempt, even after his slow and heroic construction of a life for himself, he felt undeserving. And this feeling was intertwined, ultimately to the point of indistinguishability, with the thought of suicide, which was the one sure way out of his imprisonment; surer than addiction, surer than fiction, and surer, finally, than love.

We who were not so pathologically far out on the spectrum of self-involvement, we dwellers of the visible spectrum who could imagine how it felt to go beyond violet but were not ourselves beyond it, could see that David was wrong not to believe in his lovability and could imagine the pain of not believing in it. How easy and natural love is if you are well! And how gruesomely difficult—what a philosophically daunting contraption of self-interest and self-delusion love appears to be—if you are not! And yet one of the lessons of David's work (and, for me, of being his friend) is that the difference between well and not well is in more respects a difference of degree than of kind. Even though David laughed at my much milder addictions and liked to tell me that I couldn't even conceive of how moderate I was, I can still extrapolate from these addictions, and from the secretiveness and solipsism and radical isolation and raw animal craving that accompany them, to the extremity of his. I can imagine the sick mental pathways by which suicide comes to seem like the one consciousness-quenching substance that nobody can take away from you. The need to have something apart from other people, the need for a secret, the need for some last-ditch narcissistic validation of the self's primacy, and then the voluptuously self-hating anticipation of the last grand score, and the final severing of contact with the world that would deny you the enjoyment of your self-involved pleasure: I can follow David there.

It is, admittedly, harder to connect with the infantile rage and displaced homicidal impulses visible in certain particulars of his death. But even here I can discern a funhouse-mirror Wallace logic, a perverse sort of yearning for intellectual honesty and consistency. To deserve the death sentence he'd passed on himself, the execution of the sentence had to be deeply injurious to someone. To prove once and for all that he truly didn't deserve to be loved, it was necessary to betray as hideously as possible those who loved him best, by killing himself at home and making them firsthand witnesses to his act. And the same was true of suicide as a career move, which was the kind of adulation-craving calculation that he loathed in himself and would deny (if he thought he could get away with it) that he was conscious of making, and would then (if you called him on it) laughingly or wincingly admit that, yeah, okay, he was indeed capable of making. I imagine the side of David that advocated going the Kurt Cobain route speaking in the seductively reasonable voice of the devil in *The Screwtape Letters*, which was one of David's favorite books, and pointing out that death by his own hand would simultaneously satisfy his loathsome hunger for career advantage and, because it would represent a capitulation to the side of himself that his embattled better side perceived as evil, further confirm the justice of his death sentence.

This is not to say that he spent his last months and weeks in lively intellectual conversation with himself, à la Screwtape or the Grand Inquisitor. He was so sick, toward the end, that every new waking thought of his, on whatever subject, immediately corkscrewed into the same conviction of his worthlessness, causing him continual dread and pain. And yet one of his own favored tropes, articulated especially clearly in his story "Good Old Neon" and in his treatise on Georg Cantor, was the infinite divisibility of a single instant in time. However continually he was suffering in his last summer, there was still plenty of room, in the interstices between his identically painful thoughts, to entertain the idea of suicide, to flash forward through its logic, and to set in motion the practical plans (of which he eventually made at least four) for effectuating it. When you decide to do something very bad, the intention and the reasoning for it spring into existence simultaneously and fully formed; any addict who's about to fall off the wagon can tell you this. Though suicide itself was painful to contemplate, it became—to echo the title of another of David's stories—a sort of present to himself.

Adulatory public narratives of David, which take his suicide as proof that (as Don McLean sang of van Gogh) "this world was never meant for one as beautiful as you," require that there have been a unitary David, a beautiful and supremely gifted human being who, after quitting the antidepressant Nardil, which he'd been taking for twenty years, succumbed to major depression and was therefore *not himself* when he committed suicide. I will pass over the question of diagnosis (it's possible he was not simply depressive) and the question of how such a beautiful human being had come by such vividly intimate knowledge of the thoughts of hideous men. But bearing in mind his fondness for Screwtape and his demonstrable penchant for deceiving himself and others—a penchant that his years in recovery held in check but never eradicated—I can imagine a narrative of ambiguity and ambivalence truer to the spirit of his work. By his own account to me, he had never ceased to live in fear of returning to the psych ward, where his early suicide attempt had landed him. The allure of suicide, the last big score, may go underground, but it never entirely disappears. Certainly, David had "good" reasons to go off Nardil—his fear that its long-term physical effects might shorten the good life he'd managed to make for himself; his suspicion that its psychological effects might be interfering with the best things in his life (his work and his relationships)—and he also had less "good" reasons of ego: a perfectionist wish to be less substance-dependent, a narcissistic aversion to seeing himself as permanently mentally ill. What I find hard to believe is that he didn't have very bad reasons as well. Flickering beneath his beautiful moral intelligence and his lovable human weakness was the old addict's consciousness, the secret self, which, after decades of suppression by the Nardil, finally glimpsed its chance to break free and have its suicidal way.

This duality played out in the year that followed his quitting Nardil. He made strange and seemingly self-defeating decisions about his care, engaged in a fair amount of bamboozlement of his shrinks (whom one can only pity for having drawn such a brilliantly complicated case), and in the end created an entire secret life devoted to suicide. Throughout that year, the David whom I knew well and loved immoderately was struggling bravely to build a more secure foundation for his work and his life, contending with heartbreaking levels of anxiety and pain, while the David whom I knew less well, but still well enough to have always disliked and distrusted, was methodically plotting his own destruction and his revenge on those who loved him.

That he was blocked with his work when he decided to quit Nardil—was bored with his old tricks and unable to muster enough excitement about his new novel to find a way forward with it—is not inconsequential. He'd loved writing fiction, *Infinite Jest* in particular, and he'd been very explicit, in our many discussions of the purpose of novels, about his belief that fiction is a solution, the *best* solution, to the problem of existential solitude. Fiction was his way off the island, and as long as it was working for him—as long as he'd been able to pour his love and passion into preparing his lonely dispatches, and as long as these dispatches were coming as urgent and fresh and honest news to the mainland—he'd achieved a measure of happiness and hope for himself. When his hope for fiction died, after years of struggle with the new novel, there was no other way out but death. If boredom is the soil in which the seeds of addiction sprout, and if the phenomenology and the teleology of suicidality are the same as those of addiction, it seems fair to say that David died of boredom. In his early story "Here and There," the brother of a perfection-seeking young man, Bruce, invites him to consider "how *boring* it would be to be perfect," and Bruce tells us:

> I defer to Leonard's extensive and hard-earned knowledge about being boring, but do point out that since being boring is an imperfection, it would by definition be impossible for a perfect person to be boring.

It's a good joke; and yet the logic is somehow strangulatory. It's the logic of "everything and more," to echo yet another of David's titles, and everything and more is what he wanted from and for his fiction. This had worked for him before, in *Infinite Jest*. But to try to add more to what is already everything is to risk having nothing: to become boring to yourself.

A funny thing about Robinson Crusoe is that he never, in twenty-eight years on his Island of Despair, becomes bored. He speaks, yes, of the drudgery of his early labors, he later admits to becoming "heartily tir'd" of searching the island for cannibals, he laments not having any pipes in which to smoke the tobacco he finds on the island, and he describes his first year of company with Friday as the "pleasantest year of all the life I led in this place." But the modern craving for *stimulation* is wholly absent. (The novel's most astonishing detail may be that Robinson makes "three large runlets of rum or spirits" last a quarter century; I would have drunk all three in a month, just to be done with them.) Although he never ceases to dream of escape, he soon comes to take "a secret kind of pleasure" in his absolute ownership of the island:

> I look'd now upon the world as a thing remote, which I had nothing to do with, no expectation from, and indeed no desires about: In a word, I had nothing indeed to do with it, nor was ever like to have; so I thought it look'd as we may perhaps look upon it hereafter.

Robinson is able to survive his solitude because he's lucky; he makes peace with his condition because he's ordinary and his island is concrete. David, who was extraordinary, and whose island was virtual, finally had nothing but his own interesting self to survive on, and the problem with making a virtual world of oneself is akin to the problem with projecting ourselves onto a cyberworld: there's no end of virtual spaces in which to seek stimulation, but their very endlessness, the perpetual stimulation without satisfaction, becomes imprisoning. To be everything and more is the Internet's ambition, too.

The vertiginous point where I turned back in the rain was less than a mile from La Cuchara, but the return hike took two hours. The rain was now not just horizontal but heavy, and I was having trouble staying upright in the wind. The GPS unit was giving me "Low Battery" messages, but I had to keep turning it on, because visibility was so poor that I couldn't maintain a straight line. Even when the unit showed that the *refugio* was 150 feet away, I had to walk farther before I could make out its roofline.

I tossed my drenched knapsack into the *refugio*, ran down to my tent, and found it a basin of rainwater. I managed to wrestle out the foam mattress and get it back to the *refugio*, and then I went back and unstaked the tent and poured off the water and gathered the whole thing in my arms, trying to keep the things inside it halfway dry, and hustled it back uphill through the horizontal rain. The *refugio* was a disaster zone of soaked clothes and equipment. I spent two hours on various drying projects, followed by an hour of searching the promontory, to no avail, for a critical piece of tent hardware that I'd lost in my mad dash. And then, in a matter of minutes, the rain ended and the clouds blew off and I realized I'd been staying in the most dramatically beautiful spot I'd ever seen.

It was late afternoon, and the wind was blowing out over the insanely blue ocean, and it was time. La Cuchara seemed more suspended in the air than attached to the earth. There was a feeling of near-infinity, the sun eliciting from the hillsides more shades of green and yellow than I'd suspected the visible spectrum of containing, a dazzling near-infinity of colors, and the sky so immense that I wouldn't have been surprised to see the mainland on the eastern horizon. White shreds of remnant cloud came barreling down from the summit, whipped past me, and vanished. The wind was blowing out, and I began to cry, because I knew it was time and I hadn't prepared myself; had managed to forget. I went to the *refugio* and got the little box of David's ashes, the "booklet"—to use the term he'd amusingly applied to his not-short book about mathematical infinity—and walked back down the promontory with it, the wind at my back.

I was doing a lot of different things at every moment. Even as I was crying, I was also scanning the ground for the missing piece of my tent, and taking my camera out of my pocket and trying to capture the celestial beauty of the light and the landscape, and damning myself for doing this when I should have been purely mourning, and telling myself that it was *okay* that I'd failed in my attempt to see the rayadito in what would surely be my only visit to the island—that it was better this way, that it was time to accept finitude and incompleteness and leave certain birds forever unseen, that the ability to accept this was the gift I'd been given and my beloved dead friend had not.

At the end of the promontory, I came to a pair of matching boulders that together formed a kind of altar. David had chosen to leave the people who loved him and give himself to the world of the novel and its readers, and I was ready to wish him well in it. I opened the box of ashes and threw them up into the wind. Some bits of gray bone came down on the slope below me, but the dust was caught in the wind and vanished into the blue vault of the sky, blowing out across the ocean. I turned and wandered back up the hill toward the *refugio*, where I would have to spend the night, because my tent was disabled. I felt done with anger, merely bereft, and done with islands, too.

Riding with me on the boat back to Robinson Crusoe were twelve hundred lobsters, a couple of skinned goats, and an old lobsterman who, after the anchor had been weighed, shouted to me that the sea was very rough. Yeah, I agreed, it was a little rough. "*No poco!*" he shouted seriously. "*Mucho!*" The boat's crew were tossing around the bloody goats, and I realized that instead of heading straight back toward Robinson we were angling forty-five degrees to the south, to keep from capsizing. I staggered down into a tiny, fetid bunkroom beneath the bow and heaved myself onto a bunk and there—after an hour or two of clutching the sides of the bunk to avoid becoming airborne, and trying to think about something, anything, that wasn't seasickness, and sweating off (as I later discovered) the antiseasickness patch I'd stuck behind my ear, and listening to water slosh and hammer against the hull—I threw up into a Ziploc bag. Ten hours later, when I ventured back out on deck, I was expecting the harbor to be in sight, but the captain had done so much tacking that we were still five hours away. I couldn't face returning to the bunk, and I was still too sick to look at seabirds, and so I stood for five hours and did little but imagine changing my return flight, which I'd booked for the following week to allow for delays, and going home early.

I hadn't felt so homesick since, possibly, the last time I'd camped by myself. In three days, the Californian woman I live with would be going out to watch the Super Bowl with friends of ours, and when I thought of sitting beside her on a sofa and drinking a martini and rooting for the Green Bay quarterback Aaron Rodgers, who'd been a star at Berkeley, I felt *desperate* to escape the islands. Before leaving for Masafuera, I'd already seen Robinson's two endemic land-bird species, and the prospect of another week there, with no chance of seeing something new, seemed suffocatingly boring—an exercise in deprivation from the very busyness that I'd been so intent on fleeing, a busyness whose pleasurability I appreciated only now.

Back on Robinson, I enlisted my innkeeper, Ramón, to try to get me on one of the following day's flights. Both flights turned out to be full, but while I was eating lunch the local agent of one of the air companies happened to walk into the inn, and Ramón pressed her to let me fly on a third, cargo-only, flight. The agent said no. But what about the copilot seat? Ramón asked her. Couldn't he sit in the copilot seat? No, the agent said, the copilot seat, too, would be filled with cartons of lobster.

And so, although I no longer wanted it, or because I didn't want it, I had the experience of being truly stranded on an island. I ate the same bad Chilean white bread at every meal, the same nondescript fish served without sauce or seasoning at every lunch and dinner. I lay in my room and finished *Robinson Crusoe*. I wrote postcards in reply to the stack of mail I'd brought along. I practiced mentally inserting into Chilean Spanish the *s*'s that its speakers omitted. I got better views of the Juan Fernández firecrown, a splendid large cinnamon-colored hummingbird severely endangered by invasive plant and animal species. I hiked over the mountains to a grassland where the island's annual cattle-branding festival was being held, and I watched horseback riders drive the village's herd into a corral. The setting was spectacular—sweeping hills, volcanic peaks, whitecapped ocean—but the hills were denuded and deeply gouged by erosion. Of the hundred-plus cattle, at least ninety were malnourished, the majority of them so skeletal it seemed remarkable that they could even stand up. The herd had historically been a reserve source of protein, and the villagers still enjoyed the ritual of roping and branding, but couldn't they see what a sad travesty their ritual had become?

With three more days to fill and my knees worn out by downhill hiking, I had no choice but to start reading Samuel Richardson's first novel, *Pamela*, which I'd brought along mainly because it's a lot shorter than *Clarissa*. All I'd known about *Pamela* was that Henry Fielding had satirized it in *Shamela*, his own first venture into novel writing. I hadn't known that *Shamela* was only one of many works published in immediate response to *Pamela*, and that *Pamela*, indeed, had been possibly the biggest news of any kind in London in 1741. But as soon as I started reading it I could see why: the novel is compelling and electric with sex and class conflicts, and it details psychological extremes at a level of specificity like nothing before it. Pamela Andrews isn't everything and more. She's simply and uniquely Pamela, a beautiful servant girl whose virtue is under sustained and ingenious assault by the son of her late employer. Her story is told through her letters to her parents, and when she finds out that these letters are being intercepted and read by her would-be seducer, Mr. B., she continues to write them *while knowing that Mr. B. will read them*. Pamela's piousness and self-dramatizing hysterics were bound to infuriate a certain kind of reader (one of the books published in response satirized Richardson's subtitle, "Virtue Rewarded," as "Feign'd Innocence Detected"), but underneath her strident virtue and Mr. B.'s lascivious machinations is a fascinatingly rendered love story. The realistic power of this story was what made the book such a groundbreaking sensation. Defoe had staked out the territory of radical individualism, which has remained a fruitful subject for novelists as late as Beckett and Wallace, but it was Richardson who first granted full fictional access to the hearts and minds of individuals whose solitude has been overwhelmed by love for someone else.

Exactly halfway through *Robinson Crusoe*, when Robinson has been alone for fifteen years, he discovers a single human footprint on the beach and is literally made crazy by *"the fear of man."* After concluding that the footprint is neither his own nor the Devil's but, rather, some cannibal intruder's, he remakes his garden island into a fortress, and for several years he can think of little but concealing himself and repelling imagined invaders. He marvels at the irony that

> I whose only affliction was, that I seem'd banish'd from human society, that I was alone, circumscrib'd by the boundless ocean, cut off from mankind, and condemn'd to what I call'd silent life . . . that I should now tremble at the very apprehensions of seeing a man, and was ready to sink into the ground at but the shadow, or silent appearance of a man's having set his foot in the island.

Nowhere was Defoe's psychology more acute than in his imagination of Robinson's response to the rupture of his solitude. He gave us the first realistic portrait of the radically isolated individual, and then, as if impelled by novelistic truth, he showed us how sick and crazy radical individualism really is. No matter how carefully we defend our selves, all it takes is one footprint of another real person to recall us to the endlessly interesting hazards of living relationships. Even Facebook, whose users collectively spend billions of hours renovating their self-regarding projections, contains an ontological exit door, the Relationship Status menu, among whose options is the phrase "It's complicated." This may be a euphemism for "on my way out," but it's also a description of all the other options. As long as we have such complications, how dare we be bored?

THE GREATEST FAMILY
EVER STORIED

[on Christina Stead's The Man Who Loved Children*]*

------►

There are any number of reasons you shouldn't read *The Man Who Loved Children*. It's a novel, for one thing; and haven't we all secretly sort of come to an agreement, in the last year or two or three, that novels belonged to the age of newspapers and are going the way of newspapers, only faster? As an old English professor friend of mine likes to say, novels are a curious moral case, in that we feel guilty about not reading more of them but also guilty about doing something as frivolous as reading them; and wouldn't we all be better off with one less thing in the world to feel guilty about?

To read *The Man Who Loved Children* would be an especially frivolous use of your time, since, even by novelistic standards, it's about nothing of world-historical consequence. It's about a family, and a very extreme and singular family at that, and the few parts of it that aren't about this family are the least compelling parts. The novel is also rather long, sometimes repetitious, and undeniably slow in the middle. It requires you, moreover, to learn to read the family's private language, a language created and imposed by the eponymous father, and though the learning curve is nowhere near as steep as with Joyce or Faulkner, you're still basically being asked to learn a language good for absolutely nothing but enjoying this one particular book.

Even the word *enjoying*: Is that the right word? Although its prose ranges from good to fabulously good—is lyrical in the true sense, every observation and description bursting with feeling, meaning, subjectivity—and although its plotting is unobtrusively masterly, the book operates at a pitch of psychological violence that makes *Revolutionary Road* look like *Everybody Loves Raymond*. And, worse yet, can never stop making fun of that violence! Who needs to read this kind of thing? Isn't the nuclear family, at least the psychologically violent side of it, the thing we're all trying to escape from—the infernal reactor into which, when outright escape is not an option, we've learned to stick our new gadgetry and entertainments and after-school activities like graphite rods, to cool the reaction down? *The Man Who Loved Children* is so retrograde as to accept what we would call "abuse" as a natural feature of the familial landscape, and a potentially comic feature at that, and to posit a gulf between adults and children far wider than their differing consumer tastes. The book intrudes on our better-regulated world like a bad dream from the grandparental past. Its idea of a happy ending is like no other novel's, and probably not at all like yours.

And then there's your e-mail: shouldn't you be dealing with your e-mail?

It will be seventy years this October since Christina Stead published her masterpiece to lackluster reviews and negligible sales. Mary McCarthy wrote an especially caustic notice for *The New Republic*, finding fault with the novel's anachronisms and its imperfect grasp of American life. Stead had in fact arrived in the United States less than four years earlier, with her companion, William Blake, an American Marxist and writer and businessman who was trying to obtain a divorce from his wife. Stead had grown up in Australia and fled the country decisively in 1928, at the age of twenty-five. She and Blake had lived in

London, Paris, Spain, and Belgium while she was writing her first four books; her fourth, *House of All Nations*, was a gargantuan, impenetrable novel about international banking. Soon after she arrived in New York, Stead undertook to clarify her feelings about her unbelievable Australian childhood by way of fiction. She wrote *The Man Who Loved Children* on East Twenty-second Street, near Gramercy Park, in less than eighteen months. According to her biographer, Hazel Rowley, Stead set the novel in Washington, D.C., at the insistence of her publisher, Simon & Schuster, which didn't think American readers would care about Australians.

Anyone trying to revive interest in the novel at this late date will labor under the shadow of the poet Randall Jarrell's long and dazzling introduction to its 1965 reissue. Not only can nobody praise the book more roundly and minutely than Jarrell already did, but if an appeal as powerful as his couldn't turn the world on to the book, back in the day when our country still took literature halfway seriously, it seems highly unlikely that anybody else can now. Indeed, one very good reason to read the novel is that you can then read Jarrell's introduction and be reminded of what outstanding literary criticism used to look like: passionate, personal, fair-minded, thorough, and intended for ordinary readers. If you still care about fiction, it might make you nostalgic.

Jarrell, who repeatedly linked Stead with Tolstoy, was clearly taking his best shot at installing her in the Western canon, and in this he clearly failed. A 1980 study of the hundred most-cited literary writers of the twentieth century, based on scholarly citations from the late 1970s, found Margaret Atwood, Gertrude Stein, and Anaïs Nin on the list, but not Christina Stead. This would be less puzzling if Stead and her best novel didn't positively *cry out* for academic criticism of every stripe. Especially confounding is that *The Man Who Loved Children* has failed to become a core text in every women's studies program in the country.

At its most basic level, the novel is the story of a patriarch, Sam Pollit—Samuel Clemens Pollit—who subjugates his wife, Henny, by impregnating her six times, and who seduces and beguiles his progeny with endless torrents of private language and crackpot household schemes and rituals that cumulatively serve to make him the sun (he is radiantly white, with yellow hair) around which the Pollit world revolves. By day, Sam is a striving, idealistic bureaucrat in FDR's Washington. By night and on weekends, he's the hyperkinetic lord of the family's run-down house in Georgetown; he's the great I-Am (Henny's words), the Great Mouthpiece (Henny again), Mr. Here-There-and-Everywhere (Henny); he's the Sam-the-Bold (his own name for himself) who insinuates himself into every pore of his children's beings. He lets them run naked, he spits chewed-up sandwich into their mouths (to strengthen their immune systems), he's unfazed by the news that his youngest is eating his own excrement (because it's "natural"). To his sister, a schoolteacher, he says, "It's not even right they should be forced to go to school when they have a father like me." To the children themselves he says things like "You are myself" and "When I say, 'Sun, you can shine!' doesn't it shine?"

To a wild degree, Sam makes his children accessories of and to his narcissism. There isn't a more hilarious narcissist in all of literature, and, in good narcissistic fashion, while Sam imagines himself a prophet of "world peace, world love, world under-standing," he remains happily blind to the squalor and misery of his circumstances. He is a perfect instance of the Western-rationalist male boogeyman stalked by a certain kind of literary critic. Through the fine accident of being forced to set the novel in America, Stead was also able to map his imperialism and his innocent faith in his own good intentions directly onto those of the city he works in. He is literally the Great White Father, he is literally Uncle Sam. He's the kind of misogynist who adores femininity in the abstract but feels himself "dragged down to earth—no, into the slime" by an actual flesh-and-blood woman, and who believes that women are too crazy to be allowed to vote. And yet, though monstrous, he isn't a monster. It's Stead's genius to make palpable on page after page the childlike need and weakness at the core of his overbearing masculinity, and to make the reader pity him and like him and, therefore, find him funny. The language he speaks at home, not baby talk exactly, something weirder, is an endlessly inventive cascade of alliteration, nonsensical rhymes, puns, running jokes, clashing diction levels, and private references; quotation out of context can't do it justice. As his best friend says to him, admiringly, "Sam, when you talk, you know you create a world." His children are at once enthralled by his words and more sensibly grown-up than he is. When he's ecstatically describing a future form of travel, *projection by dematerialization*, in which passengers "will be shot into a tube and decomposed," his oldest son dryly declares: "No one would travel."

The immovable objects opposed to Sam's irresistible force are Henny and her stepdaughter, Louie, the child of his dead first wife. Henny is the spoiled, amoral, and now operatically suffering daughter of a wealthy Baltimore family. The hatred between husband and wife is heightened by the determination of each not to let the other leave and take the children. Their all-out war, aggravated by their deepening money troubles, is the novel's narrative engine, and here again what saves their hatred from being monstrous—makes it comic instead—is its very extremity. Neurasthenic, worn-out, devious Henny, given to "black looks" and blacker moods, is the household "hag" (her word) who pours reality-based poison into her children's eagerly open ears. Her language is as full of neurotic pain and darkness as Sam's is full of unrealistic love and optimism. As the narrator notes, "He called a spade the predecessor of modern agriculture, she called it a muck dig: they had no words between them intelligible." Or, as Henny says, "He only wants the truth, but he wants my mouth shut." And: "He talks about human equality, the rights of man, nothing but that. How about the rights of woman, I'd like to scream at him." But she doesn't scream it at him directly, because the two of them haven't been on speaking terms for years. She instead leaves terse notes addressed to "Samuel Pollit," and both of them use the children as emissaries.

While Sam and Henny's war takes up the novel's foreground, its less and less secret arc is Sam's deteriorating relationship with his eldest child, Louie. Many good novelists produce entire good *oeuvres* without leaving us one indelible, archetypal character. Christina Stead, in one book, gives us three, of which Louie is the most endearing and miraculous. She is a big, fat, clumsy girl who believes herself to be a genius; "I'm the ugly duckling, you'll see," she shouts at her father when he's tormenting her. As Randall Jarrell noted, while many if not most writers were ugly ducklings as children, few if any have ever conveyed as honestly and completely as Stead does the pain of the experience of being one. Louie is forever covered with cuts and bruises from her bumblings, her clothes forever stained and shredded from her accidents. She's befriended only by the queerest of neighbors (for one of whom, old Mrs. Kydd, in one of the novel's hundred spectacular little scenes, she consents to drown an unwanted cat in the bathtub). Louie is constantly reviled by both parents for her slovenliness: that she isn't pretty is a terrible blow to Sam's narcissism, while, to Henny, her oblivious self-regard is an intolerable seconding of Sam's own ("She crawls, I can hardly touch her, she reeks with her slime and filth—she doesn't notice!"). Louie keeps trying to resist being drawn into her father's insane-making games, but because she's still a child, and because she loves him, and because he really is irresistible, she keeps humiliating herself by surrendering.

More and more clearly, though, Louie emerges as Sam's true nemesis. She begins by challenging him on the field of spoken language, as in the scene in which he's expatiating on the harmonious oneness of future mankind:

> "My system," Sam continued, "which I invented myself, might be called *Monoman* or *Manunity*!"
>
> Evie [Sam's younger, favored daughter] laughed timidly, not knowing whether it was right or not. Louisa said, "You mean Monomania."
>
> Evie giggled and then lost all her color, became a stainless olive, appalled at her mistake.
>
> Sam said coolly, "You look like a gutter rat, Looloo, with that expression. Monoman would only be the condition of the world after we had weeded out the misfits and degenerates." There was a threat in the way he said it.

Later, as she enters adolescence, Louie begins to keep a diary and fills it not with scientific observations (as Sam has suggested) but with veiled accusations of her father, elaborately enciphered. When she falls in love with one of her high school teachers, Miss Aiden, she embarks on composing what she calls the Aiden Cycle, consisting of poems to Miss Aiden in "every conceivable form and also every conceivable meter in the English language." As a present for her father on his fortieth birthday, she writes a one-act tragedy, *Herpes Rom*, in which a young

THE GREATEST FAMILY EVER STORIED / 61

woman is strangled by her father, who seems to be part snake; since Louie doesn't know a foreign language yet, she uses a language of her own invention.

While the novel is building to various cataclysms at the plot level (Henny is finally losing her long war), its inner story consists of Sam's efforts to hold on to Louie and crush her separate language. He keeps vowing to break her spirit, claiming to have direct telepathic access to her thoughts, insisting that she'll become a scientist and support him in his altruistic mission, and calling her his "foolish, poor little Looloo." In front of the assembled children, he forces her to decipher her diary, so that she can be laughed at. He recites poems from the Aiden Cycle and laughs at these, too, and when Miss Aiden comes to dinner with the Pollits he takes her away from Louie and talks to her non-stop. After *Herpes Rom* has been performed, ridiculously, incomprehensibly, and Louie has presented Sam with the English translation, he pronounces his judgment: "Damn my eyes if I've ever seen anything so stupid and silly."

In a lesser work, this might all read like a grim, abstract feminist parable, but Stead has already devoted most of the book to making the Pollits specific and real and *funny*, and to establishing them as capable of saying and doing just about anything, and she has particularly established what a problem love is for Louie (how much, in spite of everything, she yearns for her father's adoration), and so the abstraction becomes inescapably concrete, the warring archetypes are given sympathetic flesh: you can't help being dragged along through Louisa's bloody soul-struggle to become her own person, and you can't help cheering for her triumph. As the narrator remarks, matter-of-factly, "That was family life." And telling the story of this inner life is what novels, and only novels, are for.

Or used to be, at least. Because haven't we left this stuff behind us? High-mindedly domineering males? Children as accessories to their parents' narcissism? The nuclear family as a free-for-all of psychic abuse? We're tired of the war between the sexes and the war between the generations, because these wars are so ugly, and who wants to look into the mirror of a novel and see such ugliness? How much better about ourselves we'll feel when we stop speaking our embarrassing private family languages! The absence of literary swans seems like a small price to pay for a world in which ugly ducklings grow up to be big ugly ducks whom we can then agree to call beautiful.

And yet the culture isn't monolithic. Although *The Man Who Loved Children* is probably too difficult (difficult to stomach, difficult to allow into your heart) to gain a mass following, it's certainly less difficult than other novels common to college syllabuses, and it's the kind of book that, if it is for you, is *really* for you. I'm convinced that there are tens of thousands of people in this country who would bless the day the book was published, if only they could be exposed to it. I might never have found my way to it myself had my wife not discovered it in the public library in Somerville, Mass., in 1983, and pronounced it the truest book she'd ever read. Every time I've been away from it for some years and am thinking of reading it again, I worry that I must have been wrong about it, since the literary and academic and book-club worlds make so little of it. (For example, as I'm writing this, there are 177 Amazon customer reviews of *To the Lighthouse*, 312 for *Gravity's Rainbow*, and 409 for *Ulysses*; for *The Man Who Loved Children*, a much more accessible book, there are 14.) I open the book with trepidation, and then I read five pages and am right back into it and realize that I wasn't wrong at all. I feel as if I've come home again.

I suspect that one reason *The Man Who Loved Children* remains exiled from the canon is that Christina Stead's ambition was to write not "like a woman" but "like a man": her allegiances are too dubious for the feminists, and she's not *enough* like a man for everybody else. The novel's precursor, *House of All Nations*, more resembles a Gaddis novel, even a Pynchon novel, than it does any novel by a twentieth-century woman. Stead wasn't content to make a separate peace for herself, in a room of her own. She was competitive like a son, not a daughter, and she needed to go back, in her best novel, to her life's primal scenes and beat her eloquent father at his own game. And this, too, is an embarrassment, since, however central competition may be to the free-enterprise system we live in, to cop to it personally and speak of it nakedly is very unflattering (athletic competition being the exception that proves the rule).

Stead, in the interviews she gave, was sometimes frank about how directly and completely autobiographical her novel was. Basically, Sam Pollit *is* her father, David Stead. Sam's ideas and voice and domestic arrangements are all David's, transposed from Australia to America. And where Sam is infatuated with an innocent girl-woman, Gillian, the daughter of a colleague, the real-life David fell for a pretty girl the same age as Christina, Thistle Harris, with whom he briefly had an affair, later lived with, and eventually, after many years, married. Thistle was the beautiful acolyte and flattering mirror who Christina herself could never be for David, if only because, although she wasn't fat like Louie, she also wasn't remotely good-looking. (Rowley's biography has pictures to prove it.)

In the novel, Louie's lack of good looks is a blow to her own narcissism. Her fatness and plainness are, arguably, what rescue her from her father's delusions, impel her toward honesty, and save her. But the pain that Louie experiences in not being pleasing to anybody's eyes, least of all to her father's, is surely drawn from Christina Stead's own pain. Her best novel feels finally like a daughter's offering of love and solidarity to her father—you see, I *am* like you, I've achieved a language equal to yours, *superior* to yours—which is also, of course, an offering of white-hot competitive hatred. When Louie tells her father that she's never told anybody what her home life is like, the reason she gives is that "no one would believe me!" But the grown-up Stead found a way to make readers believe her. The fully mature writer created a faithful mirror of everything her father and Sam Pollit least wanted to see; and when the novel was published, the person in Australia to whom she sent a copy wasn't David Stead but Thistle Harris. The inscription read: "To dear Thistle. A Strindberg Family Robinson. In some respects might be considered a private letter to Thistle from Christina Stead." Whether David himself ever read the book remains unknown.

HORNETS

-------▶

In the early nineties, when I reached the point of having no money at all, I began to borrow people's houses. The first house I sat belonged to a professor at my alma mater. He and his wife were afraid that their son, a student at the college, would throw parties in their absence, and so they urged me to consider the house my private and exclusive home. This was already something of a struggle, because it's in the nature of a borrowed house that its closets will be hung with someone else's bathrobes, its refrigerator glutted with someone else's condiments, its shower drain plugged with someone else's hair. And when, inevitably, the son showed up at the house and began to run around barefoot, and then invited his friends over and partied late into the night, I felt sick with powerlessness and envy. I must have been a repellent specter of silent grievance indeed, because one morning, in the kitchen, without my having said a word, the son looked up from his bowl of cold cereal and brutally set me straight: "This is *my* house, Jonathan."

A few summers later, having less than no money at all, I borrowed the grand stucco house of two older friends, Ken and Joan, in Media, Pennsylvania. My orientation occurred one evening over martinis that Ken gently chided Joan for having "bruised" with melting ice. I sat with them on their mossy rear terrace while they enumerated, with a kind of mellow resignation, their house's problems. The foam mattress in their master bedroom was crumbling and cratered; their beautiful carpets were being reduced to dust by an apparently unstoppable moth infestation. Ken made himself a second martini, and then, gazing up at a part of the roof that leaked during thunderstorms, he delivered a self-summation that offered me an unexpected glimpse of how I might live more happily, a vision of potential liberation from the oppressive sense of financial responsibility that my parents had bequeathed me. Holding his martini glass at a casual angle, Ken reflected to no one in particular, "We have . . . *always* lived beyond our means."

The only thing I had to do to earn my keep in Media was mow Ken and Joan's extensive lawn. Mowing lawns has always seemed to me among the most despair-inducing of human activities, and, by way of following Ken's example of living beyond one's means, I delayed the first mowing until the grass was so long that I had to stop and empty the clippings bag every five minutes. I delayed the second mowing even longer. By the time I got around to it, the lawn had been colonized by a large clan of earth-burrowing hornets. They had bodies the size of double-A batteries and were even more aggressively proprietary than the son in the first house I'd borrowed. I called Ken and Joan at their summer place, in Vermont, and Ken told me that I needed to visit the hornet homes, one by one, after dark, when the inhabitants were sleeping, and pour gasoline into the burrows and set them on fire.

I knew enough to be afraid of gasoline. On the night I ventured out to the lawn with a flashlight and a gas can, I took care to recap the can after I'd poured gas into a burrow, and to take the can some distance away before returning to throw a lighted match at the hole. In a few of the holes, I heard a piteous feeble buzzing before I set off the inferno, but my empathy with the hornets was outweighed by my pyromaniac pleasure in the explosions and by the satisfaction of ridding my home of intruders. Eventually, I got careless with the gas can, not bothering to recap it between killings, and there came then, naturally, a match that refused to be lit. While I struck it on the box, again and again, and then fumbled for a better match, gasoline vapors were flowing invisibly back down the slope toward where I'd left the can. When I finally managed to ignite the burrow and run down the slope, I found myself pursued and overtaken by a river of flame. It expired just short of the can, but it was an hour before I could stop shaking. I'd nearly burned myself out of a home, and the home wasn't even mine. However modest my means were, it was seeming preferable, after all, to live within them. I never house-sat again.

THE UGLY MEDITERRANEAN

-------►

The southeastern corner of the Republic of Cyprus has been heavily developed for foreign tourism in recent years. Large medium-rise hotels, specializing in vacation packages for Germans and Russians, overlook beaches occupied by sunbeds and umbrellas in orderly ranks, and the Mediterranean is nothing if not extremely blue. You can spend a very pleasant week here, driving the modern roads and drinking the good local beer, without suspecting that the area harbors the most intensive songbird-killing operations in the European Union.

On the last day of April, I went to the prospering tourist town of Protaras to meet four members of a German bird-protection organization, the Committee Against Bird Slaughter (CABS), that runs seasonal volunteer "camps" in Mediterranean countries. Because the peak season for songbird trapping in Cyprus is autumn, when southbound migrants are loaded up with fat from a northern summer's feasting, I was worried that we might not see any action, but the first orchard we walked into, by the side of a busy road, was full of lime sticks: straight switches, about thirty inches long, that are coated with the gluey gum of the Syrian plum and deployed artfully, to provide inviting perches, in the branches of low trees. The CABS team, which was led by a skinny, full-bearded young Italian named Andrea Rutigliano, fanned into the orchard, taking down the sticks, rubbing them in dirt to neutralize the glue, and breaking them in half. All the sticks had feathers on them. In a lemon tree, we found a male collared flycatcher hanging upside down like a piece of animal fruit, its tail and its legs and its black-and-white wings stuck in glue. While it twitched and futilely turned its head, Rutigliano videoed it from multiple angles, and an older Italian volunteer, Dino Mensi, took still photographs. "The photos are important," said Alex Heyd, a sober-faced German who is the organization's general secretary, "because you win the war in the newspapers, not in the field."

In hot sunshine, the two Italians worked together to free the flycatcher, gently liberating individual feathers, applying squirts of diluted soap to soften the resistant gum, and wincing when a feather was lost. Rutigliano then carefully groomed gum from the bird's tiny feet. "You have to get every bit of lime off," he said. "The first year I was doing this, I left a bit on the foot of one bird and saw it fly and get stuck again. I had to climb the tree." Rutigliano put the flycatcher in my hands, I opened them, and it flew off low through the orchard, resuming its northward journey.

We were surrounded by traffic noise, melon fields, housing developments, hotel complexes. David Conlin, a beefy British military veteran, threw a bundle of disabled sticks into some weeds and said, "It's shocking—that you can stop anywhere around here and find these." I watched Rutigliano and Mensi work to free a second bird, a wood warbler, a lovely yellow-throated thing. It felt wrong to be seeing at such close range a species that ordinarily requires careful work with binoculars to get a decent view of. It felt literally disenchanting. I wanted to say to the wood warbler what Saint Francis of Assisi is said to have said when he saw a captured wild animal: "Why did you let yourself be caught?"

As we were leaving the orchard, Rutigliano suggested that Heyd turn his CABS T-shirt inside out, so that we would look more like ordinary tourists taking a walk. In Cyprus, it's permissible to enter any private land that isn't fenced, and all forms of songbird trapping have been criminal offenses since 1974, but what we were doing still felt to me high-handed and possibly dangerous. The team, in its black and drab clothing, looked more like commandos than like tourists. A local woman, perhaps the orchard's owner, watched without expression as we headed inland on a dirt lane. Then a man in a pickup truck passed us, and the team, fearing that he might be going ahead to take down lime sticks, followed him at a trot.

In the man's back yard, we found two pairs of twenty-foot-long metal pipes propped up in parallel on lawn chairs: a small-scale lime-stick factory of the sort that can provide good income for the mostly older Cypriot men who know the trade. "He's manufacturing them and keeping a few for himself," Rutigliano said. He and the others strolled brazenly around the man's chicken coop and rabbit cages, taking down a few empty sticks and laying them on the pipes. We then trespassed up a hillside and back down into an orchard crisscrossed by irrigation hoses and full of trapped birds. "*Questo giardino è un disastro!*" said Mensi, who spoke only Italian.

A female blackcap had torn most of its tail off and was stuck not only by both legs and both wings but also by the bill, which sprang open as soon as Rutigliano unglued it; it began to cry out furiously. When the bird was freed altogether, he squirted a little water in its mouth and set it on the ground. It fell forward and flopped piteously, pushing its head into the mud. "It's been hanging so long that its leg muscles are overstretched," he said. "We'll keep it tonight, and it can fly tomorrow."

"Even without a tail?" I said.

"Certainly." He scooped up the bird and stowed it in an outer pocket of his backpack.

Blackcaps are one of Europe's most common warblers and the traditional national delicacy of Cyprus, where they're known as *ambelopoulia*. They are the main target of Cypriot trappers, but the bycatch of other species is enormous: rare shrikes, other warblers, larger birds like cuckoos and golden orioles, even small owls and hawks. Stuck in lime in the second orchard were five collared flycatchers, a house sparrow, and a spotted flycatcher (formerly widespread, now becoming rare in much of northern Europe), as well as three more blackcaps. After the team members had sent them on their way, they wrangled about the tally of lime sticks at the site and settled on a figure of fifty-nine.

A little farther inland, in a dry and weedy grove with a view of the blue sea and the golden arches of a new McDonald's, we found one active lime stick with one living bird hanging from it. The bird was a thrush nightingale, a gray-plumaged species that I had seen only once before. It was deeply tangled in lime and had broken a wing. "The break is between two bones, so it cannot recover," Rutigliano said, palpating the joint through feathers. "Unfortunately, we need to kill this bird."

It seemed likely that the thrush nightingale had been caught on a stick overlooked by a trapper who had taken down his other sticks that morning. While Heyd and Conlin discussed whether to get up before dawn the next day and try to "ambush" the trapper, Rutigliano stroked the head of the thrush nightingale. "He's so beautiful," he said, like a little boy. "I can't kill him."

"What should we do?" Heyd said.

"Maybe give him a chance to hop around on the ground and die on his own."

"I don't think there's a good chance for it," Heyd said.

Rutigliano put the bird on the ground and watched as it scurried, looking more mouselike than birdlike, under a small thornbush. "Maybe in a few hours he can walk better," he said, unrealistically.

"Do you want me to make the decision?" Heyd said.

Rutigliano, without answering, wandered up the hill and out of sight.

"Where did it go?" Heyd asked me.

I pointed at the shrub. Heyd reached into it from two sides, captured the bird, held it gently in his hands, and looked up at me and Conlin. "Are we agreed?" he said, in German.

I nodded, and with a twist of his wrist he tore the bird's head off.

The sun had expanded its reach across the entire sky, killing its blue with whiteness. As we scouted for an approach from which to ambush the grove, it was already hard to say how many hours we'd been walking. Every time we saw a Cypriot in a truck or a field, we had to duck down and backtrack over rocks and pants-piercing thistles, for fear that somebody would alert the owner of the trapping site. There was nothing larger at stake here than a few songbirds, there were no land mines on the hillside, and yet the blazing stillness had a flavor of wartime menace.

Lime-stick trapping has been traditional and widespread in Cyprus since at least the sixteenth century. Migratory birds were an important seasonal source of protein in the countryside, and older Cypriots today remember being told by their mothers to go out to the garden and catch some dinner. In more recent decades, *ambelopoulia* became popular with affluent, urbanized Cypriots as a kind of nostalgic treat—you might bring a friend a jar of pickled birds as a house gift, or you might order a platter of them fried in a restaurant for a special occasion. By the mid-nineties, two decades after the country had outlawed all forms of bird trapping, as many as ten million songbirds a year were being killed. To meet the restaurant demand, traditional lime-stick trapping had been augmented by large-scale netting operations, and the Cypriot government, which was trying to clean up its act and win membership in the European Union, cracked down hard on the netters. By 2006, the annual take had fallen to around a million.

In the past few years, however, with Cyprus now comfortably ensconced in the EU, signs advertising illicit *ambelopoulia* have begun to reappear in restaurants, and the number of active trapping sites is rising. The Cypriot hunting lobby, which represents the republic's fifty thousand hunters, is this year supporting two parliamentary proposals to relax antipoaching laws. One would reduce lime-stick use to a misdemeanor; the other would decriminalize the use of electronic recordings to attract birds. Opinion polls show that, while most Cypriots disapprove of bird trapping, most also don't think it's a serious issue, and that many enjoy eating *ambelopoulia*. When the country's Game Fund organized raids on restaurants serving the birds, the media coverage was roundly negative, leading with an account of food being pulled from the hands of a pregnant female diner.

"Food is sacred here," said Martin Hellicar, the campaigns manager of BirdLife Cyprus, a local organization more averse to provocation than CABS is. "I don't think you'll ever get someone convicted for eating these things."

Hellicar and I had spent a day touring netting sites in the country's southeast corner. Any small olive grove can be used for netting, but the really big sites are in plantations of acacia, an alien species there's no reason to irrigate if you're not trapping birds. We saw these plantations everywhere. Long runners of cheap carpeting are laid down between rows of acacias; hundreds of meters of nearly invisible "mist" nets are strung from poles that are typically anchored in old car tires filled with concrete; and then, in the night, birdsong is played at high volume to lure migrants to rest in the lush acacias. In the morning, at first light, the poachers throw handfuls of pebbles to startle the birds into the nets. (A telltale sign of trapping is a mound of these pebbles dumped by the side of the road.) Since it's a superstition among poachers that letting birds go free ruins a site, the unmarketable species are torn up and dropped on the ground or left to die in the nets. The marketable birds can fetch up to five euros apiece, and a well-run site can yield a thousand birds or more a day.

The worst area in Cyprus for poaching is the British military base on Cape Pyla. The British may be the bird-lovingest people in Europe, but the base, which leases its extensive firing ranges to Cypriot farmers, is in a delicate position diplomatically; after one recent enforcement sweep by the army, twenty-two Sovereign Base Area signs were torn down by angry locals. Off the base, enforcement is hampered by logistics and politics. Poachers employ lookouts and night guards and have learned to erect little shacks on their sites, because Game Fund officers are required to get a warrant to search any "domicile," and in the time it takes to do this the poachers can take down their nets and hide their electronic equipment. Because large-scale poachers are nowadays straight-up criminals, the officers are also afraid of violent attacks. "The biggest problem is that no one in Cyprus, not even the politicians, comes out and says that eating *ambelopoulia* is wrong," the director of the Game Fund, Pantelis Hadjigerou, told me. Indeed, the record holder for most *ambelopoulia* eaten in one sitting (fifty-four) was a popular politician in north Cyprus.

"Our ideal would be to find a well-known personality to come out and say, 'I don't eat *ambelopoulia*, it's wrong,'" the director of BirdLife Cyprus, Clairie Papazoglou, said to me. "But there's a little pact here that says that if anything bad happens it has to stay on the island, we can't look bad to the outside world."

"Before Cyprus joined the EU," Hellicar said, "the trappers said, 'We'll pull back for a while.' Now, for eighteen- and nineteen-year-olds, there's a kind of patriotic machismo to poaching. It's a symbol of resistance to Big Brother EU."

What seemed Orwellian to me was Cyprus's internal politics. It's been thirty-six years since Turkey occupied the northern part of the island, and the ethnically Greek south has prospered immensely since then, but the national news is still dominated, seven days a week, by the Cyprus Problem. "Every other issue is swept under the carpet, everything else is insignificant," the Cypriot social anthropologist Yiannis Papadakis told me. "They say, 'How dare you take us to European Court for something as stupid as birds? We're taking Turkey to court!' There was never any serious debate about joining the EU—it was simply the means by which we were going to solve the Cyprus Problem."

The European Union's most powerful instrument of conservation is its landmark Birds Directive, which was issued in 1979 and requires member states to protect all European bird species and preserve sufficient habitat for them. Since joining the EU, in 2004, Cyprus has received repeated warnings from the European Commission for infringement of the directive, but it has so far avoided judgments and fines; if a member state's environmental laws accord on paper with the directive, the commission is reluctant to interfere with sovereign enforcement.

Cyprus's nominally Communist ruling party ardently embraces private development. The tourism ministry is touting plans to build fourteen new residential golf complexes (the island currently has three), even though the country has very limited supplies of fresh water. Anyone who owns land reachable by road can build on it, and, as a result, the countryside is remarkably fragmented. I visited four of the southeast's most important nature preserves, all of them theoretically due special protection under EU regulations, and was uniformly depressed by their condition. The big seasonal lake at Paralimni, for example, near where I was patrolling with the CABS people, is a noisy dust bowl commandeered for an illegal shooting range and an illegal motocross course, carpeted with shotgun shells, and extensively littered with construction debris, discarded large appliances, and household trash.

And yet birds still come to Cyprus; they have no choice. Returning to town at some less white-skied hour, the CABS patrol stopped to admire a black-headed bunting, a jewel of gold and black and chestnut, that was singing from the top of a bush. For a moment, our tension abated, and we were all just bird-watchers exclaiming in our native languages. *"Ah, che bello!"*

"Fantastic!"

"Unglaublich schön!"

Before we quit for the day, Rutigliano wanted to make one last stop, at an orchard where the previous year a CABS volunteer had been roughed up by trappers. As we were turning, in the team's rental car, off the main highway and up a dirt track, a red four-seater pickup truck was coming down the track, and its driver made a neck-slicing gesture at us. After the truck had moved onto the highway, two of its passengers leaned out of windows to give us the finger.

Heyd, the sober German, wanted to turn around and leave immediately, but the others argued that there was no reason to think the men were coming back. We proceeded up to the orchard and found it hung with four collared flycatchers and one wood warbler, which, because it couldn't get airborne, Rutigliano gave to me to put in my backpack. When all the lime sticks had been destroyed, Heyd again, more nervously, suggested that we leave. But there was another grove in the distance which the two Italians wanted to investigate. "I don't have a bad feeling," Rutigliano said.

"There's an English expression, 'Don't press your luck,'" Conlin said.

At that moment, the red pickup sped back into sight, fifty yards down the slope from us, and stopped with a lurch. Three men jumped out and began running toward us, picking up baseball-size rocks and hurling them at us as they ran. I would have guessed that it was easy to dodge a few flying rocks, but it wasn't so easy, and Conlin and Heyd were hit by them. Rutigliano was shooting video, Mensi was taking pictures, and there was a lot of confused shouting—"Keep shooting, keep shooting!" "Call the police!" "What the hell is the number?" Mindful of the warbler in my backpack, and not eager to be mistaken for a CABS member, I followed Heyd as he retreated up the slope. From a not very safe distance, we stopped and watched two men attacking Mensi, trying to pull his backpack from his shoulders and his camera from his hands. The men, who were in their thirties and deeply suntanned, were shouting, "Why do you do this? Why do you make photos?" Mensi, keening terribly, his muscles bulging, was clutching the camera to his stomach. The men picked him up, threw him down, and fell on him; there ensued a blur of fighting. I couldn't see Rutigliano but later learned that he was being hit in the face, knocked to the ground, and kicked in the legs and the ribs. His video camera was smashed on a rock; Mensi was also hit in the head with it. Conlin was standing amid the fray with formidable military bearing, holding two cell phones and trying to dial the police. He said to me, later, that he'd told the attackers that he would drag them through every court in the country if they touched him.

Heyd had continued to retreat, which seemed to me a good idea. When I saw him look back and go pale and break into a dead run, I panicked, too.

Running from danger is like no other kind of running—it's hard to look where you're going. I jumped a stone fence and dashed through a field full of brambles, found myself stumbling into a ditch and getting hit in the chin by a piece of metal fencing, and decided: That's enough of that. I was worried about the warbler I was carrying. I saw Heyd running on up through a large garden, speaking to a middle-aged man, and then, looking frightened, continuing to run. I walked up to the garden's owner and tried to explain the situation, but he spoke only Greek. Seeming at once concerned and suspicious, he fetched his daughter, who was able to tell me, in English, that I'd blundered into the yard of the district director of Greenpeace. She gave me water and two plates of cookies and told my story to her father, who responded with one angry word. "Barbarians!" the daughter translated.

Back down by the rental car, under clouds threatening rain, Mensi was touching his ribs gently and dabbing at the cuts and abrasions that covered his arms; both his camera and his backpack had been stolen. Conlin showed me the smashed video camera, and Rutigliano, who had lost his glasses and was limping heavily, confessed to me, with matter-of-fact fanaticism, "I wanted something like this to happen. Just not this bad."

A second CABS team had arrived and was milling around with grim expressions. In its car was an empty wine carton into which, as a police cruiser was pulling up, I was able to transfer the wood warbler, which was looking subdued but no worse for the wear. I would have felt better about its rescue had there not been, on my cell phone, a new text message from a Cypriot friend of mine, confirming our clandestine date to eat *ambelopoulia* the following night. I was managing to half convince myself that I could simply be a good journalistic observer and not personally have to eat one; but it wasn't at all clear how I could avoid it.

Every spring, some five billion birds come flooding up from Africa to breed in Eurasia, and every year as many as a billion are killed deliberately by humans, most notably on the migratory flyways of the Mediterranean. As its waters are fished clean by trawlers with sonar and efficient nets, its skies are vacuumed clean of migrants by the extremely effective technology of birdsong recordings. Since the 1970s, as a result of the Birds Directive and various other conservation treaties, the situation of some of the most endangered bird species has improved somewhat. But hunters throughout the Mediterranean are now seizing on this marginal improvement and pushing back. Cyprus recently experimented with a spring season on quail and turtledove; Malta, in April, opened its own spring season; and Italy's parliament, in May, passed a law that extends the fall season there. While Europeans may think of themselves as models of environmental enlightenment—they certainly lecture the United States and China on carbon emissions as if they were—the populations of many resident and migratory birds in Europe have been collapsing alarmingly in the past ten years. You don't have to be a birdwatcher to miss the calling of the cuckoo, the circling of lapwings over fields, the singing of corn buntings from utility poles. A world of birds already battered by habitat loss and intensive agriculture is being hastened toward extinction by hunters and trappers. Spring in the Old World is liable to fall silent far sooner than in the New.

The Republic of Malta, which consists of several densely populated chunks of limestone with collectively less than twice the area of the District of Columbia, is the most savagely bird-hostile place in Europe. There are twelve thousand registered hunters (about three percent of the country's population), a large number of whom consider it their birthright to shoot any bird unlucky enough to migrate over Malta, regardless of the season or the bird's protection status. The Maltese shoot bee-eaters, hoopoes, golden orioles, shearwaters, storks, and herons. They stand outside the fences of the international airport and shoot swallows for target practice. They shoot from urban rooftops and from the side of busy roads. They stand in closely spaced cliffside bunkers and mow down flocks of migrating hawks. They shoot endangered raptors, such as lesser spotted eagles and pallid harriers, that governments farther north in Europe are spending millions of euros to conserve. Rarities are stuffed and added to trophy collections; nonrarities are left on the ground or buried under rocks, so as not to incriminate their shooters. When birdwatchers in Italy see a migrant that's missing a chunk of its wing or its tail, they call it "Maltese plumage."

In the 1990s, in the run-up to Malta's accession to the EU, the government began to enforce an existing law against shooting nongame species, and Malta became a cause célèbre among groups as far-flung as the U.K.'s Royal Society for the Protection of Birds, which sent volunteers to assist with law enforcement. As a result, in the words of a British volunteer I spoke to, "the situation has gone from being diabolical to merely atrocious." But Maltese hunters, who argue that the country is too small for its shooting to make a meaningful dent in European bird populations, fiercely resent what they see as foreign interference in their "tradition." The national hunters' organization, the Federazzjoni Kaċċaturi Nassaba Konservazzjonisti, said in its April 2008 newsletter, "FKNK believes that the police's work should only be done by Maltese police and not by arrogant foreign extremists who think Malta is theirs because it's in the EU."

When, in 2006, the local bird group BirdLife Malta hired a Turkish national, Tolga Temuge, a former Greenpeace campaigns director, to launch an aggressive campaign against illegal hunting, hunters were reminded of Malta's siege by the Turks in 1565 and reacted with explosive rage. The FKNK's general secretary, Lino Farugia, inveighed against "the Turk" and his "Maltese lackeys," and there ensued a string of threats and attacks on BirdLife's property and personnel. A BirdLife member was shot in the face; three cars belonging to BirdLife volunteers were set on fire; and several thousand young trees were uprooted at a reforestation site that hunters resent for its competition with the main island's only other forest, which they control and shoot roosting birds in. As a widely read hunters' magazine explained in August 2008, "There is a limit to what extent one can expect to stretch the strong moral ties and values of Maltese families and stop their Latin blood from boiling over and expect them to give up their land and culture in a cowardly retreat."

And yet, in contrast to Cyprus, Maltese public opinion is strongly antihunting. Along with banking, tourism is Malta's main industry, and the newspapers frequently print angry letters from tourists who have been menaced by hunters or have witnessed avian atrocities. The Maltese middle class itself is unhappy that the country's very limited open space is overrun by trigger-happy hunters who post NO TRESPASSING signs on public land. Unlike BirdLife Cyprus, BirdLife Malta has succeeded in enlisting prominent citizens, including the owner of the Radisson Hotel group, in a media campaign called "Reclaiming YOUR Countryside."

Malta is a two-party country, however, and because its national elections are typically decided by a few thousand votes, neither the Labour Party nor the Nationalists can afford to alienate their hunting constituents so much that they stay away from the polls. Enforcement of hunting laws therefore continues to be lax: minimal manpower is devoted to it, many local police are friendly with hunters, and even the good police can be lethargic in responding to complaints. Even when offenders are prosecuted, Maltese courts have been reluctant to fine them more than a few hundred euros.

This year, the Nationalist government opened the country's spring season on quail and turtledove in defiance of a European Court of Justice ruling last fall. The EU Birds Directive permits member states to apply "derogations" and allow the killing of small numbers of protected species for "judicious use," such as control of bird flocks around airports, or subsistence hunting by traditional rural communities. The Maltese government had sought a derogation for continuing the "tradition" of spring hunting, which the directive normally forbids, and the Court had ruled that Malta's proposal failed three of four tests provided by the directive: strict enforcement, small numbers, and parity with other EU member states. Regarding the fourth test, however—whether an "alternative" exists—Malta presented evidence, in the form of bag counts, that autumn hunting of quail and turtledove was not a satisfactory alternative to spring hunting. Although the government was aware that the bag counts were unreliable (the FKNK's general secretary himself once publicly admitted that the actual bag might be ten times higher than the reported count), the European Commission has a policy of trusting the data presented by the governments of member states. Malta further argued that, because quail and turtledove aren't globally threatened species (they're still plentiful in Asia), they didn't merit absolute protection, and the commission's lawyers failed to point out that what counted was the species' status within the EU, where, in fact, their populations are in serious decline. The Court therefore, while ruling against Malta and forbidding a spring hunt, did allow that it had passed one of the four tests. And the government, at home, proclaimed a "victory" and proceeded, in early April, to authorize a hunt.

I joined Tolga Temuge, a ponytailed man who likes to swear, on an early-morning patrol on the first day of the season. We weren't expecting to see much shooting, because the FKNK, angered by the government's terms—the season would last only six half-days, instead of the traditional six to eight weeks, and only 2,500 licenses would be granted—had organized a boycott of the season, threatening to "name and shame" any hunter who applied for a license. "The European Commission *failed*," Temuge said as we drove the dark, dusty labyrinth of Malta's road system. "The European hunting organization and BirdLife International did a lot of hard work to arrive at sustainable hunting limits, and then Malta joins the EU, as the smallest member state, and threatens to bring down the whole edifice of the excellent Birds Directive. Malta's disregard for it is setting a bad precedent for other member states, especially in the Mediterranean, to behave the same way."

When the sky lightened, we stopped in a rough limestone lane, amid walled fields of golden hay, and listened for gunshots. I heard dogs barking, a cock crowing, trucks shifting gears, and, somewhere nearby, electronic quailsong playing. Patrolling elsewhere on the island were six other of Temuge's teams, staffed mainly by foreign volunteers, with a few hired Maltese security men. As the sun came up, we began to hear distant gunshots, but not many; the country seemed essentially bird-free that morning. We proceeded through a village in which a couple of shots rang out—"Fucking unbelievable!" Temuge cried. "This is a residential area! Fucking unbelievable!"—and back into the stony maze of walls that passes for countryside in Malta. Further gunshots led us to a small field in which two men in their thirties were standing with a handheld radio. As soon as they saw us, they picked up hoes and began tending lush plantings of beans and onions. "Once you're in the area, they know," Temuge said. "Everybody knows. If they have radios, it's ninety percent sure they're hunters." It did indeed seem awfully early to be out doing hoe-work, and as long as we were standing by the field we heard no more shots. Four blazing male golden orioles flashed by, unlucky to have chosen Malta as a migratory stopover but lucky that we were standing there. In a low tree I spotted a female chaffinch, which is one of the most common birds in Europe and is all but absent in Malta, owing to the country's widespread illegal finch trapping. Temuge became very excited when I called it out. "A chaffinch!" he said. "That would be incredible, if we're starting to have breeding chaffinch here again." It was like somebody in North America being amazed to see a robin.

Maltese hunters are in the weak position of wanting something that would get Malta into real, punishable trouble with the EU: the legal right to shoot birds bound for their breeding grounds. Their leaders at the FKNK thus have little choice but to adopt uncompromising positions, such as this spring's boycott, which raises false hopes in the FKNK rank and file, fostering frustration and feelings of betrayal when, inevitably, the government disappoints them. I met with the FKNK's spokesman, Joseph Perici Calascione, a nervous but articulate man, at the organization's cramped, cluttered headquarters. "How could anybody, in their wildest imagination, expect us to be satisfied with a spring season that left eighty percent of hunters unable to get a license?" Perici Calascione said. "We've already gone two years without a season that was part of our tradition, part of our living. We weren't looking for a season as it was three years ago, but still a reasonable season, which the government had promised us in no uncertain terms before accession to the EU."

I brought up the matter of illegal shooting, and Perici Calascione offered me a scotch. When I declined, he poured himself one. "We're completely against the illegal shooting of protected species," he said. "We're prepared to have hunting marshals in place to spot these individuals, and take away their membership. And this would have been in place, had we been given a good season." Perici Calascione conceded that he was uncomfortable with the more incendiary statements of the FKNK's general secretary, but he himself became visibly distressed as he tried to convey how much hunting mattered to him; he sounded strangely like a victimized environmentalist. "Everybody is frustrated," he said, with a tremor in his voice. "Psychiatric incidents have increased, we've had suicides among our membership—our culture is threatened."

Just how much Maltese-style shooting is a "culture" and a "tradition" is debatable. While spring hunting and the killing and taxidermy of rare birds are unquestionably traditions of long standing, the phenomenon of indiscriminate slaughter seems not to have arisen until the 1960s, when Malta achieved its independence and began to prosper. Malta, indeed, represents a stark refutation of the theory that a society's affluence leads to better environmental stewardship. Affluence in Malta brought more sophisticated weapons, more money to pay taxidermists, and more cars and better roads, which made the countryside more easily accessible to hunters. Where hunting had once been a tradition handed down from father to son, it now became the pastime of young men who went out in unruly groups.

On a piece of land belonging to a hotel that hopes to build a golf course on it, I met with an old-fashioned hunter who is disgusted with his countrymen's bad behavior and with the FKNK's tolerance of it. He told me that undisciplined shooting is in the Maltese "blood," and that it was unreasonable to expect hunters to suddenly change after the country joined the EU. ("If you were born of a prostitute," he said, "you won't become a nun.") But he also put much of the blame on younger hunters and said that Malta's lowering of the hunting age from twenty-one to eighteen had made matters worse. "And now that they've changed the spring-hunting law," he said, "law-abiding people can't go out, but the indiscriminate shooters still go out, because there's not enough law enforcement. I've been in the country for three weeks this spring, and I've seen one police car."

Spring was always the main hunting season in Malta, and the hunter said that if the season is closed permanently he will probably keep hunting in the fall only as long as his two dogs live, and then quit and be just a birdwatcher. "Something else is happening," he said. "Because where are the turtledoves? When I was young and going out with my father, we'd look up at the sky and see thousands of them. Now it's peak season, and I was out all day yesterday and saw twelve. I haven't seen a nightjar in two years. I haven't seen a rock thrush in five years. Last autumn, I went out every morning and afternoon looking for woodcock, with my dogs, and I saw three of them and didn't fire once. And that's part of the problem: people get frustrated. 'I don't find a woodcock, so let's shoot a kestrel.'"

Late on a Sunday afternoon, from a secluded height, Tolga Temuge and I used a telescope to spy on two men who were scanning the sky and fields with binoculars. "They're definitely hunters," Temuge said. "They keep their guns hidden until something comes by for them to shoot." But, as an hour passed and nothing came by, the men picked up rakes and began weeding a garden, only occasionally returning to their binoculars, and then another hour passed and they worked harder in the garden, because there were no birds.

Italy is a long, narrow gauntlet for a winged migrant to run. Poachers in Brescia, in the north, trap a million songbirds annually for sale to restaurants offering *pulenta e osei*—polenta with little birds. The woods of Sardinia are full of wire snares, the Venetian wetlands are a slaughtering ground for wintering ducks, and Umbria, the home of Saint Francis, has more registered hunters per capita than any other region. Hunters in Tuscany pursue their quotas of woodcock and wood pigeon and four legally shootable songbirds, including song thrush and skylark; but at dawn, in the mist, it's hard to distinguish legal from illegal quarry, and who's keeping track, anyway? To the south, in Campania, much of which is controlled by the Camorra (the local mafia), the most inviting habitat for migratory waterfowl and waders is in fields flooded by the Camorra and rented to hunters for up to a thousand euros a day; songbird wholesalers from Brescia bring down refrigerated trucks to collect the take from small-time poachers; entire Campanian provinces are blanketed with traps for seven tuneful European finch species, and flush Camorristi pay handsomely for well-trained singers at the illegal bird markets there. Farther south, in Calabria and Sicily, the highly publicized springtime hunting of migrating honey buzzards has been reduced by intensive law enforcement and volunteer monitoring, but Calabria, especially, is still full of poachers who, if they can get away with it, will shoot anything that flies.

A curious old statute in Italy's civil code, enacted by the Fascists to encourage familiarity with firearms, gives hunters, and only hunters, the right to enter private property, regardless of who owns it, in pursuit of game. By the 1980s, there were more than two million licensed hunters running wild in the Italian countryside, which had emptied out as the population flowed into the cities. Most urban Italians dislike hunting, however, and in 1992 the Italian parliament passed one of Europe's more restrictive hunting laws, which included, most radically, a declaration that all wild fauna belong exclusively to the Italian state, thereby reducing hunting to a special concession. In the two decades since then, the populations of some of Italy's most lovable megafauna, including wolves, have rebounded spectacularly, while the number of licensed hunters has fallen below eight hundred thousand. These two trends have prompted Franco Orsi, a Ligurian senator from Silvio Berlusconi's party, to propose a law that would liberalize the use of decoy birds and expand the times and places in which hunting is permitted. A second, "communitary" law, intended to bring Italy into compliance with the Birds Directive and thereby avoid hundreds of millions of euros in fines pending against it, has just been passed by the parliament and includes at least one clear victory for hunters: a shifting of the hunting season for certain bird species into February.

I met with Orsi at his party's offices in Genoa, on the eve of regional elections that brought fresh gains for Berlusconi's coalition. Orsi, a handsome, soft-eyed man in his forties, is a passionate hunter who chooses vacation destinations on the basis of what he can shoot in them. His argument for updating the 1992 law is that it has led to an explosive increase of harmful species; that Italian hunters should be allowed to do whatever French and Spanish hunters do; that private landowners could manage land for game better than the state does; and that hunting is a socially and spiritually beneficial activity. He showed me a newspaper picture of wild boar running down a Genoese street; he described the menace posed by starlings at airports and in vineyards. But when I agreed that controlling boar and starlings is a good idea, he went on to say that hunters don't like killing boar in the season the authorities want them to. "And, anyway, I can't accept that hunting is only for wild boar, nutria, and starlings," he said. "That's something the army can do."

I asked Orsi whether he favored hunting every bird species to the maximum compatible with sustaining existing numbers.

"Let's imagine fauna as capital that every year produces interest," he said. "If I spend the interest, I can still keep the capital, and the future of the species and of hunting will be preserved."

"But there's also the investment strategy of reinvesting part of the interest, to grow the capital," I said.

"That depends on each species. There's an optimal density for each one, and some have a density that's larger than optimal, others smaller. So hunting has to regulate the balance."

My impression, from earlier visits to Italy, was that its avian populations are pretty much all suboptimal. Since Orsi didn't seem to share it, I asked him how he thought hunting harmless birds benefited society. To my surprise, he quoted Peter Singer, the author of *Animal Liberation*, to the effect that, if every man had to kill the animals he eats, we would all be vegetarians. "In our urban society, we've lost the relationship between man and animal which has elements of violence," Orsi said. "When I was fourteen, my grandfather made me kill a chicken, which was the family tradition, and now every time I eat chicken I remember that it was an animal. To go back to Peter Singer, the overconsumption of animals in our society corresponds to an overconsumption of resources. Huge amounts of space are devoted to wasteful, industrialized farming, because we've lost a sense of rural identity. We shouldn't think that hunting is the only form of human violence against the environment. And hunting, in this sense, is educational."

I thought Orsi had a point, but, to the Italian environmentalists I spoke with, his rhetoric proved only that he was skilled at handling journalists. Behind the national push to liberalize hunting laws, the *ambientalisti* all see the hand of Italy's large arms and munitions industry. As one of them said to me, "When somebody asks you what your business produces, do you say, 'Land mines that blow up Bosnian children,' or do you say, 'Traditional shotguns for people who enjoy waiting at dawn in a wetland for the ducks to come'?"

It's impossible to know how many birds are shot in Italy. The annual reported take of song thrushes, for example, ranges from three million to seven million, but Fernando Spina, a senior scientist at Italy's environmental-protection agency, considers these numbers "hugely conservative," since only the most conscientious hunters fill out their game cards correctly, local game authorities lack the manpower to police the hunters, the provincial databases are largely uncomputerized, and most local Italian hunting authorities routinely ignore requests for data. What is known is that Italy is a crucial migratory flyway. Banded birds have been recovered there from every country in Europe, thirty-eight countries in Africa, and six in Asia. And return migration begins in Italy very early, in some cases as early as late December. The EU's Birds Directive protects all birds on return migration, permitting hunting only within limits of natural autumn mortality, and most responsible hunters therefore believe that the season should end on December 31. Italy's new communitary law goes the other way, however, and extends the season into February. Since early-return migrants tend to be the fittest of their species, the new law makes targets of precisely those birds with the best chance of breeding success. A longer season also shields poachers of protected species, because an illegal gunshot sounds just like a legal one. And without good data nobody can say whether a region's annual bag limit on a species falls within natural mortality. "The bag limit is an arbitrary number, set by local officials," Spina said. "It has no relation to actual census numbers."

Although habitat loss is the biggest reason that European bird populations are collapsing, Italian-style hunting (*caccia selvaggia*, "wild hunting," its detractors call it) adds particular insult to the injury. When I asked Fulco Pratesi, a former big-game hunter who founded WWF Italy and who now considers hunting "a mania," why Italian hunters are so wild to kill birds, he cited his countrymen's love of weapons, their attachment to an "attitude of virility," their delight in breaking laws, and, strangely, their love of being in nature. "It's like a rapist who loves women but expresses it in a violent and perverse way," Pratesi said. "Birds that weigh twenty-two grams are being shot with thirty-two-gram ammunition." Italians, he added, more easily feel affection for "symbolic" animals like wolves and bears, and have actually done a better job of protecting them than the rest of Europe has. "But birds are invisible," he said. "We don't see them, we don't hear them. In northern Europe, the arrival of migrating birds is visible and audible, and it moves people. Here, people live in cities and large housing complexes, and birds are literally up in the air."

For most of its history, Italy was visited every spring and fall by unimaginable numbers of packets of flying protein, and, unlike in northern Europe, where people learned to see the correlation between overharvesting and diminishing returns, supplies seemed limitless in the Mediterranean. A poacher from Reggio di Calabria, still bitter about being forbidden to shoot honey buzzards, said to me, "We were only killing about twenty-five hundred a spring in Reggio, out of a total passage of sixty to a hundred thousand—it wasn't a big deal." The only way he could understand the banning of his sport was in terms of money. He told me, in all seriousness, that certain organizations that wanted to tap into state money had set themselves up as antipoachers, and that it was their need for poachers to oppose which had led to the writing of antipoaching laws. "And now these people are getting rich with money from the state," he explained.

In one of the southern provinces, I got to know an impishly boyish ex-poacher named Sergio. He'd been well into middle age before giving up poaching, feeling that he'd finally outgrown that stage of life, and he now tells stories of his "sins of youth" for comic effect. Going hunting at night was always illegal but never a problem, Sergio said, if your poaching companions were the parish priest and the brigadier of the local carabinieri. The brigadier was especially helpful in discouraging forest rangers from patrolling in their neighborhood. One night, when Sergio was out hunting with him, they froze a barn owl in the head-lights of the brigadier's jeep. The brigadier told Sergio to shoot it. When Sergio demurred, the brigadier took out a shovel, walked around behind the owl, and whacked it on the head. Then he put it in the rear compartment of the jeep.

"Why?" I asked Sergio. "Why did he want to kill the owl?"

"Because we were poaching!"

At the end of the night, when the brigadier opened the rear compartment, the owl, which had only been stunned, flew up and attacked him—Sergio spread his arms and made a ridicu-lously ferocious face to show me how.

For Sergio, the point of poaching had always been eating. He taught me a rhyme in his local dialect which approximately translates: *For meat of the feather, eat a crow; for a heart that's kind, love a crone.* "You can cook crow for six days, and it's still tough," he told me. "But it's not bad in a broth. I also ate badger and fox—I ate everything." The only bird that no Italian seems interested in eating is the seagull. Even the honey buzzard, although southern families traditionally kept one specimen stuffed and mounted in the best room of their house (its local nickname is *adorno*, for "adornment"), was eaten as a springtime treat; the poacher in Reggio gave me his recipe for fricasseeing it with sugar and vinegar.

Italian wild hunters who, unlike Sergio, haven't outgrown the pursuit, and who are frustrated by declining game populations and increasing state restrictions, have learned to go elsewhere in the Mediterranean for a thrill. On the Campanian seacoast, I spoke with a gap-toothed, gleefully unrepentant young-old poacher who, now that he can no longer set up a blind on the beach and shoot unlimited numbers of arriving migrants, contents himself with looking forward to vacations in Albania, where you can still shoot as much as you can find of whatever you want, whenever you want, for a very low fee. Although hunters from all nations go abroad, the Italians are widely considered to be the worst. The wealthiest of them go to Siberia to shoot woodcock during their springtime display flights, or to Egypt, where, I was told, you can hire a local police officer to fetch your kills while you shoot ibises and globally threatened duck species until your arms are tired; there are pictures on the Internet of visiting hunters standing beside meter-high piles of bird carcasses.

The responsible hunters in Italy hate the wild ones; they hate Franco Orsi. "We have a culture clash in Italy between two visions of hunting," Massimo Canale, a young hunter in Reggio di Calabria, told me. "One side, Orsi's side, says, 'Let's just open it up.' On the other side are people with a sense of responsibility for where they live. To become a selective hunter, you need more than just a license. You need to study biology, physics, ballistics. You become selective for boar and deer—you have a role to play."

Canale discovered his predatory instinct as a child, while hunting indiscriminately with his grandfather, and he feels fortunate to have met people who taught him a better way. "I don't mind not killing something on any given day," he said, "but killing is the goal, and I'd be lying if I said it wasn't. I have a conflict between my predatory instinct and my rationality, and my way of trying to tame my instinct is through selective hunting. In my opinion, it's the only way to hunt in 2010. And Orsi doesn't know or care about it."

The two visions of hunting correspond broadly to Italy's two faces. There's the frankly criminal Italy of the Camorra and its allies and the quasi-criminal Italy of Berlusconi's cronies, but there is also, still, *l'Italia che lavora*—"the Italy that works [i.e., labors]." The Italians who combat poaching are motivated by disgust with their country's lawlessness, and they rely heavily on tips from responsible hunters, like Canale, who become frustrated when, for example, they're unable to find quail to shoot because all the birds have been attracted to illegal recordings. In Salerno, the least disorderly of Campania's provinces, I joined a squad of WWF guards who took me out to an artificial pond, now drained, where they had recently stalked the president of a regional hunters' association and caught him illegally using electronic recordings to attract birds. Looming near the pond, amid fields rendered desolate by white plastic crop covers, was a disintegrating mountain of "ecoballs"—shrink-wrapped bales of Neapolitan garbage that had been dumped all over the Campanian countryside and become a symbol of Italy's environmental crisis. "It was the second time in two years that we'd caught the guy," the squad leader said. "He was part of the committee that regulates hunting in the region, and he'd remained president in spite of having been charged. There are other regional presidents who do the same thing but are harder to catch."

One shining example of the Italy that works has been the suppression of honey-buzzard poaching at the Strait of Messina. Every year since 1985, the national forest police have assigned an extra team with helicopters to patrol the Calabrian side of the Strait. Although the Calabrian situation has lately deteriorated somewhat—this year's team was smaller than in the past and stayed for fewer days, and the estimated death toll was four hundred, double the number in recent years—the Sicilian side of the Strait is the domain of a famous crusader, Anna Giordano, and remains essentially free of poachers. Beginning as a fifteen-year-old, in 1981, Giordano undertook surveillance of the concrete blinds from which raptors were being shot by the thousands as they sailed in low over the mountains above Messina. Unlike the Calabrians, who ate the buzzards, the Sicilians shot purely for the sake of tradition, for competition with one another, and for trophies. Some of them shot everything; others restricted themselves to honey buzzard ("The Bird," they called it) unless they saw a real rarity, like golden eagle. Giordano hurried from the blinds to the nearest pay phone, from which she summoned the forest police, and then back to the blinds. Although her cars were vandalized, and although she was constantly threatened and vilified, she was never physically harmed, probably because she was a young woman. (The Italian word for "bird," *uccello*, is also slang for "penis" and lent itself to dirty jibes about her, but a poster I saw on the wall of her office flipped these jibes around: "Your Virility? A Dead Bird.") With increasing success, especially after the advent of cell phones, Giordano compelled the forest police to crack down on the poachers, and her growing fame brought media attention and legions of volunteers. In recent years, her teams have reported seasonal gunshot totals in the single digits.

"In the early years," Giordano said when I joined her on a

hilltop to look at passing hawks, "we didn't even dare raise our binoculars when we were counting raptors, because the poachers would watch us and start shooting if they saw us looking at something. Our logs from back then show lots of 'unidentified raptors.' And now we can stand up here all afternoon, comparing the markings of first-calendar-year female harriers, and not hear a shot. A couple of years ago, one of the worst poachers, a violent, stupid, vulgar guy who'd always been in our face wherever we went, drove up to me and asked if we could talk. I was, like, 'Heh-heh-heh-heh, okay.' He asked me if I remembered what I'd said to him twenty-five years ago. I said I couldn't remember what I said yesterday. He said, 'You said the day would come when I would love the birds instead of killing them. I just came up here to tell you you were right. I used to say to my son, when we were going out, "Have you got the gun?" Now I say, "Have you got the binoculars?"' And I handed him my own binoculars—to a poacher!—so he could see a honey buzzard that was flying over."

Giordano is small, dark, and zealous. She has lately been attacking the local government for failing to regulate housing development around Messina, and, as if to ensure that she has too much to do, she also helps operate a wildlife rescue center. I'd already visited one Italian animal hospital, on the grounds of a shuttered psychiatric hospital in Naples, and seen an X-ray of a hawk heavily dotted with lead shot, several recovering raptors in large cages, and a seagull whose left leg was blackened and shriveled from having stepped in acid. At Giordano's center, on a hill behind Messina, I watched her feed scraps of raw turkey to a small eagle that had been blinded by a shotgun pellet. She grasped the eagle's taloned legs in one hand and cradled the bird against her belly. Its tail feathers sadly bedraggled, its gaze stern but impotent, it suffered her to open its bill and stuff in meat until its gullet bulged. The bird seemed to me at once all eagle and no longer an eagle at all. I didn't know what it was.

Like most Cypriot restaurants that serve *ambelopoulia*, the one I went to with a friend and a friend of his (I'll call them Takis and Demetrios) had a small private dining room in which the little birds could be consumed discreetly. We walked through the main room, in which a TV was blaring one of the Brazilian soap operas that are popular in Cyprus, and sat down to an onslaught of Cypriot specialties: smoked pork, fried cheese, pickled caper twigs, wild asparagus and mushrooms with eggs, wine-soaked sausage, couscous. The proprietor also brought us three fried song thrushes, which we hadn't asked for, and hovered by our table as if to make sure I ate mine. I thought of Saint Francis, who had set aside his sympathy for animals once a year, on Christmas, and eaten meat. I thought of a kid named Woody, who, on a backpacking trip I'd taken as a teenager, had given me a bite of fried robin. I thought of a prominent Italian conservationist who'd admitted to me that song thrushes are "bloody tasty." The conservationist was right. The meat was dark and richly flavorful, and the bird was enough bigger than an *ambelopoulia* that I could think of it as ordinary restaurant food, more or less, and of myself as an ordinary consumer.

After the proprietor went away, I asked Takis and Demetrios what kind of Cypriots like to eat *ambelopoulia*.

"The people who do it a lot," Demetrios said, "are the same ones who go to cabarets, the lounges where there's pole dancing and Eastern European girls who make themselves available. In other words, people with not a high level of morality. Which is to say, most Cypriots. There's a saying here, 'Whatever you can stuff your mouth with, whatever your ass can grab—'"

"I.e., because life is short," Takis said.

"People come to Cyprus and think they're in a European country, because we belong to the EU," Demetrios said. "In fact, we're a Middle Eastern country that's part of Europe by accident."

The night before, at the Paralimni police station, I'd given a statement to a young detective who seemed to want me to say that the attackers of the CABS team had only been trying to get the team to stop taking pictures and video of them. "For people here," the detective explained when we were done, "it's a tradition to trap birds, and you can't change that overnight. Trying to talk to them and explain why it's wrong is more helpful than the aggressive approach of CABS." He may have been right, but I'd been hearing the same plea for patience all over the Mediterranean, and it was sounding to me like a version of modern consumerism's more general plea regarding nature: Just wait until we've used up everything, and then you nature lovers can have what's left.

While Takis and Demetrios and I waited for the dozen *ambelopoulia* that were coming, we argued about who was going to eat them. "Maybe I'll take one small bite," I said.

"I don't even like *ambelopoulia*," Takis said.

"Neither do I," Demetrios said.

"Okay," I said. "How about if I take two and you each take five?"

They shook their heads.

Dismayingly soon, the proprietor returned with a plate. In the room's harsh light, the *ambelopoulia* looked like a dozen little gleaming yellowish-gray turds. "You're the first American I've ever served," the proprietor said. "I've had lots of Russians, but never an American." I put one on my plate, and the proprietor told me that eating it was the same as taking two Viagras.

When we were alone again, my field of vision shrank to a few inches, the way it had when I'd dissected a frog in ninth-grade biology. I made myself eat the two almond-size breast muscles, which were the only obvious meat; the rest was greasy cartilage and entrail and tiny bones. I couldn't tell whether the meat's bitterness was real or the product of emotion, the killing of a blackcap's enchantment. Takis and Demetrios were making short work of their eight birds, taking clean bones from their mouths and exclaiming that *ambelopoulia* were much better than they remembered; were rather good, in fact. I trashed a second bird and then, feeling somewhat sick, wrapped my remaining two in a paper napkin and put them in my pocket. The proprietor returned and asked if I'd enjoyed the birds.

"Mm!" I said.

"If you hadn't asked for them"—this in a regretful tone—"I think you really would have liked the lamb tonight."

I made no reply, but now, as if satisfied by my complicity, the proprietor became talkative: "Young kids today don't like to eat them. It used to start young, and you'd get used to the taste. My toddler can eat ten at a time."

Takis and Demetrios exchanged skeptical glances.

"It's a shame they've been outlawed," the proprietor went on, "because they used to be a great tourist attraction. Now it's become almost like the drug trade. A dozen of them cost me sixty euros. These damned foreigners come and take down the nets and destroy them, and we've surrendered to them. Trapping *ambelopoulia* used to be one of the few ways people around here could make a good living."

Outside, by the edge of the restaurant parking lot, near some bushes in which I'd earlier heard *ambelopoulia* singing, I knelt down and scraped a hole in the dirt with my fingers. The world was feeling especially empty of meaning, and the best I could do to fight this feeling was to unwrap the two dead birds from the napkin, put them in the hole, and tamp some dirt down on them. Then Takis led me to a nearby tavern with medium-size birds grilling on charcoal outside. It was a sort of poor man's cabaret, and as soon as we'd ordered beers at the bar one of the hostesses, a heavy-legged blonde from Moldova, pulled up a stool behind us.

The blue of the Mediterranean isn't pretty to me anymore. The clarity of its water, prized by vacationers, is the clarity of a sterile swimming pool. There are few smells on its beaches, and few birds, and its depths are on their way to being empty; much of the fish now consumed in Europe comes illegally, no questions asked, from the ocean west of Africa. I look at the blue and see not a sea but a postcard, paper thin.

And yet it is the Mediterranean, specifically Italy, that gave us the poet Ovid, who in the *Metamorphoses* deplored the eating of animals, and the vegetarian Leonardo da Vinci, who envisioned a day when the life of an animal would be valued as highly as that of a person, and Saint Francis, who once petitioned the Holy Roman Emperor to scatter grain on fields on Christmas Day and give the crested larks a feast. For Saint Francis, the crested larks, whose drab brown plumage and peaked head feathers resemble the hooded brown robes of his Friars Minor, his Little Brothers, were a model for his order: wandering, as light as air, and saving up nothing, just gleaning their daily minimum of food, and always singing, singing. He addressed them as his Sister Larks. Once, by the side of an Umbrian road, he preached to the local birds, which are said to have gathered around him quietly and listened with a look of understanding, and then chastised himself for not having thought to preach to them sooner. Another time, when he wanted to preach to human beings, a flock of swallows was chattering noisily, and he said to them, either angrily or politely—the sources are unclear—"Sister Swallows, you've had your say. Now be quiet and let me have my say." According to the legend, the swallows immediately fell silent.

I visited the site of the Sermon to the Birds with a Franciscan friar, Guglielmo Spirito, who is also a passionate amateur Tolkien scholar. "Even as a child," Guglielmo said, "I knew that if I ever joined the Church it would be as a Franciscan. The main thing that attracted me, when I was young, was his relationship with animals. To me the lesson of Saint Francis is the same as that of fairy tales: that oneness with nature is not only desirable but possible. He's an example of wholeness regained, wholeness actually within our reach." There was no intimation of wholeness at the little shrine, across a busy road from a Vulcangas station, that now commemorates the Sermon to the Birds; I could hear a few crows cawing and tits twittering, but mostly just the roar of passing cars and trucks and farm equipment.

Back in Assisi, however, Guglielmo took me to two other Franciscan sites that felt more enchanted. One was the Sacred Hut, the crude stone building in which Saint Francis and his first followers had lived in voluntary poverty and invented a brotherhood. The other was the tiny chapel of Santa Maria degli Angeli, outside which, in the night, as Saint Francis lay dying, his sister larks are said to have circled and sung. Both structures are now entirely enclosed by later, larger, more ornate churches; one of the architects, some pragmatic Italian, had seen fit to plant a fat marble column in the middle of the Sacred Hut.

Nobody since Jesus has lived a life more radically in keeping with his gospel than Saint Francis did; and Saint Francis, unburdened by the weight of being the Messiah, went Jesus one better and extended his gospel to all creation. It seemed to me that if wild birds survive in modern Europe it will be in the manner of those ancient small Franciscan buildings, sheltered by the structures of a vain and powerful Church: as beloved exceptions to its rule.

THE CORN KING

[on Donald Antrim's The Hundred Brothers*]*

------►

THE COLOSSUS

The Hundred Brothers is possibly the strangest novel ever published by an American. Its author, Donald Antrim, is arguably more unlike any other living writer than any other living writer. And yet, paradoxically—in much the same way that the novel's narrator, Doug, is at once the most singular of his father's hundred sons and the one who most profoundly expresses the sorrows and desires and neuroses of the other ninety-nine—*The Hundred Brothers* is also the most representative of novels. It speaks like none of us for all of us.

Midway through his narrative, Doug spells out the fundamental fact that drives it: "I love my brothers and I hate their guts." The beauty of the novel is that Antrim has created a narrator who reproduces, in the reader, the same volatile mixture of feelings regarding the narrator himself: Doug is at once irresistibly lovable and unbearably frustrating. The genius of the novel is that it maps these contradictory feelings onto the archetypal figure of the scapegoat: the exemplary sufferer who recurs throughout human history, most notably in the person of Jesus of Nazareth, as an object of both love and homicidal rage, and who must be ritually killed in order for the rest of us to go on living with the contradictions in our lesser hearts.

In modern times, the role of the exemplary sufferer has come to be played by artists. Nonartists depend on and cherish artists for giving pleasing form to the central experiences of being human. At the same time, artists are resented, sometimes even homicidally, for the dubiety of their moral character and for bringing to consciousness painful truths that nonartists prefer to remain unconscious of. Artists will drive you crazy, and *The Hundred Brothers* is a perfect instance of the work of art that seduces you with its beauty and power and then maddens you with its craziness. It's often hilarious, but there's always a dangerous edge to the hilarity. When, for example, Doug is describing the complicated seating chart for the dinner table at which he and ninety-eight of his brothers gather in a scene reminiscent of the Last Supper, he notes that his own name, unlike all the others, is written in "bright orange," and that he's "never been able to figure out the logic behind this." The orange writing recalls the fire that several brothers are building in the book's opening pages and the flames that illuminate the primitive ritual with which the book closes; the color targets Doug like a hunted animal. And the whole comedy of his situation—he simultaneously knows and resists knowing that he's his brothers' beloved and hated scapegoat—is encapsulated in his putative inability to "figure out the logic." Is the logic that Doug is the family's devoted genealogist, the former star quarterback of the family football team, the trustworthy listener to whom others turn with questions about God, and the brother who nurses his psychically and physically wounded brothers at the expense of his own needs? Or is it (as his narrative gradually and comically reveals) that Doug is a chronic liar and an unrepentant thief of his brothers' drugs and money, has a penchant for drinking too much and misbehaving, nurtures a bizarre fetish for his brothers' footwear, and once, as the quarterback in a crucial game, fumbled away the football in his own endzone? Or is it (as seems most likely) that Doug is the family artist, the outsider who is also the family's deepest insider, the brother who has taken it upon himself to annually assume the role of Corn King and perform "the nocturnal dance of death and the life that grows out of death"?

The Hundred Brothers speaks for all of us because we all inescapably feel ourselves to be the special center of our private worlds. It's a funny novel and a sad novel because this natural solipsism of ours is belied—rendered both ridiculous and tragic—by our ties of love and kinship to private worlds that we are necessarily not the center of.

At the level of technique, the book is a marvel: *has* to be a marvel, for, without supreme authorial control of scene and sentence and detail, it would collapse under the weight of its preposterous premise. In the opening sentence, Antrim manages to name and specify, through the magic of his commas and semicolons and dashes and parentheses, all ninety-nine of the brothers who have come together for drinks and dinner, bad masculine behavior, and avoidance of the work of giving their father's funeral ashes a proper burial. (This opening sentence also contains the book's first and last reference to a particular woman, Jane, who is responsible for the disappearance of the hundredth brother; it's as if, according to the novel's logic, the mere naming of a Significant Other is enough to exclude a brother from the narrative.) The story takes place entirely in the enormous library of the family's ancestral mansion, from the windows of which the campfires of homeless people can be seen in the "forlorn valley" outside the property's walls, and the action is confined to a single night, punctuated here and there by glimpses of the family's history of brother-on-brother cruelty and violence. (Doug's recollection of the childhood game of Kill the Man with the Ball, a game that embodies the love/hatred between siblings and prefigures their latter-day scapegoating ritual, is particularly inspired.) The incidents that occur on this single night are often farcical, often frustrating to Doug and to the reader, and always intensely vivid and specific. Taken together, they amount to a dexterous feat of choreography, in which Doug, the self-appointed Corn King, is the lead dancer who engages all the others as he makes his way around the library.

The novel is a feat of exclusion and inclusion, too. Left out of it are women (including, especially, the brothers' mother or mothers), children, any reference to a particular place or year, and any realistic accounting of how there came to be so many brothers, how they all fit into a single house, and what their lives outside the house are like. Within these fantastical confines, however, can be found a remarkably complete catalogue of the things that men do and feel among men. Football, fisticuffs, food fights, chess playing, bullying, gambling, hunting, drinking, pornography, pranking, philanthropy, power tools ("Doug, I need my belt-sander back," the brother Angus says in passing), homosexual cruising, anxieties about incontinence and penis size and middle-age weight gain: it's all there. The book also, despite its brevity, contains a deftly telescoped genealogy of human knowledge and experience, reaching from prehistory up through a very belated present day in which civilization seems to be teetering at the brink of collapse. Just as a vast collection of books and periodicals on every subject and from every era is housed in a single leaky and neglected library, so the totality of human archetypes ("the primeval aspects of the Self," in Doug's phrase) are gathered together in the single heroic, failing consciousness of the narrator.

When the brothers are all seated at the dinner table, one of them makes a call for better maintenance of the library: "As some of you may know, a slow drip, directly over Philosophy of Mind, has recently waterlogged and destroyed seventy to eighty percent of Cognitive Theory." As in some kind of nightmare of paralysis, however, the brothers are able only to notice the library's decay, not seriously combat it. Chandelier lights flicker, rainwater pours in, bats fly around, furniture is broken, food scraps are ground into once-valuable carpets. The entire novel is shadowed by the insight, or fear, or premonition, that postmodernity doesn't lead us forward but backward to the primitive: that our huge and hard-won sum of knowledge will ultimately prove useless and be lost. Already in the book's early pages, describing the eighteenth-century pornography that some of the married brothers are huddled over, Doug has intimations of this loss. "The Age of Enlightenment's inattention to hygiene is well documented," he remarks. "A certain syphilitic degeneracy lurks in these bookplate etchings of rheumy aristocrats making doggy love with their hats on." In the latter half of the novel, the intimations of decay become a drumbeat, culminating in the brilliant scene in which Doug himself ecstatically, with his urine, amid the shelved works of Liberal Theologians, Antiquaries, and Bibliographers, "hoses down, as they say, a few literary masterpieces." In the despair that grips Doug after this ecstatic moment, the dissolution of the library becomes increasingly indistinguishable from what's happening to him. The man has become the world, the world has become the man; the solipsism is complete; the narrative has gone fully mad.

The craziness of *The Hundred Brothers* derives from its willingness to embrace, even celebrate, the dark fact that an individual's life consists, finally, of an accelerating march toward decay and death. The novel is a Dionysian dream in which nothing, not even sanity, can escape the corrosive chaos of this circumstance; but its form is bravely Apollonian. It renders lonely solipsism universal and humane by way of rite and archetype and artistic excellence. What Nick Carraway says about his friend Jay Gatsby could also be said of the scapegoat Doug: he turns out all right at the end. The rest of us, his brothers and sisters, awaken from the harrowing dream refreshed and better able, as Doug says with equal parts of irony and hope, to "prosper and thrive."

ON AUTOBIOGRAPHICAL
FICTION

[lecture]

-------▶

I'm going to begin by addressing four unpleasant questions that novelists often get asked at an event like this. These questions are apparently the price we have to pay for the pleasure of appearing in public. They're maddening not just because we're asked them so often but also because, with one exception, they're difficult to answer and, therefore, very much worth asking.

The first of these perennial questions is: *Who are your influences?*

Sometimes the person asking this question merely wants some book recommendations, but all too often the question seems to be intended seriously. And part of what annoys me about it is that it's always asked in the present tense: Who *are* my influences? The fact is, at this point in my life, I'm mostly influenced by my own past writing. If I were still laboring in the shadow of, say, E. M. Forster, I would certainly be at pains to pretend that I wasn't. According to Mr. Harold Bloom, whose clever theory of literary influence helped him make a career of distinguishing "weak" writers from "strong" writers, I wouldn't even be conscious of the degree to which I was still laboring in E. M. Forster's shadow. Only Harold Bloom would be fully conscious of that.

Direct influence makes sense only with very young writers, who, in the course of figuring out how to write, first try copying the styles and attitudes and methods of their favorite authors.

I personally was very influenced, at the age of twenty-one, by C. S. Lewis, Isaac Asimov, Louise Fitzhugh, Herbert Marcuse, P. G. Wodehouse, Karl Kraus, my then-fiancée, and *The Dialectic of Enlightenment*, by Max Horkheimer and Theodor Adorno. For a while, in my early twenties, I put a lot of effort into copying the sentence rhythms and comic dialogue of Don DeLillo; I was also very taken with the strenuously vivid and all-knowing prose of Robert Coover and Thomas Pynchon. And the plots of my first two novels were substantially borrowed from two movies, *The American Friend* (by Wim Wenders) and *Cutter's Way* (by Ivan Passer). But to me these various "influences" seem not much more meaningful than the fact that, when I was fifteen, my favorite music group was the Moody Blues. A writer has to begin somewhere, but where exactly he or she begins is almost random.

It would be somewhat more meaningful to say that I was influenced by Franz Kafka. By this I mean that it was Kafka's novel *The Trial*, as taught by the best literature professor I ever had, that opened my eyes to the greatness of what literature can do, and made me want to try to create some literature myself. Kafka's brilliantly ambiguous rendering of Josef K., who is at once a sympathetic and unjustly persecuted Everyman and a self-pitying and guilt-denying criminal, was my portal to the possibilities of fiction as a vehicle of self-investigation: as a method of engagement with the difficulties and paradoxes of my own life. Kafka teaches us how to love ourselves even as we're being merciless toward ourselves; how to remain humane in the face of the most awful truths about ourselves. It's not enough to love your characters, and it's not enough to be hard on your characters: you always have to try to be doing both at the same time. The stories that recognize people as they really are—the books whose characters are at once sympathetic subjects and dubious objects—are the ones capable of reaching across cultures and generations. This is why we still read Kafka.

The bigger problem with the question about influences, however, is that it seems to presuppose that young writers are lumps of soft clay on which certain great writers, dead or living, have indelibly left their mark. And what maddens the writer trying to answer the question honestly is that almost everything a writer has ever *read* leaves some kind of mark. To list every writer I've learned something from would take me hours, and it still wouldn't account for why some books matter to me so much more than other books: why, even now, when I'm working, I often think about *The Brothers Karamazov* and *The Man Who Loved Children* and never about *Ulysses* or *To the Lighthouse*. How did it happen that I did *not* learn anything from Joyce or Woolf, even though they're both obviously "strong" writers?

The common understanding of influence, whether Harold Bloomian or more conventional, is far too linear and one-directional. Art history, with its progressive narrative of influences handed down from generation to generation, is a useful pedagogical tool for organizing information, but it has very little to do with the actual experience of being a fiction writer. When I write, I don't feel like a craftsman influenced by earlier craftsmen who were themselves influenced by earlier craftsmen. I feel like a member of a single, large virtual community in which I have dynamic relationships with other members of the community, most of whom are no longer living. As in any other community, I have my friends and I have my enemies. I find my way to those corners of the world of fiction where I feel most at home, most securely but also provocatively among my friends. Once I've read enough books to have identified who these friends are—and this is where the young writer's process of active *selection*

comes in, the process of *choosing* whom to be "influenced" by—
I work to advance our common interests. By means of what I
write and how I write, I fight for my friends and I fight against
my enemies. I want more readers to appreciate the glory of the
nineteenth-century Russians; I'm indifferent to whether readers
love James Joyce; and my work represents an active campaign
against the values I dislike: sentimentality, weak narrative, overly
lyrical prose, solipsism, self-indulgence, misogyny and other
parochialisms, sterile game playing, overt didacticism, moral
simplicity, unnecessary difficulty, informational fetishes, and so
on. Indeed, much of what might be called actual "influence" is
negative: I don't want to be like this writer or that writer.

The situation is never static, of course. Reading and writing
fiction is a form of active social engagement, of conversation
and competition. It's a way of being and becoming. Somehow,
at the right moment, when I'm feeling particularly lost and forlorn, there's always a new friend to be made, an old friend to
distance myself from, an old enemy to be forgiven, a new enemy
to be identified. Indeed—and I'll say more about this later—it's
impossible for me to write a new novel without first finding
new friends and enemies. To start writing *The Corrections*, I befriended Kenzaburo Oe, Paula Fox, Halldór Laxness, and Jane
Smiley. With *Freedom*, I found new allies in Stendhal, Tolstoy,
and Alice Munro. For a while, Philip Roth was my new bitter
enemy, but lately, unexpectedly, he has become a friend as well.
I still campaign against *American Pastoral*, but when I finally got
around to reading *Sabbath's Theater* its fearlessness and ferocity
became an inspiration. It had been a long time since I'd felt as
grateful to a writer as I did when reading the scene in *Sabbath's
Theater* where Mickey Sabbath's best friend catches him in the
bathtub holding a picture of the friend's adolescent daughter and
a pair of her underpants, or the scene in which Sabbath finds a

paper coffee cup in the pocket of his army jacket and decides to abase himself by begging for money in the subway. Roth may not want to have me as a friend, but I was happy, at those moments, to claim him as one of mine. I'm happy to hold up the savage hilarity of *Sabbath's Theater* as a correction and reproach of the sentimentality of certain young American writers and not-so-young critics who seem to believe, in defiance of Kafka, that literature is about being nice.

The second perennial question is: *What time of day do you work, and what do you write on?*

This must seem, to the people who ask it, like the safest and politest of questions. I suspect that it's the question people ask a writer when they can't think of anything else to ask. And yet to me it's the most disturbingly personal and invasive of questions. It forces me to picture myself sitting down at my computer every morning at eight o'clock: to see objectively the person who, as he sits down at his computer in the morning, wants only to be a pure, invisible subjectivity. When I'm working, I don't want anybody else in the room, including myself.

Question No. 3 is: *I read an interview with an author who says that, at a certain point in writing a novel, the characters "take over" and tell him what to do. Does this happen to you, too?*

This one always raises my blood pressure. Nobody ever answered it better than Nabokov did in his *Paris Review* interview, where he fingered E. M. Forster as the source of the myth about a novelist's characters "taking over," and claimed that, unlike Forster, who let his characters sail away on their passage to India, he himself worked his characters "like galley slaves." The question obviously raised Nabokov's blood pressure, too.

When a writer makes a claim like Forster's, the best-case scenario is that he's mistaken. More often, unfortunately, I catch a whiff of self-aggrandizement, as if the writer were trying to distance his work from the mechanistic plotting of genre novels. The writer would like us to believe that, unlike those hacks who can tell you in advance how their books are going to end, *his* imagination is so powerful, and *his* characters so real and vivid, that he has no control over them. The best case here, again, is that it isn't true, because the notion presupposes a loss of authorial will, an abdication of intent. The novelist's primary responsibility is to create meaning, and if you could somehow leave this job to your characters you would necessarily be avoiding it yourself.

But let's assume, for charity's sake, that the writer who claims to be the servant of his characters isn't simply flattering himself. What might he actually mean? He probably means that, once a character has been fleshed out enough to begin to form a coherent whole, a kind of inevitability has been set in motion. He means, specifically, that the story he originally imagined for a character often turns out not to follow from the lineaments of the character he's been able to create. I may abstractly imagine a character whom I intend to make a murderer of his girlfriend, only to discover, in the actual writing, that the character I'm able to make actually work on the page has too much compassion or self-awareness to be a murderer. The key phrase here is "work on the page." Everything under the sun is imaginable and proposable in the abstract. But the writer is always limited by what he or she is actually able to make work: to make plausible, to make readable, to make sympathetic, to make entertaining, to make compelling, and, above all, to make distinctive and original. As Flannery O'Connor famously said, the fiction writer does whatever she can get away with—"and nobody ever got away with much." Once you start writing the book, as opposed to planning it, the universe of conceivable human types and behaviors shrinks drastically to the microcosm of human possibilities that you contain within yourself. A character dies on the page if you can't hear his or her voice. In a very limited sense, I suppose, this amounts to "taking over" and "telling you" what the character will and won't do. But the reason the character can't do something is that *you* can't. The task then becomes to figure out what the character *can* do—to try to stretch the narrative as far as possible, to be sure not to overlook exciting possibilities in yourself, while continuing to bend the narrative in the direction of meaning.

Which brings me to perennial question No. 4: *Is your fiction autobiographical?*

I'm suspicious of any novelist who would honestly answer no to this question, and yet my strong temptation, when I'm asked it myself, is to answer no. Of the four perennial questions, this is the one that always feels the most hostile. Maybe I'm just projecting that hostility, but I feel as if my powers of imagination are being challenged. As in: "Is this a true work of fiction, or just a thinly disguised account of your own life? And since there are only so many things that can happen to you in your life, you're surely going to use up all of your autobiographical material soon—if, indeed, you haven't used it up already!—and so you probably won't be writing any more good books, will you? In fact, if your books are just thinly disguised autobiography, maybe they weren't as interesting as we thought they were? Because, after all, what makes your life so much more interesting than anybody else's? It's not as interesting as Barack Obama's life, is it? And also, for that matter, if your work is autobiographical, why didn't you do the honest thing and write a non-fiction account of it? Why dress it up in lies? What kind of bad person are you, telling us lies to try to make your life seem more interesting and dramatic?" I hear all of these other questions in the question, and before long the very word *autobiographical* feels shameful to me.

My own strict understanding of an autobiographical novel is one in which the main character closely resembles the author and experiences many of the same scenes that the author experienced in real life. My impression is that *A Farewell to Arms*, *All Quiet on the Western Front*, *Villette*, *The Adventures of Augie March*, and *The Man Who Loved Children*—all of them masterpieces—are substantially autobiographical in this regard. But most novels, interestingly, are not. My own novels are not. In thirty years, I don't think I've published more than twenty or thirty pages of scenes drawn directly from real-life events that I participated in. I've actually tried to write a lot more pages than that, but these scenes rarely seem to work in a novel. They embarrass me, or they don't seem interesting enough, or, most frequently, they don't seem quite relevant to the story I'm trying to tell. Late in *The Corrections*, there's a scene in which Denise Lambert—who resembles me to the extent of being a youngest child—tries to teach her demented father how to do some simple stretching exercises, and then has to deal with his having wet the bed. That actually happened to me, and I took a number of the details straight from my life. Some of what Chip Lambert experiences when he's with his father in the hospital also happened to me. And I did write an entire short memoir, *The Discomfort Zone*, which consists almost entirely of scenes that I experienced firsthand. But that was nonfiction, and so I ought to be able to answer the perennial autobiography question with a resounding, unashamed NO. Or at least to answer, as my friend Elisabeth Robinson does, "Yes, seventeen percent. Next question, please?"

The problem is that, in another sense, my fiction is extremely autobiographical, and, moreover, that I consider it my job as a writer to make it ever more so. My conception of a novel is that it ought to be a personal struggle, a direct and total engagement with the author's story of his or her own life. This conception, again, I take from Kafka, who, although he was never transformed into an insect, and although he never had a piece of food (an apple from his family's table!) lodged in his flesh and rotting there, devoted his whole life as a writer to describing his personal struggle with his family, with women, with moral law, with his Jewish heritage, with his Unconscious, with his sense of guilt, and with the modern world. Kafka's work, which grows out of the nighttime dreamworld in Kafka's brain, is *more* autobiographical than any realistic retelling of his daytime experiences at the office or with his family or with a prostitute could have been. What is fiction, after all, if not a kind of purposeful dreaming? The writer works to create a dream that is vivid and has meaning, so that the reader can then vividly dream it and experience meaning. And work like Kafka's, which seems to proceed directly from dream, is therefore an exceptionally pure form of autobiography. There's an important paradox here that I would like to stress: the greater the autobiographical content of a fiction writer's work, the *smaller* its superficial resemblance to the writer's actual life. The deeper the writer digs for meaning, the more the random particulars of the writer's life become *impediments* to deliberate dreaming.

And this is why writing good fiction is almost never easy. The point at which fiction seems to become easy for a writer—and I'll let everyone supply his or her own examples of this—is usually the point at which it's no longer necessary to read that writer. There's a truism, at least in the United States, that every person has one novel in him. In other words, one autobiographical novel. For people who write more than one, the truism can probably be amended to say: every person has one easy-to-write novel in him, one ready-made meaningful narrative. I'm obviously not talking here about writers of entertainments, not P. G. Wodehouse or Elmore Leonard, the pleasure of whose books is not diminished by their similarity to one another; we read them, indeed, for the reliable comforts of their familiar worlds. I'm talking about more complicated work, and it's a prejudice of mine that literature cannot be a mere performance: that unless the writer is personally at risk—unless the book has been, in some way, for the writer, an adventure into the unknown; unless the writer has set himself or herself a personal problem not easily solved; unless the finished book represents the surmounting of some great resistance—it's not worth reading. Or, for the writer, in my opinion, worth writing.

This seems to me all the more true in an age where there are so many other fun and inexpensive things a reader can do besides picking up a novel. As a writer, nowadays, you owe it to your readers to set yourself the most difficult challenge that you have some hope of being equal to. With every book, you have to dig as deep as possible and reach as far as possible. And if you do this, and you succeed in producing a reasonably good book, it means that the next time you try to write a book, you're going to have to dig even deeper and reach even farther, or else, again, it won't be worth writing. And what this means, in practice, is that you have to become a different person to write the next book. The person you already are already wrote the best book you could. There's no way to move forward without changing yourself. Without, in other words, working on the story of your own life. Which is to say: your autobiography.

I'd like to devote the remainder of my remarks to the idea of becoming the person who can write the book you need to write. I recognize that by talking about my own work, and telling a story of my progress from failure to success, I run the risk of seeming to congratulate myself or of seeming inordinately fascinated with myself. Not that it's so strange or damning if a writer feels proud of his best work and spends a lot of time examining his own life. But does he also have to *talk* about it? For a long time, I would have answered no, and it may very well say something bad about my character that I'm now answering yes. But I'm going to talk about *The Corrections* anyway, and describe a few of the struggles I had to become its author. I will note in advance that much of the struggle consisted—as I think it always will for writers fully engaged with the problem of the novel—in overcoming shame, guilt, and depression. I'll also note that I'll be experiencing some fresh shame as I do this.

The first thing I had to do in the early nineties was get out of my marriage. Breaking the oath and the emotional bonds of loyalty is rarely an easy thing for anyone to do, and in my case it was particularly complicated by my having married another writer. I was dimly aware that we were too young and inexperienced to be making a lifetime vow of monogamy, but my literary ambition and my romantic idealism prevailed. We got married in the fall of 1982, when I had just turned twenty-three, and we set about working as a team to produce literary masterworks. Our plan was to work side by side all our lives. It didn't seem necessary to have a fallback plan, because my wife was a gifted and sophisticated New Yorker who seemed bound to succeed, probably long before I did, and I knew that I could always take care of myself. And so we both proceeded to write novels, and we were both surprised and disappointed when my wife couldn't sell hers. When I did sell mine, in the fall of 1987, I felt simultaneously excited and very, very guilty.

There was nothing for us to do then but start running, to various towns and cities on two continents. Somehow, amid all the running, I managed to write and publish a second novel. The fact that I was having some success while my wife was struggling to write her own second novel I attributed to the general injustice and unfairness of the world. We were a team, after all—it was us against the world—and my job as a husband was to believe in my wife. And so, instead of taking pleasure in my accomplishments, I felt angry and bitter with the world. My second novel, *Strong Motion*, was an attempt to convey how it felt to be the two of us living in that bitter world. Looking back, although I'm still proud of that novel, I can now see the ways in which its ending was deformed by my wishful thinking about my marriage: by my loyalty. And it only made me feel guiltier that my wife didn't see it this way herself. She once claimed, memorably, that I had stolen from her soul to write it. She also asked me, fairly enough, why my main female characters kept getting killed or severely wounded by gunfire.

Nineteen ninety-three was the worst year of my life. My father was dying, my wife and I had run out of money, and we were both increasingly depressed. Hoping to get rich quick, I wrote a screenplay about a young couple, very much like the two of us, who start committing burglaries together, *almost* have affairs with other people, but end up blissfully united in a triumph of eternal love. By this point, even I could see that my work was being deformed by my loyalty to the marriage. But this didn't stop me from plotting a new novel, *The Corrections*, in which a young midwestern man like myself goes to prison for twenty years for a murder committed by his wife.

Fortunately, before my wife and I ended up killing ourselves or somebody else, reality intervened. This reality took several forms. One was our undeniable inability to tolerate living together. Another was the handful of close literary friendships I finally made outside my marriage. A third form of reality, the most important of all, was our pressing need for money. Since Hollywood didn't seem interested in a screenplay that reeked of Personal Issues (and that bore a fatally strong resemblance to *Fun with Dick and Jane*), I was forced to start doing journalism, and before long *The New York Times* assigned me to write a magazine piece about the parlous state of American fiction. While researching this piece, I got to know some of my old heroes, including Don DeLillo, and I became aware of belonging not just to the two-person team of me and my wife but to a much larger and still-vital community of readers and writers. To whom, as I discovered, crucially, I also had responsibilities and owed loyalty.

Once the hermetic seal on my marriage had been broken in these ways, things fell apart quickly. By the end of 1994, we each had our own apartment in New York and were finally leading the single lives we probably should have had in our twenties. This ought to have been fun and a liberation, but I was still feeling nightmarishly guilty. Loyalty, especially to family, is a foundational value for me. Loyalty unto death had always given meaning to my life. I suspect that people less encumbered by loyalty have an easier time being fiction writers, but all serious writers struggle, to some extent, at some point in their lives, with the conflicting demands of good art and good personhood. As long as I was married, I'd tried to avoid this conflict by remaining technically *anti*autobiographical—there's not a single scene drawn from life in either of my first two novels—and by constructing plots that were preoccupied with intellectual and social concerns.

When I went back to writing *The Corrections*, in the midnineties, I was still working with an absurdly overcomplicated plot that I'd developed while trying to work safely within my loyalty. I had many reasons to want to write a Big Social Novel, but probably the most important was my wish to be all intellect, all worldly expertise, so as to avoid the messy business of my private life. I tried for another year or two to keep writing that Big Social Novel, but eventually it became apparent, from the less and less deniable falseness of the pages, that I would have to become a different kind of writer to produce another novel. In other words, a different kind of person.

The first thing that had to go was the novel's main character, a man in his mid-thirties named Andy Aberant. He'd been a fixture of the story from the very beginning, when I'd imagined him in jail for a murder his wife had committed, and he'd since undergone numerous metamorphoses, finally ending up as a lawyer for the United States government, investigating cases of insider stock trading. I'd written about him in third person and then, at great length, and with absolutely no success, in first person. Along the way, I'd taken several long, enjoyable vacations from Andy Aberant in order to write about two other characters, Enid and Alfred Lambert, who'd appeared out of nowhere and were not unlike my parents. The chapters about them had poured out of me quickly and—compared with the torture of trying to write about Andy Aberant—effortlessly. Since Andy wasn't the Lamberts' son and, for complicated plot reasons, *couldn't* be their son, I was now trying to invent even more complicated ways to tie his story to theirs.

Although it's obvious to me now that Andy didn't belong in the book, it was anything but obvious at the time. I'd spent a number of really bad years of marriage becoming intimately and encyclopedically acquainted with depression and guilt, and since Andy Aberant was *defined* by his depression and guilt (especially regarding women, and especially regarding women's biological clocks), it seemed unthinkable not to make use of my hard-won knowledge and keep him in the book. The only problem was—as I wrote again and again in my novel notes—I couldn't see the humor in him. He was creepy and self-conscious and remote and depressing. Almost every day, for seven months, I struggled to write some Andy pages that I liked. Then, in my notes, for another two months, I wrestled with whether or not to give him the boot. What exactly I was thinking and feeling during all these months is no more accessible to me now than the misery of the flu is after I've recovered from it. I only know that what finally gave me the resolve to lose him was (1) sheer exhaustion, (2) a general lifting of my depression, and (3) a sudden easing of my guilt about my wife. I still felt plenty guilty, but I'd achieved enough distance from her to see that I was not to blame for *everything*. And I had lately fallen for a woman who was slightly older, which, ridiculous though it may sound, made me feel less villainous for having left my wife childless in her late thirties. My new friend came out from California and spent a week with me in New York, and at the end of that extremely happy week I was ready to recognize that Andy Aberant had no place in the book. I drew a little tombstone for him in my notes and gave him an epitaph from *Faust II*: *"Den können wir erlösen."* I honestly don't think I understood what I meant then in saying, "Him we can redeem." But it makes sense to me now.

With Andy gone, I was left with the Lamberts and their three grown children, who'd been haunting the novel's margins all along. I will skip over the many further contractions and subtractions the story had to undergo to become writable, and mention just two other obstacles I had to surmount, at least partially, to become the person who could write it.

The first of these obstacles was shame. By my mid-thirties, I was ashamed of almost everything I'd done in my personal life for the previous fifteen years. I was ashamed of having married so early, ashamed of my guilt, ashamed of the years of moral contortions I'd undergone on my way to divorce, ashamed of my sexual inexperience, ashamed of my longtime social isolation, ashamed of what an outrageous and judgmental mother I had, ashamed of being a bleeding and undefended person instead of a tower of remoteness and command and intellect like DeLillo or Pynchon, ashamed to be writing a book that seemed to want to turn on the question of whether an outrageous midwestern mother will get one last Christmas at home with her family. I wanted to write a novel about the big issues of my day, and instead, like Josef K., who is dismayed and maddened by having to deal with his trial while his colleagues all pursue their professional advantage, I was mired in shame about my innocence.

Much of this shame became concentrated in the character of Chip Lambert. I worked for a full year to get his story going, and at the end of that year I had about thirty usable pages. In the last days of my marriage, I'd had a brief relationship with a young woman I'd met when I was teaching. She wasn't a student and had never been my student, and she was much sweeter and more patient than the girl Chip Lambert gets involved with. But it was a very awkward and unsatisfactory relationship, a relationship that I now literally *writhed with shame* to think about, and for some reason it seemed necessary to incorporate it into Chip's story. The problem was that every time I tried to put Chip into a situation like mine, he became horribly repellent to me. To make his situation plausible and understandable, I kept trying to invent a backstory for him that bore some resemblance to my own, but I couldn't stop hating my own innocence. When I tried to make Chip less innocent, more worldly-wise and sexually experienced, the story simply seemed dishonest and uninteresting. I was haunted by the ghost of Andy Aberant, haunted also by two early novels of Ian McEwan, *The Innocent* and *The*

Comfort of Strangers, both of which were so powerfully *icky* that I'd wanted to take a hot shower after reading them. They were my prime example of what I didn't want to write but couldn't seem to help writing. Every time I held my breath for a few days and produced a new batch of Chip pages, I ended up with stuff that made me want to take a shower. The pages would start out funny but quickly devolve into a confession of shame. There seemed to be simply no way to translate my singular weird experience into a more general and forgiving and entertaining narrative.

A lot happened to me in that year of struggling with Chip Lambert, but two things that people said to me that year stand out in particular. One was said by my mother, on the last afternoon I spent with her, when we knew she was going to die soon. A piece of *The Corrections* had appeared in *The New Yorker*, and although my mother, to her immense credit, had chosen not to read the piece while she was dying, I decided to confess some things I'd always kept secret from her. They weren't terribly dark secrets—this was simply my attempt to explain why I hadn't turned out to have the kind of life she'd wanted for me. I wanted to reassure her that, strange though my life might look to her, I was still going to be okay after she was gone. And, as with the *New Yorker* story, she mostly didn't want to hear about all the times I'd climbed out of my bedroom window at night, and how sure I'd always been of wanting to be a writer, even when I'd pretended otherwise. But late in the afternoon she made it clear that she had been listening. She nodded and said, in a kind of vague summation: "Well, you're an eccentric." This was, partly, her best effort to recognize and forgive who I was. But the statement was mainly, in its vague and summary quality—its almost dismissive tone—her way of saying that it finally didn't *matter* to her what kind of person I was. That my life was more important to me than it was to her. That what mattered most to her now was her own life, which was about to end. And this was one of her last gifts to me: the implicit instruction not to worry so much about what she, or anybody else, might think of me. To be myself, as she, in her dying, was being herself.

The other really helpful comment came from my friend David Means a few months later, when I was complaining to him about how mad I was being driven by the problem of Chip Lambert's sexual history. David is a true artist, and his most insightful comments tend also to be his most opaque and mysterious. He said to me, on the subject of shame: "You don't write *through* shame, you write around it." I still couldn't tell you exactly what he meant by these contrasting prepositions, but it was immediately clear to me that those two early McEwan novels were examples of somebody writing *through* shame, and that my task, with Chip Lambert, was to find some way to include shame in the narrative without being overcome by it: some way to isolate and quarantine shame as an object, ideally as an object of comedy, rather than letting it permeate and poison every sentence. From here it was a short step to imagining that Chip Lambert, while having his dalliance with his student, takes an illegal drug whose primary effect is to eliminate shame. Once I had that idea, and could finally begin to *laugh* at shame, I wrote the rest of the Chip section in a few weeks and the rest of the novel in a year.

The biggest remaining problem during that year was loyalty. It arose particularly in the writing of the chapter about Gary Lambert, who bore a certain superficial resemblance to my oldest brother. There was, for example, Gary's project of assembling an album of his favorite family photographs: my brother was involved with a project like that himself. And since my brother is the most sensitive and sentimental person in my family, I didn't see how I could use details from his life without hurting him and jeopardizing our good relations. I felt afraid of his anger, guilty about laughing at real-life details that weren't funny to him, disloyal to be airing private family matters in a public narrative, and all-around morally dubious to be appropriating, for my own professional purposes, the private life of a nonwriter. These were all reasons I'd resisted "autobiographical" fiction in the past. And yet the details were too meaningful not to use, and it wasn't as if I'd ever concealed from my family that I was a writer listening carefully to everything they said. So I went around and around and finally ended up discussing the matter with a wise older friend of mine. To my surprise, she became angry with me and reproached me for my narcissism. What she said was akin to my mother's message on our last afternoon together. She said, "Do you think your brother's life revolves around *you*? Do you think he's not an adult with a life of his own, full of things more important than you are? Do you think you're so powerful that something you write in a novel is going to *harm* him?"

All loyalties, both in writing and elsewhere, are meaningful only when they're tested. Being loyal to yourself as a writer is most difficult when you're just starting out—when being a writer hasn't yet given you enough of a public return to justify your loyalty to it. The benefits of being on good terms with your friends and family are obvious and concrete; the benefits of writing about them are still largely speculative. There comes a point, though, when the benefits begin to equalize. And the question then becomes: Am I willing to risk alienating somebody I love in order to continue becoming the writer I need to be? For a long time, in my marriage, my answer to this was no. Even today there are relationships so important to me that I'm at pains to write around them, rather than through them. But what I've learned is that there's potential value, not only for your writing but also for your relationships, in taking autobiographical risks: that you may, in fact, be doing your brother or your mother or your best friend a favor by giving them the opportunity to rise to the occasion of being written about—by trusting them to love the whole you, including the writer part. What turns out to matter most is that you write as truthfully as possible. If you really love the person whose material you're writing about, the writing has to reflect that love. There's still always a risk that the person won't be able to see the love, and that your relationship may suffer, but you've done what all writers finally reach the point of having to do, which is to be loyal to themselves.

I'm happy to report, in closing, that my brother and I are now on better terms than ever. When I was about to send him an advance copy of *The Corrections*, I told him, on the phone, that he might hate the book and might even hate *me*. His reply, for which I remain deeply grateful, was "Hating you is not an option." The next time I heard from him, after he'd read the book, he began by saying, "Hello, Jon. It's your brother—*Gary*." He has since gone on, when talking to his friends about the book, to make no secret of the resemblance. He has his own life, with its own trials and satisfactions, and having a writer for a brother is just another piece of his own story. We love each other dearly.

I JUST CALLED TO SAY
I LOVE YOU

-------▸

One of the great irritations of modern technology is that when some new development has made my life palpably worse and is continuing to find new and different ways to bedevil it, I'm still allowed to complain for only a year or two before the peddlers of coolness start telling me to get over it already, Grampaw—this is just the way life is now.

I'm not opposed to technological developments. Digital voice mail and caller ID, which together destroyed the tyranny of the ringing telephone, seem to me two of the truly great inventions of the late twentieth century. And how I love my BlackBerry, which lets me deal with lengthy, unwelcome e-mails in a few breathless telegraphic lines for which the recipient is nevertheless obliged to feel grateful, because I did it with my thumbs. And my noise-canceling headphones, on which I can blast frequency-shifted white noise that drowns out even the most determined woofing of a neighbor's television set. And the whole wonderful world of DVD technology and high-definition screens, which have already spared me from so many sticky theater floors, so many rudely whispering cinemagoers, so many openmouthed crunchers of popcorn.

Privacy, to me, is not about keeping my personal life hidden from other people. It's about sparing me from the intrusion of other people's personal lives. And so, although my very favorite gadgets are actively privacy-enhancing, I look kindly on pretty much any development that doesn't force me to interact with it. If you choose to spend an hour every day tinkering with your Facebook profile, or if you don't see any difference between reading Jane Austen on a Kindle and reading her on a printed page, or if you think *Grand Theft Auto IV* is the greatest *Gesamtkunstwerk* since Wagner, I'm very happy for you, as long as you keep it to yourself. The developments I have a problem with are the insults that keep on insulting, the injuries of yesteryear that keep on giving pain. Airport TV, for example: it seems to be actively watched by about one traveler in ten (unless there's football on) while creating an active nuisance for the other nine. Year after year; in airport after airport; a small but apparently permanent diminution in the quality of the average traveler's life. Or, another example, the planned obsolescence of great software and its replacement by bad software. I'm still unable to accept that the best word-processing program ever written, WordPerfect 5.0 for DOS, won't even run on any computer I can buy now. Oh, sure, in theory you can still run it in Windows' little DOS-emulating window, but the tininess and graphical crudeness of that emulator are like a deliberate insult on Microsoft's part to those of us who would prefer not to use a feature-heavy behemoth. WordPerfect 5.0 was hopelessly primitive for desktop publishing but unsurpassable for writers who wanted only to write. Elegant, bug-free, negligible in size, it was bludgeoned out of existence by the obese, intrusive, monopolistic, crash-prone Word. If I hadn't been collecting old cast-off computers in my office closet, I wouldn't be able to use WordPerfect at all by now. And already I'm down to my last spare computer! And yet people have the nerve to be annoyed with me if I won't send them texts in a format intelligible to all-powerful Word. We live in a Word world now, Grampaw. Time to take your GOI pill.

But these are mere annoyances. The technological development that has done lasting harm of real social significance—the development that, despite the continuing harm it does, you risk ridicule if you publicly complain about today—is the cell phone.

Just ten years ago, New York City (where I live) still abounded with collectively maintained public spaces in which citizens demonstrated respect for their community by not inflicting their banal bedroom lives on it. The world ten years ago was not yet fully conquered by yak. It was still possible to see the use of Nokias as an ostentation or an affectation of the affluent. Or, more generously, as an affliction or a disability or a crutch. There was unfolding, after all, in New York in the late nineties, a seamless citywide transition from nicotine culture to cellular culture. One day the lump in the shirt pocket was Marlboros, the next day it was Motorola. One day the vulnerably unaccompanied pretty girl was occupying her hands and mouth and attention with a cigarette, the next day she was occupying them with a very important conversation with a person who wasn't you. One day a crowd gathered around the first kid on the playground with a pack of Kools, the next day around the first kid with a color screen. One day travelers were clicking lighters the second they were off an airplane, the next day they were speed-dialing. Pack-a-day habits became hundred-dollar monthly Verizon bills. Smoke pollution became sonic pollution. Although the irritant changed overnight, the suffering of a self-restrained majority at the hands of a compulsive minority, in restaurants and airports and other public spaces, remained eerily constant. Back in 1998, not long after I'd quit cigarettes, I would sit on the subway and watch other riders nervously folding and unfolding phones, or nibbling on the teatlike antennae that all the phones then had, or just quietly clutching their devices like a mother's hand, and I would feel something close to sorry for them. It still seemed to me an open question how far the trend would go: whether New York truly wanted to become a city of phone addicts sleepwalking down the sidewalks in off-putting little clouds of private life, or whether the notion of a more restrained public self might somehow prevail.

Needless to say, there wasn't any contest. The cell phone wasn't one of those modern developments, like Ritalin or oversize umbrellas, for which significant pockets of civilian resistance hearteningly persist. Its triumph was swift and total. Its abuses were lamented and bitched about in essays and columns and letters to various editors, and then lamented and bitched about more trenchantly when the abuses seemed only to be getting worse, but that was the end of it. The complaints had been registered, some small token adjustments had been made (the "quiet car" on Amtrak trains; discreet little signs poignantly pleading for restraint in restaurants and gyms), and cellular technology was then free to continue doing its damage without fear of further criticism, because further criticism would be unfresh and uncool. Grampaw.

But just because the problem is familiar to us now doesn't mean steam stops issuing from the ears of drivers trapped behind a guy chatting on his phone in a passing lane and staying perfectly abreast of a vehicle in the slow lane. And yet: everything in our commercial culture tells the chatty driver that he is in the right and tells everybody else that we are in the wrong—that we are failing to get with the attractively priced program of freedom and mobility and unlimited minutes. Commercial culture tells us that if we're sore with the chatty driver it must be because we're not having as good a time as he is. *What is wrong with us, anyway?* Why can't we lighten up a little and take out our own phones, with our own Friends and Family plans, and start having a better time ourselves, right there in the passing lane?

Socially retarded people don't suddenly start acting more adult when social critics are peer-pressured into silence. They only get ruder. One currently worsening national plague is the shopper who remains engrossed in a call throughout a transaction with a checkout clerk. The typical combination in my own neighborhood, in Manhattan, involves a young white woman, recently graduated from someplace expensive, and a local black or Hispanic woman of roughly the same age but fewer advantages. It is, of course, a liberal vanity to expect your checkout clerk to interact with you or to appreciate the scrupulousness of your determination to interact with her. Given the repetitive and low-paying nature of her job, she's allowed to treat you with boredom or indifference; at worst, it's unprofessional of her. But this does not relieve you of your own moral obligation to acknowledge her existence as a person. And while it's true that some clerks don't seem to mind being ignored, a notably large percentage do become visibly irritated or angered or saddened when a customer is unable to tear herself off her phone for even two seconds of direct interaction. Needless to say, the offender herself, like the chatty freeway driver, is blissfully unaware of pissing anybody off. In my experience, the longer the line behind her, the more likely it is she'll pay for her $1.98 purchase with a credit card. And not the tap-and-go microchip kind of credit card, either, but the wait-for-the-printed-receipt-and-then-(only-then)-with-zombiesh-clumsiness-begin-shifting-the-cell-phone-from-one-ear-to-the-other-and-awkwardly-pin-the-phone-with-ear-to-shoulder-while-signing-the-receipt-and-continuing-to-express-doubt-about-whether-she-really-feels-like-meeting-up-with-that-Morgan-Stanley-guy-

Zachary-at-the-Etats-Unis-wine-bar-again-tonight kind of credit card.

There is, to be sure, one positive social consequence of this worsening misbehavior. The abstract notion of civilized public spaces, as rare resources worth defending, may be all but dead, but there's still consolation to be found in the momentary ad hoc microcommunities of fellow sufferers which bad behavior creates. To look out your car window and see the steam coming out of another driver's ears, or to meet the eyes of a pissed-off check-out clerk and to shake your head along with her: it makes you feel a little less alone. Which is why, of all the worsening varieties of bad cell-phone behavior, the one that most deeply irritates me is the one that seems, because it is ostensibly victimless, to irritate nobody else. I'm talking about the habit, uncommon ten years ago, now ubiquitous, of ending cell-phone conversations by braying the words "LOVE YOU!" Or, even more oppressive and grating: "I LOVE YOU!" It makes me want to go and live in China, where I don't understand the language.

The cellular component of my irritation is straightforward. I simply do not, while buying socks at the Gap, or standing in a ticket line and pursuing my private thoughts, or trying to read a novel on a plane that's being boarded, want to be imaginatively drawn into the sticky world of some nearby human being's home life. The very essence of the cell phone's hideousness, as a social phenomenon—the bad news that stays bad news—is that it enables and encourages the inflicting of the personal and individual on the public and communal. And there is no higher-caliber utterance than "I love you"—nothing worse that an individual can inflict on a communal public space. Even "Fuck you, dickhead" is less invasive, since it's the kind of thing that angry people do sometimes shout in public, and it can just as easily be directed at a stranger.

My friend Elisabeth assures me that the new national plague of love-yous is a good thing: a healthy reaction against the repressed family dynamics of our Protestant childhoods some decades ago. What could be wrong, Elisabeth asks, with telling your mother that you love her, or with hearing from her that she loves you? What if one of you dies before you can speak again? Isn't it nice that we can say these things to each other so freely now?

I do here admit the possibility that, compared with everyone else on the airport concourse, I am an extraordinarily cold and unloving person; that the sudden overwhelming sensation of *loving* somebody (a friend, a spouse, a parent, a sibling), which to me is such an important and signal sensation that I'm at pains not to wear out the phrase that best expresses it, is for other people so common and routine and easily achieved that it can be reexperienced and reexpressed many times in a single day without significant loss of power.

It's also possible, however, that too-frequent habitual repetition empties phrases of their meaning. Joni Mitchell, in the last verse of "Both Sides Now," referenced the solemn amazement of saying I love you "right out loud": of giving vocal birth to such intensity of feeling. Stevie Wonder, in lyrics written seventeen years later, sings of calling somebody up on an ordinary afternoon simply to say "I love you," and, being Stevie Wonder (who probably really is a more loving person than I am), he half succeeds in making me believe in his sincerity—at least until the last line of the chorus, where he finds it necessary to add: "And I mean it from the bottom of my heart." Avowing sincerity is more or less diagnostic of insincerity.

And, just so, when I'm buying those socks at the Gap and the mom in line behind me shouts "I love you!" into her little phone, I am powerless not to feel that something is being performed;

overperformed; publicly performed; defiantly inflicted. Yes, a lot of domestic things get shouted in public which really aren't intended for public consumption; yes, people get carried away. But the phrase "I love you" is too important and loaded, and its use as a sign-off too self-conscious, for me to believe I'm being made to hear it accidentally. If the mother's declaration of love had genuine, private emotional weight, wouldn't she take at least a little care to guard it from public hearing? If she truly meant what she was saying, from the bottom of her heart, wouldn't she have to say it *quietly*? Overhearing her, as a stranger, I have the feeling of being made party to an aggressive assertion of entitlement. At a minimum, the person seems to be saying to me and to everyone else present: "*My* emotions and *my* family are more important to me than your social comfort." And also, often enough, I suspect: "I want you all to know that unlike many people, including my cold bastard of a father, *I* am the kind of person who always tells my loved ones that I love them."

Or am I, in my admittedly now rather lunatic-sounding irritation, simply projecting all this?

The cell phone came of age on September 11, 2001. Imprinted that day on our collective consciousness was the image of cell phones as conduits of intimacy for the desperate. In every too-loud I-love-you that I hear nowadays, as in the more general national orgy of connectedness—the imperative for parents and children to connect by phone once or twice or five or ten times daily—it's difficult not to hear an echo of those terrible, entirely appropriate I-love-yous uttered on the four doomed planes and in the two doomed towers. And it's precisely this echo, the fact that it's an echo, the sentimentality of it, that so irritates me.

My own experience of 9/11 was anomalous for the lack of television in it. At nine in the morning, I got a phone call from my book editor, who, from his office window, had just seen the second plane hit the towers. I did immediately go to the nearest TV, in the conference room of the real estate office downstairs from my apartment, and watch with a group of agents as first one tower and then the other went down. But then my girlfriend came home and we spent the rest of the day listening to the radio, checking the Internet, reassuring our families, and watching from our roof and from the middle of Lexington Avenue (which was filled with pedestrians streaming uptown) as the dust and smoke at the bottom of Manhattan diffused into a sickening pall. In the evening, we walked down to Forty-second Street and met up with an out-of-town friend and found a restaurant in the West Forties which happened to be serving dinner. Every table was packed with people drinking heavily; the mood was wartime. I got another brief glimpse of a TV screen, this one showing the face of George W. Bush, as we were departing through the restaurant's bar. "He looks like a scared mouse," somebody said. Sitting on a 6 train at Grand Central, waiting for it to move, we watched a New York commuter angrily complain to a conductor about the lack of express service to the Bronx.

Three nights later, from 11:00 p.m. to nearly 3:00 a.m., I sat in a frigid room at ABC News from which I could see my fellow New Yorker David Halberstam and speak by video link to Maya Angelou and a couple of other out-of-town writers while we waited to offer Ted Koppel a literary perspective on Tuesday morning's attacks. The wait was not short. Footage of the attacks and the ensuing collapses and fires was shown again and again, interspersed with long segments on the emotional toll on ordinary citizens and their impressionable children. Every once in a while, one or two of us writers would have sixty seconds to say something writerly before the coverage reverted to more carnage and wrenching interviews with friends and family of the dead and the missing. I spoke four times in three and a half hours. The second time, I was asked to confirm widespread reports that Tuesday's attacks had profoundly changed the personality of New Yorkers. Thinking of the angry commuter, I could not confirm these reports. I talked about the people I'd seen shopping in the stores in my neighborhood on Wednesday afternoon, buying fall clothes. Ted Koppel, in his response, made clear that I'd failed at the task I'd been waiting half the night to perform. With a frown, he said that his own impression was very different: that the attacks had indeed profoundly changed the personality of New York City.

Naturally, I assumed that I was speaking truth and Koppel merely retransmitting received opinion. But Koppel had been watching TV and I had not. I didn't understand that the worst damage to the country was being done not by the pathogen but by the immune system's massive overresponse to it, because I didn't have a TV. I was mentally comparing Tuesday's death toll with other tallies of violent death—three thousand Americans killed in traffic accidents in the thirty days preceding September 11—because, not seeing the images, I thought the numbers mattered. I was devoting energy to imagining, or resisting imagining, the horror of sitting in a window seat while your plane came in low along the West Side Highway, or of being trapped on the ninety-fifth floor and hearing the steel structure below you begin to groan and rumble, while the rest of the country was experiencing *actual real-time trauma* by watching the same footage over and over. And so I was not in need of—was, for a while, not even aware of—the national televised group therapy session, the vast techno-hug-a-thon, that unfolded in the following days and weeks and months in response to the trauma of exposure to televised images.

What I *could* see was the sudden, mysterious, disastrous sentimentalization of American public discourse. And just as I can't help blaming cellular technology when people pour parental or filial affection into their phones and rudeness onto every stranger within earshot, I can't help blaming media technology for the national foregrounding of the personal. Unlike in, say, 1941, when the United States responded to a terrible attack with collective resolve and discipline and sacrifice, in 2001 we had terrific visuals. We had amateur footage and could break it down frame by frame. We had screens to bring the violence raw into every bedroom in the country, and voice mail to record the desperate final calls of the doomed, and late-model psychology to explicate and heal our trauma. But as for what the attacks actually signified, and what a sensible response to them might look like, opinions varied. This was the wonderful thing about digital technology: no more hurtful censoring of anybody's feelings! Everybody entitled to express his or her own opinion! Whether or not Saddam Hussein had personally bought plane tickets for the hijackers therefore remained open to lively debate. What everybody agreed to agree on, instead, was that the families of 9/11's victims had a right to approve or veto plans for the memorial at Ground Zero. And everybody could share in the pain experienced by the families of the fallen cops and firefighters. And everybody agreed that irony was dead. The bad, empty irony of the nineties was simply "no longer possible" post-9/11; we'd stepped forward into a new age of sincerity.

On the plus side, Americans in 2001 were a lot better at saying "I love you" to their children than their fathers or grandfathers had been. But competing economically? Pulling together as a nation? Defeating our enemies? Forming strong international alliances? Perhaps a bit of a minus side there.

My parents met two years after Pearl Harbor, in the fall of 1943, and within a few months they were exchanging cards and letters. My father worked for the Great Northern Railway and was often on the road, in small towns, inspecting or repairing bridges, while my mother stayed in Minneapolis and worked as a receptionist. Of the letters from him to her in my possession, the oldest is from Valentine's Day 1944. He was in Fairview, Montana, and my mother had sent him a Valentine's card in the style of all her cards in the year leading up to their marriage: sweetly drawn babies or toddlers or baby animals voicing sweet sentiments. The front of her valentine (which my father likewise saved) shows a pigtailed little girl and a blushing little boy standing beside each other with their eyes bashfully averted and their hands tucked bashfully behind their backs.

> I wish I were a little rock,
> 'Cause then when I grew older,
> Maybe I would find some day
> I was a little "boulder."

Inside the card is a drawing of the same two kids, but holding hands now, with my mother's cursive signature ("Irene") at the feet of the little girl. A second verse reads:

> And that would really help a lot
> It sure would suit me fine,
> For I'd be "bould" enough to say,
> "Please be my Valentine."

My father's letter in response was postmarked Fairview, Montana, February 14.

Tuesday Evening

Dear Irene,

I'm sorry to have disappointed you on Valentine's Day; I did remember but after not being able to get one at the drugstore, I felt a little foolish about asking at the grocery or hardware store. I'm sure they have heard about Valentine's Day out here. Your card fit the situation out here perfectly and I'm not sure if it were intentional or accidental, but I guess I did tell about our rock troubles. Today we ran out of rock so I'm wishing for little rocks, big rocks or any kind of rocks as there is nothing we can do until we get some. There is little enough for me to do when the contractor is working and now there is nothing at all. Today I hiked out to the bridge where we are working just to kill time and get a little exercise; it's about four miles which is far enough with a sharp wind blowing. Unless we get rock on the freight in the morning, I'm going to sit right here and read philosophy; it hardly seems right that I should get paid for putting in that kind of day. About the only other pastime around here is to sit in the hotel lobby and take in the town gossip, and the old timers who haunt the place can sure put it out. You would get a kick out of it because there is sure a broad cross section of life represented here—from the local doctor down to the town drunk. And the last is probably the most interesting; I heard that he taught at the University of N.D. at one time, and he seems really to be quite an intelligent person, even when drunk. Normally the talk is pretty rough, about like Steinbeck must have used for a pattern, but this evening there came in a great big woman who made herself right at home. It all sort of makes me realize how sheltered a life we city people live. I grew up

*in a small town and feel quite at home here but I somehow now
seem to view things differently. You will hear more of this.*

*I hope to get back to St. Paul on Saturday night but cannot
tell for certain now. I'll call you when I get in.*

*With all my love,
Earl*

My father had recently turned twenty-nine. It's impossible
to know how my mother, in her innocence and optimism, received his letter at the time, but in general, considering the
woman I grew up knowing, I can say that it was absolutely not
the sort of letter she would have wanted from her romantic interest. Her valentine's cutely punning conceit taken literally as a
reference to *track ballast*? And she, who spent her whole life
shuddering free of the hotel bar where her father had worked as
a bartender, *getting a kick out of* hearing "rough talk" from the
town drunk? Where were the endearments? Where were the
dreamy discussions of love? It was obvious that my father still
had a lot to learn about her.

To me, though, his letter seems full of love. Love for my
mother, certainly: he's tried to get her a valentine, he's read her
card carefully, he wishes she were with him, he has ideas he
wants to share with her, he's sending all his love, he'll call her as
soon as he's back. But love, too, for the larger world: for the varieties of people in it, for small towns and big cities, for philosophy and literature, for hard work and fair pay, for conversation,
for thinking, for long walks in a sharp wind, for carefully chosen words and perfect spelling. The letter reminds me of the
many things I loved in my father, his decency, his intelligence,
his unexpected humor, his curiosity, his conscientiousness, his
reserve and dignity. Only when I place it alongside the valentine from my mother, with its big-eyed babies and preoccupa-

tion with pure sentiment, does my focus shift to the decades of mutual disappointment that followed my parents' first few years of half-seeing bliss.

Late in life, my mother complained to me that my father had never told her that he loved her. And it may literally be true that he never spoke the big three words to her—I certainly never heard him do it. But it's definitely not true that he never wrote the words. One reason it took me years to summon the courage to read their old correspondence is that the first letter of my father's that I glanced at, after my mother died, began with an endearment ("Irenie") that I had never heard him utter in the thirty-five years I knew him, and it ended with a declaration ("I love you, Irene") that was more than I could stand to see. It sounded nothing like him, and so I buried all the letters in a trunk in my brother's attic. More recently, when I retrieved them and managed to read through them all, I discovered that my father had in fact declared his love dozens of times, using the big three words, both before and after he married my mother. But maybe, even then, he'd been incapable of saying the words out loud, and maybe this was why, in my mother's memory, he'd never "said" them at all. It's also possible that his written declarations had sounded as strange and untrue to his character in the forties as they now sound to me, and that my mother, in her complaints, was remembering a deeper truth now concealed by his seemingly affectionate words. It's possible that, in guilty response to the onslaught of sentiment he was getting from her notes to him ("I love you with all my heart," "With oh so much love," etc.), he'd felt obliged to perform romantic love in return, or to try to perform it, the way he'd tried (sort of) to buy a valentine in Fairview, Montana.

———

"Both Sides Now," in the Judy Collins version, was the first pop song that ever stuck in my head. It was getting heavy radio play when I was eight or nine, and its reference to declaring love "right out loud," combined with the crush I had on Judy Collins's voice, helped to ensure that for me the primary import of "I love you" was sexual. I did eventually live through the seventies and become capable, in rare accesses of emotion, of telling my brothers and many of my best male friends that I loved them. But throughout grade school and junior high, the words had only one meaning for me. "I love you" was the phrase I wanted to see scrawled on a note from the cutest girl in the class or to hear whispered in the woods on a school picnic. It happened only a couple of times, in those years, that a girl I liked actually said or wrote this to me. But when it did happen, it came as a shot of pure adrenaline. Even after I got to college and started reading Wallace Stevens and found him making fun, in "Le Monocle de Mon Oncle," of indiscriminately love-seeking people like me—

> *If sex were all, then every trembling hand*
> *Could make us squeak, like dolls, the wished-for words*

—those wished-for words continued to signify the opening of a mouth, the offering of a body, the promise of intoxicating intimacy. And so it was highly awkward that the person I constantly heard these words from was my mother. She was the only woman in a house of males, and she lived with such an excess of unrequitable feeling that she couldn't help reaching for romantic expressions of it. The cards and endearments that she bestowed on me were identical in spirit to the ones she'd once bestowed on my father. Long before I was born, her effusions had come to seem intolerably babyish to my father. To me, though, they weren't nearly babyish enough. I went to elaborate lengths to avoid reciprocating them. I survived many stretches of my childhood, the long weeks in which the two of us were alone in the house together, by clinging to crucial distinctions in intensity between the phrases "I love you"; "I love you, too"; and "Love you." The one thing that was vital was never, ever to say "I love you" or "I love you, Mom." The least painful alternative was a muttered, essentially inaudible "Love you." But "I love you, too," if pronounced rapidly enough and with enough emphasis on the "too," which implied rote responsiveness, could carry me through many an awkward moment. I don't remember that she ever specifically called me out on my mumbling or gave me a hard time if (as sometimes happened) I was incapable of responding with anything more than an evasive grunt. But she also never told me that saying "I love you" was simply something she enjoyed doing because her heart was full of feeling, and that I shouldn't feel I had to say "I love you" in return every time. And so, to this day, when I'm assaulted by the shouting of "I love you" into a cell phone, I hear coercion.

My father, despite writing letters filled with life and curiosity, saw nothing wrong with consigning my mother to four decades of cooking and cleaning at home while he was enjoying his agency out in the world of men. It seems to be the rule, in both the small world of marriage and the big world of American life, that those without agency have sentimentality, and vice versa. The various post-9/11 hysterias, both the plague of I-love-yous and the widespread fear and hatred of the ragheads, were hysterias of the powerless and overwhelmed. If my mother had had greater scope for accomplishment, she might have tailored her sentiments more realistically to their objects.

Cold or repressed or sexist though my father may appear by contemporary standards, I'm grateful that he never told me, in so many words, that he loved me. My father loved privacy, which is to say: he respected the public sphere. He believed in restraint and protocol and reason, because without them, he believed, it was impossible for a society to debate and make decisions in its best interest. It might have been nice, especially for me, if he'd learned how to be more demonstrative with my mother. But every time I hear one of those brayed parental cellular I-love-yous nowadays, I feel lucky to have had the dad I did. He loved his kids more than anything. And to know that he felt it and couldn't say it; to know that he could trust me to know he felt it and never expect him to say it: this was the very core and substance of the love I felt for him. A love that I in turn was careful never to declare out loud to him.

And yet: this was the easy part. Between me and the place where my dad is now—i.e., dead—nothing but silence can be transmitted. Nobody has more privacy than the dead. My dad and I aren't saying a whole lot less to each other now than we did in many a year when he was alive. The person I find myself actively missing—mentally arguing with, wanting to show stuff to, wishing to see in my apartment, making fun of, feeling remorse about—is my mother. The part of me that's angered by cellular intrusions comes from my father. The part of me that loves my BlackBerry and wants to lighten up and join the world comes from my mother. She was the more modern of the two of them, and although he, not she, was the one with agency, she ended up on the winning side. If she were still alive and still living in St. Louis, and if you happened to be sitting next to me in Lambert Airport, waiting for a New York–bound flight, you might have to suffer through hearing me tell her that I love her. I would keep my voice down, though.

DAVID FOSTER WALLACE

[memorial service remarks, October 23, 2008]

- - - - - - - ▶

Like a lot of writers, but even more than most, Dave loved to be in control of things. He was easily stressed by chaotic social situations. I only ever saw him twice go to a party without Karen. One of them, hosted by Adam Begley, I almost physically had to drag him to, and as soon as we were through the front door and I took my eye off him for one second, he made a U-turn and went back to my apartment to chew tobacco and read a book. The second party he had no choice but to stay for, because it was celebrating the publication of *Infinite Jest*. He survived it by saying thank you, again and again, with painfully exaggerated formality.

One thing that made Dave an extraordinary teacher was the formal structure of the job. Within those confines, he could safely draw on his enormous native store of kindness and wisdom and expertise. The structure of interviews was safe in a similar way. When Dave was the subject, he could relax into taking care of his interviewer. When he was the journalist himself, he did his best work when he was able to find a technician—a cameraman following John McCain, a board operator on a radio show—who was thrilled to meet somebody genuinely interested in the arcana of his job. Dave loved details for their own sake, but details were also an outlet for the love bottled up in his heart: a way of connecting, on relatively safe middle ground, with another human being.

Which was, approximately, the description of literature that he and I came up with in our conversations and correspondence in the early nineties. I'd loved Dave from the very first letter I ever got from him, but the first two times I tried to meet him in person, up in Cambridge, he flat-out stood me up. Even after we did start hanging out, our meetings were often stressful and rushed—much *less* intimate than exchanging letters. Having loved him at first sight, I was always straining to prove that I could be funny enough and smart enough, and he had a way of gazing off at a point a few miles distant which made me feel as if I were failing to make my case. Not many things in my life ever gave me a greater sense of achievement than getting a laugh out of Dave.

But that "neutral middle ground on which to make a deep connection with another human being": this, we decided, was what fiction was for. "A way out of loneliness" was the formulation we agreed to agree on. And nowhere was Dave more totally and gorgeously able to maintain control than in his written language. He had the most commanding and exciting and inventive rhetorical virtuosity of any writer alive. Way out at word number 70 or 100 or 140 in a sentence deep into a three-page paragraph of macabre humor or fabulously reticulated self-consciousness, you could smell the ozone from the crackling precision of his sentence structure, his effortless and pitch-perfect shifting among levels of high, low, middle, technical, hipster, nerdy, philosophical, vernacular, vaudevillian, hortatory, tough-guy, brokenhearted, lyrical diction. Those sentences and those pages, when he was able to be producing them, were as true and safe and happy a home as any he had during most of the twenty years I knew him. So I could tell you stories about the bickering little road trip he and I once took, or I could tell you about the wintergreen scent that his chew gave to my apartment whenever he stayed with me, or I could tell you about the awkward chess games we played and the even more awkward tennis rallying we sometimes did—the comforting structure of the games versus the weird deep fraternal rivalries boiling along underneath—but truly the main thing was the writing. For most of the time I knew Dave, the most intense interaction I had with him was sitting alone in my armchair, night after night, for ten days, and reading the manuscript of *Infinite Jest*. That was the book in which, for the first time, he'd arranged himself and the world the way he wanted them arranged. At the most microscopic level: Dave Wallace was as passionate and precise a punctuator of prose as has ever walked this earth. At the most global level: he produced a thousand pages of world-class jest which, although the mode and quality of the humor never wavered, became less and less and less funny, section by section, until, by the end of the book, you felt the book's title might just as well have been *Infinite Sadness*. Dave nailed it like nobody else ever had.

And so now this handsome, brilliant, funny, kind midwestern man with an amazing spouse and a great local support network and a great career and a great job at a great school with great students has taken his own life, and the rest of us are left behind to ask (to quote from *Infinite Jest*), "So yo then, man, what's *your* story?"

One good, simple, modern story would go like this: "A lovely, talented personality fell victim to a severe chemical imbalance in his brain. There was the person of Dave, and then there was the disease, and the disease killed the man as surely as cancer might have." This story is at once sort of true and totally inadequate. If you're satisfied with this story, you don't need the stories that Dave wrote—particularly not those many, many stories in which the duality, the separateness, of person and disease is problematized or outright mocked. One obvious paradox, of course, is that Dave himself, at the end, did become, in a sense, satisfied with this simple story and stopped connecting with any of those more interesting stories he'd written in the past and might have written in the future. His suicidality got the upper hand and made everything in the world of the living irrelevant.

But this doesn't mean there are no more meaningful stories for us to tell. I could tell you ten different versions of how he arrived at the evening of September 12, some of them very dark, some of them very angering to me, and most of them taking into account Dave's many adjustments, as an adult, in response to his near-death of suicide as a late adolescent. But there is one particular not-so-dark story that I know to be true and that I want to tell now, because it's been such a great happiness and privilege and endlessly interesting challenge to be Dave's friend.

People who like to be in control of things can have a hard time with intimacy. Intimacy is anarchic and mutual and definitionally incompatible with control. You seek to control things because you're afraid, and about five years ago, very noticeably, Dave stopped being so afraid. Part of this came of having settled into a good, stable situation at Pomona College. Another really huge part of it was his finally meeting a woman who was right for him and who, for the first time, opened up the possibility of his having a fuller and less rigidly structured life. I noticed, when we spoke on the phone, that he'd begun to tell me he loved me, and I suddenly felt, on my side, that I didn't have to work so hard to make him laugh or to prove that I was smart. Karen and I managed to get him to Italy for a week, and instead of spending his days in his hotel room, watching TV, as he might have done a few years earlier, he was having lunch on the terrace and eating octopus and trudging along to dinner parties and actually enjoying hanging out with other writers casually. He surprised everyone, and maybe most of all himself. Here was a genuinely fun thing he might well have done again.

About a year later, he decided to get himself off the medication that had lent stability to his life for more than twenty years. Again, there are a lot of different stories about why exactly he decided to do this. But one thing he made very clear to me, when we talked about it, was that he wanted a chance at a more ordinary life, with less freakish control and more ordinary pleasure. It was a decision that grew out of his love for Karen, out of his wish to produce a new and more mature kind of writing, and out of having glimpsed a different kind of future. It was an incredibly scary and brave thing for him to try, because Dave was full of love, but he was also full of fear—he had all too ready access to those depths of infinite sadness.

So the year was up and down, and he had a crisis in June, and a very hard summer. When I saw him in July he was skinny again, like the late adolescent he'd been during his first big crisis. One of the last times I talked to him after that, in August, on the phone, he asked me to tell him a story of how things would get better. I repeated back to him a lot of what he'd been saying to me in our conversations over the previous year. I said he was in a terrible and dangerous place because he was trying to make real changes as a person and as a writer. I said that the last time he'd been through near-death experiences, he'd emerged and written, very quickly, a book that was light-years beyond what he'd been doing before his collapse. I said he was a stubborn control freak and know-it-all—"So are you!" he shot back at me—and I said that people like us are so afraid to relinquish control that sometimes the only way we can force ourselves to open up and change is to bring ourselves to an access of misery and the brink of self-destruction. I said he'd undertaken his change in medication because he wanted to grow up and have a better life. I said I thought his best writing was ahead of him. And he said: "I like that story. Could you do me a favor and call me up every four or five days and tell me another story like it?"

Unfortunately I only had one more chance to tell him the story, and by then he wasn't hearing it. He was in horrible, minute-by-minute anxiety and pain. The next times I tried to call him, after that, he wasn't picking up the phone or returning messages. He'd gone down into the well of infinite sadness, beyond the reach of story, and he didn't make it out. But he had a beautiful, yearning innocence, and he was trying.

THE CHINESE PUFFIN

The puffin was a Christmas present from my brother Bob. It came in an unmarked plastic bag and appeared to be some sort of puppet or plush toy. It had a fleece-lined body and a big, orange, squeeze-inviting beak, and its eyes were set in triangles of black fur that lent it an expression of sorrow or anxiety or incipient disapproval. I warmed to the bird right away. I gave it a funny voice and personality and used it to entertain the Californian I live with. I sent Bob an enthusiastic thank-you note, in reply to which he informed me that the puffin was not a toy at all but a golf accessory. He'd bought it in the pro shop at Bandon Dunes, a golf resort in southwest Oregon, to remind me of the fun I could have golfing and birding in Oregon, where he lives. The puffin was a head cover for a golf driver.

My difficulty with golf is that, although I play it once or twice a year to be sociable, I dislike almost everything about it. The point of the game seems to be the methodical euthanizing of workday-size chunks of time by well-off white men. Golf eats land, drinks water, displaces wildlife, fosters sprawl. I dislike the self-congratulations of its etiquette, the self-important hush of its television analysts. Most of all, I dislike how badly I play the game. Spelled backward, golf is flog.

I do own a cheap set of clubs, but there was no way I was going to impale my puffin on one of them. For one thing, the Californian had taken to clutching it in bed every night. The puffin had quickly established itself as a minor household character. Out in the world of nature, real puffins (and many other pelagic birds) were suffering badly from overfishing of the oceans and degradation of their nest sites, but nature could be a cold and abstract thing to love from the middle of New York City. The toy was furry and immediate.

In Jane Smiley's great novel *The Greenlanders*, there's a tale about a Norse farmer who brings a polar bear cub into his house and raises it as his son. Although the bear learns to read, it can't help remaining a bear, with a bear's huge appetite, and eventually it begins to eat up all the farmer's sheep. The farmer knows he has to get rid of the bear, but he can never quite bring himself to do it, because (according to the story's refrain) the bear has such beautiful soft fur and such beautiful dark eyes. Metaphorically, for Smiley, the bear represents a destructive passion too pleasurable to resist. But the story also works as a straightforward warning about sentimental idolatry. *Homo sapiens* is the animal that wants to believe, in defiance of harsh natural law, that other animals are part of its family. I can make a pretty good ethical argument for our responsibility to other species, and yet I sometimes wonder whether, at root, my concern for biodiversity and animal welfare might be a kind of regression to my childhood bedroom and its community of plush toys: a fantasy of cuddliness and interspecies harmony. Smiley's smitten farmer is finally driven to offer the flesh of his own arm to his insatiable bear-child.

Late last fall, while the *Times* was running a series of long articles about the crisis of pollution, water shortages, desertification, species loss, and deforestation in China and I was managing to read no more than fifty words of any of them, a terrific new Jeep commercial was airing during football games. You know: the one where a squirrel, a wolf, two horned larks, and an

SUV driver join together in song while rolling down an empty highway through pristine forest. I especially enjoyed the moment when the wolf gulps down one of the larks, receives a disapproving look from the SUV driver, spits the lark back out unharmed, and bursts into song. I knew perfectly well that SUVs were even more hostile to horned larks than wolves were; I knew that my domestic appetites were part of the same beast that was devouring the natural world in China and elsewhere in Asia; and yet I loved the Jeep ad. I loved the worried eyes and soft fur of my golf accessory. I didn't want to know what I knew. And yet: I couldn't stand not knowing, either. One afternoon, with a kind of grim foreboding, I went to the bedroom and grabbed the puffin by its wings and stuck it underneath a bright lamp and turned it inside out, and there, sure enough, was the label: HANDMADE IN CHINA.

I decided to visit the part of the world where the puffin came from. The industrial system that had created the fake bird was destroying real birds, and I wanted to be in a place where this connection couldn't be concealed. Basically, I wanted to know how bad things were.

I called up the American company on the puffin's label—Daphne's Headcovers, of Phoenix, Arizona—and spoke to its president, Jane Spicer. I was afraid she'd be reticent about her Chinese sources, especially in light of the recent Chinese toy scandals, but she was the opposite of reticent. In our first phone conversation, she told me about her golden retriever, Aspen, her found cat, Mango, her late mother, Daphne (with whom, at the age of ten, she'd started the company), her husband, Steve, who ran the production end of things, and her most famous customer, Tiger Woods, whose furry tiger head cover, nicknamed Frank, had costarred in a series of Nike television ads in 2003 and 2004. She told me that Daphne, herself an immigrant from

England, had made a point of hiring immigrants to sew the head covers, and that she, Jane, had once lent some workers to a woman who manufactured cat toys and had lost her own workers and was desperate to get her orders filled, and that, years later, in the mysterious way of karma, after the woman had struck it rich and Jane had forgotten all about her, she'd called up Jane and said, "Remember me? You saved my business. I've been looking for a way to repay you, and I'd like you to meet some friends of mine from China."

Daphne's is the world leader in animal head covers. When I went to visit its headquarters, in Phoenix, Jane introduced me to workers she referred to as "the zoo crew," who inspect the head covers and sort them by species in plastic-lined boxes. She helped me locate the puffins, which, piled in their box, looked about as cute and animate as laundry. In the sample room, she showed me boxes of unauthorized knockoffs with sheaves of legal documents stacked on top. "The vast majority of our lawsuits are against American companies," she said. "Often the Chinese manufacturers don't even know they're infringing." Her tiger and her gopher (with its *Caddyshack* associations) were especially popular targets of intellectual piracy. There was also a walrus head cover made from the dense brown pelt of some actual animal. "This should still be on the animal that wore it," Jane said severely. "Karma's going to get the guy who did this, but our attorney's going to get him first."

When I asked her if I could possibly meet with her suppliers in China, Jane said maybe. She wanted me to know, in any case, that the suppliers' workers in China were averaging twice, or nearly twice, the local minimum wage. "We wanted to pay for perfection," she said, "and we wanted good karma there—wanted happy workers in a happy factory." She and Steve still do some design, but they've come to trust their Chinese partners to do more and more of it. Steve can e-mail a sketch from Phoenix and have a plush prototype in hand a week later. When he travels to China, the team there can produce a prototype before lunch and a revised prototype by the end of the workday. Language is mostly not a problem, although Steve did have trouble explaining a gray whale's "barnacles" to the Chinese team, and an employee once came to him with a strange question: "You said you want all the animals to be *angry*. Why?" Steve replied that, no, to the contrary, he and Jane wanted their animals to look happy and to make people happy to touch them. The word that had been mistranslated as *angry* was *realistic*.

"Work first, *then* pleasure," David Xu cheerfully admonished me on my first official day in China. Xu was from the foreign-affairs office in the booming city of Ningbo, a hundred miles due south of Shanghai, and our "work" consisted of racing from one factory to another in a hired van. From the back of the van, it seemed to me that every inch of Greater Ningbo was under construction or reconstruction simultaneously. My extremely new hotel had been built in the rear yard of a merely very new hotel, a few feet away. The roads were modern but heavily divoted, as if it were understood that they would all be torn up again soon anyway. The countryside seethed with improvement; in some villages, it was hard to find a house that didn't have a pile of sand or a stack of bricks in front of it. Farm fields were sprouting factories while, outside the less-new factories, the support columns of coming viaducts went up behind scaffolds. The growth rate that Ningbo had sustained in recent years—about fourteen percent—quickly became exhausting just to look at.

As if to reenergize me, Xu twisted around in the front seat and emphasized, with a big smile, that "China is a *developing* country." Xu's teeth were beautiful. He had the fashionably angular eyeglasses and ingratiating eagerness of an untenured literature professor, and he was charming and frank on every imaginable subject—our driver's lack of basic road skills, the long and eventful history of homosexuality in China, the uncanny suddenness with which old neighborhoods in Ningbo were razed and replaced, even the unwisdom of the Three Gorges project on the Yangtze. Xu had also graciously refrained from asking me what I had been doing in China between my arrival in Shanghai seven days earlier and my official arrival in Ningbo the afternoon before. To repay this kindness, I tried to show keen interest in even the most obviously unrepresentative factories he took me to, such as the automobile maker Geely, a proud pioneer of green manufacturing methods like "water melt" body paint ("'Green' means friendly to the environment," Xu said), and the heavy-equipment manufacturer Haitian, where workers typically took home nine thousand dollars a year (Xu: "That's twice what I make!") and many of them commuted in private cars.

The after-work treat that Xu had promised me was a VIP tour of the almost finished Hangzhou Bay Bridge—at thirty-six kilometers, the longest sea-crossing bridge in the world. Before we got there, however, we needed to watch all-terrain-vehicle body parts being spray-painted and motorcycle wheels being milled and acrylic "cotton" fiber being extruded and ingeniously processed in the thriving municipality of Cixi, where exports last year totaled four billion dollars, and there are twenty thousand private companies and only one state-owned enterprise, and so many locals own or manage factories that the resident population is nearly equaled by the population of migrant workers who do the ordinary jobs. I'd read a lot about migrant workers, and I knew that a large percentage of them were in their teens, but I was still unprepared for how young they looked. At the acrylic-fiber plant, the four workers manning the command center might have been borrowed from a tenth-grade homeroom. They sat gazing at flat-panel screens aglow with flowcharts and streaming data, two boys and two girls in jeans and sneakers, communicating nothing so much as a wish to be left alone.

The sun was setting by the time we got to the Hangzhou Bay Bridge. Most of its total cost (about $1.7 billion) had been covered by the government of Ningbo, which was platting out a vast new industrial zone immediately to the east. The bridge will cut the driving time between Shanghai and Ningbo in half; after it officially opens, in May [of 2008], the Olympic torch will be carried across it, bound for Beijing and the Green Olympics. On our drive out and back, the only animal or plant life I saw was a pair of gulls flying rapidly away. Every five kilometers, to combat monotony, the color of the railings changed. At the bridge's midpoint, I got out and surveyed the turbid gray tide running against concrete piers on which a wayside restaurant and hotel were being built. I found myself aching to see more birds, any birds.

According to my visa application, the purpose of my trip to Ningbo was to explore the subject of Chinese manufacturing for American export, but I had taken care to let Xu know that I was very interested in birds as well. Now, trying to please me and to make our day complete, he directed our driver west from the bridge into a system of reed beds and ponds which the Cixi government had preserved as a natural area. Much of the area had recently burned, and all of it was being considered, Xu said, for conversion to a "wetland park."

I'd seen one of these wetland parks in Shanghai, earlier in the week. I did my best to sound enthusiastic.

"Red-crowned cranes are commonly seen here," Xu assured me from the front seat. "The government is planting trees to help shelter the birds from the elements."

I had the feeling that he was improvising a little bit, but I was grateful for the effort. We drove past tidal flats of such barrenness that they appeared to predate multicellular life. We crossed over a broad canal on which I thought I glimpsed four sitting ducks or grebes, but they were only plastic bottles. We passed an "eco-farm" consisting of fish ponds surrounded by vacation cottages. Finally, in failing light, we roused a flock of night herons from a densely vegetated marsh. We got out of the van and stood watching as they circled and drifted closer to us. David Xu was beside himself with joy. "Jonathan!" he cried. "They know you're a birdwatcher! They're welcoming you!"

The week before, when I'd arrived in Shanghai, my first impression of China had been that it was the most *advanced* place I'd ever seen. The scale of Shanghai, which from the sky had presented a dead-flat vista of tens of thousands of neatly arrayed oblong houses—each of which, a closer look revealed, was in fact a large apartment block—and then, on the ground, the brutally new skyscrapers and the pedestrian-hostile streets and the artificial dusk of the smoke-filled winter sky: it was all thrilling. It was as if the gods of world history had asked, "Does somebody want to get into some really unprecedentedly deep shit?" and this place had raised its hand and said, "Yeah!"

One afternoon, I'd ridden north from Shanghai in a rented car with three homegrown Chinese birdwatchers. The artificial dusk had been gathering for hours, but night didn't actually fall until the moment we all piled out of the car, on the fringes of Yancheng National Nature Reserve, and followed the bird guide known as M. Caribou down a little farm road. The temperature was below freezing. The only colors were various dark bluish grays. An utterly unidentifiable bird flushed out of some weeds and flew deeper into the night.

"Some kind of bunting," Caribou speculated.

"It's pretty dark," I said, shivering.

"We want to use the last light," the beautiful young woman who called herself Stinky said.

It got even darker. Right in front of me, the young man named Shadow flushed what he said was a pheasant. I heard it and looked around wildly, trying to distinguish shapes. Caribou was leading us past the car, where our hired driver sat with the heat blasting. We ran blindly down an embankment into a grove of sticklike trees whose pale bark made the undergrowth even darker.

"And what are we doing here?" I said.

"Could be woodcock," Caribou said. "They like wet ground where the trees aren't too close together."

We crashed around in the dark, hoping for woodcock. Up on the road, thirty feet away from us, minibuses and small trucks rushed by, swerving and honking and raising dust that I tasted but couldn't see. We stopped and listened intently to a twittering song that turned out to be the bearings of an approaching bicycle.

Stinky and Shadow and M. Caribou all went by their Web names when speaking English. Stinky was the mother of a five-year-old and had taken up birding two years ago. Via e-mail, she and I had arranged to visit Yancheng, the largest nature reserve on the Chinese coast, and she had talked me into avoiding official guidance and employing her friend Caribou, who charged seventy dollars a day to find birds. I'd asked Stinky if she really wanted me to call her Stinky, and she'd said yes. She'd come to my hotel wearing a black fleece hat, a nylon shell, and nylon adventure pants. Her friend Shadow, a biology student with a borrowed wildlife camera and time on his hands, was dressed in a down parka and thin corduroys. The first half of our drive took us up through the heart of the Yangtze River Delta, which had lately accounted for nearly twenty percent of China's GDP. One vast plain of industry and medium-rise housing and isolated shards of agriculture was succeeded by another. Always, on the southern horizon, mirage-like in the winter light, was some mythically outsize structure—some power plant, some glass-clad temple of finance, some steroidally bulked-up restaurant-hotel complex, some . . . grain elevator?

Caribou, in the front seat, was scanning the sky with a vaguely irritable alertness. "The word *eco* is very popular in China now, you see it everywhere," he commented. "But it's not real eco."

"There was no birding at all in China until four or five years ago," Stinky said.

"No—longer," Shadow said. "Ten years!"

"But only four or five years in Shanghai," Stinky said.

North of the Yangtze, in the region known as Subei, we drove through crowded, run-down urban outskirts for a long time before I understood that these weren't outskirts, this was just what Subei looked like. The houses were blocky, unpainted, blatant; only in the rooflines, which never failed to end in a vestigial Far Eastern upturning, was there a breath of aesthetic relief. We drove alongside canals frosted with thick layers of floating trash and lined on either side with even thicker deposits; white and red were the leading trash colors, but there existed sun-bleached plastic equivalents of every other major color as well. Very rarely did I see a tree more than eight inches in diameter. Vegetables were planted in tight rows on road embankments, in the aisles between the regiments of stick trees, on traffic triangles, and right up to the walls of every building.

When even Caribou had admitted that night had fallen, we left the reserve and drove into the village of Xinyanggang. The buildings there were two-story and made of unadorned concrete or brick. The light consisted mainly of spillage from low-wattage fixtures inside open-fronted stores. Over dinner, in a room where a ceiling-mounted heater blew freezing air, Caribou told me how he'd come to be one of the first professional bird guides born in the People's Republic. As a kid, he said, he'd liked animals, and as a college student he'd sometimes sketched birds and e-mailed his nature notes to his classmates. But it was impossible to be a real birdwatcher without a complete, illustrated field guide to Chinese birds, and the first of these, by John MacKinnon and Karen Phillipps, wasn't published until 2000. Caribou bought his copy in 2001. Two years later, he took a job as an air-traffic controller in Shanghai. "It was a *great* job," Stinky told me. But Caribou himself hadn't thought so. He'd hated the long nights and the constant arguing with pilots and airline directors; he'd even had to argue with passengers who called him on their cell phones. His biggest complaint, though, was that the job was incompatible with full-time birding. "Sometimes, for a week or even two weeks," he said, "I wouldn't get any sleep at all, it was just birding and work."

"But you could fly to other cities for free!" Stinky said.

This was true, Caribou admitted. But his schedule had never allowed him more than one full day in any given city, and so he'd quit. For the last two and a half years, he'd made his living as a freelance bird researcher and guide. Stinky, who had recently discovered Facebook, was trying to get Caribou to set up a page to advertise himself abroad. A lot of Europeans and Americans, she said, were unaware that there was even such a thing as Chinese birdwatchers, let alone Chinese bird guides. When I asked Caribou how many days he'd worked as a guide in 2007, he frowned and calculated. "Less than fifteen," he said.

At six-thirty the next morning, after stopping for a breakfast of noodles and rice buns filled with savory greens, Stinky and Shadow and Caribou and I headed back to the reserve. Like many Chinese reserves, Yancheng is divided into a highly protected "core area" and a larger "outer area," where visitors with binoculars are tolerated and local people are permitted to live and work. There is very little pristine habitat anywhere in eastern China, and certainly none to be seen in Yancheng. Every last hectare of the outer area seemed to be in use for fish farming, paddy building, road grading, ditchdigging, reed cutting, house rebuilding, and miscellaneous major earthmoving and concrete pouring. Caribou led us to red-crowned cranes (bushy-tailed, majestic, endangered), reed parrotbills (tiny, funny-faced, threatened), and, by my count, seventy-four other species of bird. We searched for buntings along a channel that was being widened and paved by a brigade of workers who buzzed up on motorcycles and asked if we were hunting pheasants. This is a common question in China, where birders also get used to being mistaken for surveyors, to being informed, "There are no birds here," and to being asked, "Is the bird you're looking at expensive?"

We saw a Chinese gray shrike near a billboard ominously urging DEVELOP THE LAND, PRESERVE THE WETLANDS, CONTRIBUTE TO THE ECONOMY and a peasant digging a barn foundation with a shovel. We invaded the yard of a family that had come outside to watch two men tinker with an electrical substation while, twenty feet away, near a pile of cinder blocks, a fantastic, prison-striped, crazily crested hoopoe foraged in dead grass. At the site of a reservoir where, just two months earlier,

Caribou had seen waterfowl, we pulled up face-to-face with a very handsome man who sat straddling his motorcycle and smiled at us implacably while Caribou determined that the site had been bulldozed for fish farming and was now devoid of birds. We ended the day by combing through trees and brush near the reserve's tourist center. Here, for free, on one side of the road, you could see a solitary ostrich, while, on the other side, for four dollars, you could see a few tame red-crowned cranes, listless in a pen, with yellow grass and dirty water, and climb a tower from which the reserve's core area was distantly visible.

"It's a wasteland, not a wetland," Caribou said bitterly, of the visitor center. "The problem with nature reserves in China is that local people don't support them. People who live near them think, We can't get richer, we can't build factories, we can't build power plants, because of the protections. They don't know what a reserve is, or what a wetland is. Yancheng should open part of the core area to the public, to get them interested. To help them get to know the red-crowned crane. Then they can support it."

The fine for trespassing in the core area is nominally forty dollars but can run as high as seven hundred dollars, depending on the mood of the policeman. In theory, the core area is closed in order to minimize human disturbance to rare migratory birds, but if you were to go ahead and enter it anyway, some morning in late February, you would see long, loud convoys of blue trucks bouncing down networks of dirt roads in clouds of dust and diesel exhaust. The trucks go in empty and come out stacked house-high and road-wide with harvested reeds. You'd have an easy time finding threatened species like the reed parrotbill, because their populations are driven into narrow strips of vegetation beside vast mud flats—square miles of them, stretching to the horizon—that have been clear-cut to the ground. If you're lucky, you might also see one of the world's two thousand or so remaining black-faced spoonbills, feeding in shallow water alongside endangered Oriental storks and endangered cranes, while, on a spit of land directly behind them, workers pitch bundles of reed onto a truck.

According to an administrator at the reserve, local regulations allow reeds to be cut before and after migratory birds come through. When the reserve was established, in the 1980s, the central government hadn't given it enough funds to operate, and it had charged peasants a fee to cut reeds; nowadays, the cutting is justified as a fire-prevention measure. "Global NGOs want China to do conservation the Western way, but they don't want every Chinese to drive a car," the director of another coastal reserve told me. "That's why we have to do things the Chinese way." It wasn't obvious to me that fire posed a greater risk to Yancheng's red-crowned cranes than the semiannual clear-cutting of the core area, but I knew that much of China still operates under the national watchword of the eighties, "Development first, then environment." I asked Caribou if, as China's economy continued to expand, things were simply going to get worse for birds.

"Definitely," Caribou said. He listed some of the species—Baikal teal, scaly-sided merganser, Baer's pochard, black-headed ibis, Japanese yellow bunting, hooded crane—that bred or wintered in eastern China and were disappearing. "Even just ten years ago, you could see much bigger numbers of them," he said. "The problem isn't just poaching. The biggest problem is habitat loss."

"It's a trend, there's nothing we can do about it," Stinky said.

Down the road from the visitor center, in near-darkness, Shadow called out that he'd found four teals and a snipe.

———

Stinky was officially looking for a job in marketing or PR, but she wanted a job that didn't require overtime, and in China nowadays every job required overtime. She and her husband had lived for two years in the United States. Although they'd ultimately found life there too boring and predictable, compared with China, they now felt less "flexible" than the friends of theirs who never left. "It's a little harder for the two of us to abandon our principles," Stinky said. "For example, in both China and the U.S., people say that family is the number-one priority. But in the U.S. they really mean it. In China, everything is about career now and getting ahead." She and her husband had already bought a retirement apartment in the Sichuanese city of Chengdu, where people have a reputation for knowing how to relax and enjoy life, but for now the husband was working long hours in the city of Suzhou and getting home to Shanghai only a few nights a week, and Stinky was scarcely less industrious in pursuing her new hobby. In the two years since she'd gone on a walk sponsored by the Shanghai Wild Bird Society, she'd kept financial records for the society, managed several of its outreach projects, become an active online poster of local bird counts, and, last summer, in Fujian Province, seen one of the world's rarest species, the Chinese crested tern.

I joined her on a Sunday morning at the annual meeting of the Shanghai Wild Bird Society. Forty members, including a dozen women, had gathered in a classroom on the nineteenth floor of a Forestry Bureau building. It was easy to spot the newest members—they were the shy ones trading little glossy stickers of common birds. Stinky, in stylish black jeans, her hair thick and loose on her shoulders, detached herself from a cluster of friends and gave a clear, polished financial report, using spreadsheets decorated with a cartoon of coins tumbling into a cute-faced piggy bank. (Funding in 2007 had consisted primarily of a nine-hundred-dollar gift from the Hong Kong Bird Society to pay for Shanghai's annual birding festival.) This year, for the first time, the society's board of directors was being elected directly by the membership rather than being appointed by its governmental sponsor, the Shanghai Wild Animal Protection Bureau. An older member stood up to offer roastlike mini-bios of nine nominees, including "a supermodel" (Stinky), "a student who is extremely young" (Shadow), and "a nice guy, very easy-going" (the best amateur birder in Shanghai). Members smiled for a camera as, one by one, with half-joking ceremony, they dropped pink ballots into a slotted box.

China's political system does not allow for an environmental movement in the Western, activist, integrated sense of *movement*. The Three Gorges Dam, on the Yangtze, did generate something close to an organized national resistance, but this was partly because the government itself was divided about the project and because the dam became a rallying point for political discontents in general. The government was recently shamed into addressing the pollution of Tai Lake, near the city of Wuxi, but not because of the noisy citizen (subsequently jailed) who'd blown the whistle on the problem; it was because an algal bloom had fouled Wuxi's water supply. China does have a number of prominent and outspoken environmental activists, many of them former journalists, and private citizens frequently mount NIMBY protests against specific environmental threats. But the dynamic of activists-versus-officialdom is less important than the tension between the government in Beijing, which is committed in principle to strong environmental protection, and the unequivocally progrowth local and provincial governments. Nongovernmental organizations, such as the Shanghai Wild Bird Society, are not permitted to form alliances or to take direction from a national group, and each one needs a governmental sponsor. They're a bit like what our local Audubon chapters would be if there were no national groups to the left of them—no Sierra Club agitating in Washington. Nearly all are less than ten years old, and their mission thus far is primarily educational.

Western-style conservation protests, when they do occur, are usually ad hoc, local, and ineffective. Until four years ago, the Jiangwan Wetland—eight square kilometers of diverse habitat on the site of an abandoned military airport—had been the largest natural space in central Shanghai and a magnet for local birders. When the birders learned that it was going to be developed for housing, they teamed up with local researchers, petitioned the government to abandon or modify the project, and enlisted journalists to publicize their campaign. In response, the government set aside a postage stamp of wetland on which, in Caribou's disdainful words, "you might see some blackbirds, or a little egret." Otherwise, the development had proceeded as planned.

Stinky was the leading vote-getter in the board election, mentioned on thirty-eight of the forty ballots. Extremely young Shadow was one of the two nonqualifiers. After a buffet lunch, we watched a slide show by Shanghai's nice and very easygoing best local birder, who'd recently been traveling in the lushly biodiverse province of Yunnan. ("Here," he said, clicking, "I was attacked by a leech.") Stinky was watching the presentation raptly. She herself was about to embark on a two-week birding expedition in Yunnan, leaving behind her husband and her daughter, bringing along Caribou, and hoping to see at least a hundred bird species she hadn't seen before. I'd asked her how her husband felt about her hobby. "He thinks I'm having all the fun," she said.

From the classroom windows, I could see the upper half of the Jin Mao Tower—the half that housed the hotel I was staying in. The Jin Mao had been the fifth-tallest building in the world until a few months ago, when the much taller Shanghai World Financial Center went up across the street, beginning a reign as Asia's Tallest Building which will last until the year after next, when an even taller building is scheduled to go up nearby. In my hotel room, on the seventy-seventh floor, with my eye attuned to sourcing and the sky in my windows white with coal smog, each gleaming fixture invited me to consider the energy required to extract its raw materials, process them, haul them to Shanghai, and hoist them nine hundred and something feet above the ground. The cut and polished marble, the melted glass, the plated steel. After the cold and dark of Subei, the room seemed to me outrageously luxurious, except for the tap water, which guests were advised not to drink.

"Whatever species you can't find in the forest," the top birder in Shanghai quipped, "you can go to the local market and see in a cage."

Two young men at the meeting, Yifei Zhang and Max Li, offered to show me around the Yangtze estuary the next day. Yifei was a slender, fine-featured former journalist now working for the World Wildlife Fund in Shanghai. Max was a Shanghai native who'd gone to Swarthmore to study engineering and come home as a vegan birdwatcher pursuing a career in ecology. ("I try, but it's hopeless to be a vegan here," Max said while he bought us a breakfast of omelets from a street vendor.) After a morning at a nature reserve on Chongming Island, Yifei and Max wanted me to see a wetland park on the outskirts of Shanghai. To Chinese conservationists, the phrase *wetland park* has approximately the same valence as *petting zoo*. These parks typically consist of dredged ponds and photogenic islands crisscrossed by wide wooden promenades repellent to birds. The park in Shanghai was adjacent to a military base whose firing range was so loud and close that the salvos sounded like a video arcade; I saw a tracer round cross the sky over our heads. There were also colored spotlights, fake boulders emitting Chinese pop music, and dense rectilinear plantings of pansies. Yifei looked down at the pansies and said, "Dumb."

We crossed the Yangtze in an old, slow ferry. The waters were the color of wet cement mix. As we approached the shore, hundreds of passengers pressed against the ferry's bulkheads, trying to squeeze through small doors, onto a narrow platform, and down a set of steep, narrow metal stairs. Although I liked the country's pace—the Chinese empty out of jetliners wonderfully fast, and Chinese elevator doors are hair-triggered—I didn't appreciate being jostled so close to ladder-like stairs. I was used to crowds in New York City, but not crowds like this. One difference was the alacrity with which the tiniest advantage was seized, the slightest hesitation exploited. Even more striking, though, was the self-blinkering angle at which the women pushing around me (they were mostly women) held their heads. It was the angle of looking at the ground exactly one step ahead, and the effect was not to make me feel challenged or resented (the sort of thing that raised my blood pressure on the Lexington Avenue subway line) but to render me somehow inanimate. I was nothing more than an obstacle dimly sensed.

I asked Max and Yifei about the seeming indifference of most private citizens in China to the environmental crisis, especially regarding wildlife.

"There's a long cultural tradition here of living in 'harmony with nature,'" Max said. "Those ideas persisted for thousands of years, and they can't have just evaporated. They're just temporarily lost in this generation. Under Mao, all sorts of traditional values were broken down. So now all people think is, I just want to get rich. The richer you get, the more respect you'll get. And the first people to get really rich, in the nineties, were the Cantonese. Then people in other provinces started to copy the Cantonese lifestyle, part of which is to eat a lot of seafood to show off how much money you have."

"We don't have enough researchers studying what's happening environmentally," Yifei said. "And the researchers we do have don't speak up. In all the bureaus, even at the Academy of Science, everybody is just thinking about how to say the right thing to please his boss. Instead of real information, there's a lot of fake information—you know, 'China has a wealth of natural resources.' The country's general trend is good—toward greater intellectual freedom—but it's still very limited. So, finally, everyone just cares about what he can get for himself. The goal becomes personal survival."

In Ningbo, I'd asked to see a golf-club factory, and the tireless, beautifully smiling David Xu had granted my wish. Xu was on the phone with the company president until the very minute we arrived at the factory, reassuring him that I really was a writer and that he, Xu, really did work in the foreign-affairs office. The year before, one of the company's competitors had sent spies to the factory in the guise of journalists.

Modern golf clubs may look ultra-high-tech, but they're irreducibly labor-intensive to make. The factory in Ningbo employed about five hundred workers, most of them from central and western China. They lived in the factory dormitory, they ate in the factory cafeteria, and, according to the company's young sales manager, Lawyrance Luo, they generally didn't understand much about the items they were making. Luo said that he himself went golfing only a few times a year, when the company had new products to test. Most of the clubs the factory produced were sold in sets, complete with bulky bag, at big retail outlets in America. The factory's bare concrete and basic lighting could have been one year old or fifty years old. Ditto the grease-blackened machines, operated by male workers, that rolled raw steel tubing into a taper and pressed neat rings of crimp into the resulting shaft. Female workers painted glue onto strips of graphite composite which were then rolled onto the shafts and heat-bonded to them. One heavy-duty machine stamped sheet steel into hollow driver heads; on either side of a different machine, two men used tweezers to insert and remove driver faces into which the machine pressed horizontal grooves. After stamping, the driver heads were milled in a dimly lit room full of water-cooled grinding machines and well-muscled men in masks; Luo assured me that the water here was recycled and the ventilation much better than it used to be, but the scene was still pretty infernal. Upstairs, in a room filled with shockingly intense paint fumes, tough-looking girls with big hair and extreme boots and stockings were inspecting the finish on driver shafts and buffing away small flaws. Other young people sandblasted clubheads, applied decals to shafts, hand-tinted the grooves of logos, and injected glue into driver heads to keep the residual grit in them from rattling. In a crowded ground-floor space where the finished product piled up, forests of shiny clubheads loomed above ridges of colorful bags and wide reed beds in which the stems were shafts and the heads of the reeds were cushioned grips.

Like China's nature reserves, this factory was hemmed in by difficulties. The company payroll, currently averaging about two hundred dollars a month per worker, was rising every year, and there were new federal laws that, in theory at least, increased the minimum wage and required companies to give insurance and severance pay to all but their short-term workers.

Because the central government was also bent on developing the country's interior, employers in coastal cities like Ningbo had to offer ever greater incentives to lure workers from home and retain them. Meanwhile, China's export tax credit had been made less generous, raw-material costs were increasing month by month, the American economy was slackening, the American dollar was a dog, and yet the factory couldn't pass along its increased costs to its customers—the American buyers would simply go to another factory.

"Our profit margin has become very, very small," Luo said. "It's the same as when the Taiwanese manufacturers moved over here ten years ago. We see more and more businesses moving to Vietnam now."

"Vietnam is very small," David Xu countered with an intense smile.

By the front door, as we were leaving, we came upon an enormous golf bag filled with plastic-wrapped clubs.

"These are the best clubs we make," Luo told me. "The top of the line. The president wants you to have them as a gift, because of your interest in golf."

I looked at Xu and at my translator, Miss Wang, but neither was able to give me a clear sign of what to do. As in a dream, I watched the clubs being loaded into the rear of our van. I watched the door being closed. Surely some well-known rule of journalistic ethics applied here?

"Oh, I don't know about this," I said. "I'm not at all sure about this."

The next thing I knew, Luo was waving goodbye and we were driving off into the late-morning haze. A strong, warm, smoke-laden wind had kicked up; the air was suddenly very bad. I thought I might have accomplished a refusal of the gift if only I'd felt more sure about business etiquette in China. Admittedly, though, I'd been further paralyzed, at the critical moment, by the tastiness of the phrase "top of the line" and by the thought of handling those glossy, sexy, late-model golf clubs; the extended factory tour had given me an appetite for finished product. Only now was it occurring to me that there was a lot of schlepping between Ningbo and New York. Plus: after accepting such a handsome gift, wouldn't it be rude of me to write about the intense workplace paint fumes? Plus: didn't I dislike golf?

"I'm thinking we should go back and return the clubs," I said. "Could we do that? Would the president be offended?"

"Jonathan, you must keep the clubs," Xu said. He didn't sound entirely sure of himself, though. I explained what a bother it was to travel with excess luggage, and Miss Wang, who was not much bigger than the bag of clubs, offered to carry them back to Shanghai for me and store them until I flew home. "I need to lose weight," she said.

"They will be a memento of your trip," Xu said.

"You should definitely keep them," Miss Wang agreed.

I was thinking of the trip I'd made to Oregon a month earlier. On the occasion of a major birthday of my brother's, I'd finally gone with him to Bandon Dunes. I'd seen baskets of worried-looking puffins in the pro shop, and I'd butchered, with growing impatience, eighteen gorgeous golf holes while Bob was sinking putts that seemed to cross two county lines. To get to Bandon from Bob's house, we'd taken Portland's light-rail line to the airport. If you want to feel radiantly white, male, and leisured, you can hardly do better than to trouble an ethnically diverse crowd of working people to step around your golf bags during morning rush hour.

I told David Xu that I wanted to make a present of my new clubs to him. He protested: "I've never in my life touched the gate of a golf course!" In the end, though, he had little choice but to accept. "It will help me remember you," he said philosophically. "It will be a wonderful, colorful spice to my life."

Among thousands of recent postings on the website of the Jiangsu Wild Bird Society—based in Nanjing, the capital of Jiangsu Province, which neighbors Shanghai—is a thread that began when a newcomer to the group, Xiaoxiaoge, posted bird pictures that he'd taken at a zoo and was roundly reprimanded for it. Xiaoxiaoge fired back:

> I never heard of any animal-protection organization expressing a negative opinion of zoos.... Aren't so-called "wild animal preserves" just a place set up to "imprison" animals to protect them?

He continued:

> Aren't zoos the only place one can take pictures of birds with a simple camera from close up? Otherwise, you have to spend thousands [on camera equipment] to take pictures of birds, and then isn't it like an upper-class activity? . . . These people get caught up in the pleasure of the birds' beauty and cannot get out of it; they all get caught in the pleasure of finding a new species somewhere and cannot get out of it.

If birdwatchers truly cared about birds, Xiaoxiaoge wrote, they would spend less energy on making pretty images and more time defending nature against human threats.

In reply to Xiaoxiaoge, one poster pointed out that Nanjing's very first birder had used an average set of binoculars, 200 yuan, to watch birds, and he became a nationally known expert. He insisted on using those binoculars for five years, until he finally traded them for new ones this year.

Another poster took the opportunity to lament the profit motive at Chinese zoos:

Go to Western zoos and you will realize that animals in real zoos have a much better life than in the wild. Recently, I've talked with people who've come back from overseas or friends from overseas, and I feel even more strongly that the gap in our country is: we never do a thing the way it should be done. Everything is some kind of transaction, just some self-centered transaction.

And another poster wrote of his internal conflict:

Personally, I don't like zoos and I don't like humans imprisoning animals. In my heart I want to smash the cages, but I don't have the guts. Smashing them is definitely a crime.

The longest, most patient, and most carefully reasoned response to Xiaoxiaoge's provocations came from a poster who called himself asroma13 (an Italian soccer reference). Asroma13 acknowledged that zoos can be useful, especially for novices, if they're well managed. He explained the difference between zoos and reserves: that what a reserve primarily protects is a *place*. He told Xiaoxiaoge that he, asroma13, had personally posted many photographs of "environmental destruction, bird catching, and other harmful phenomena," but that this couldn't be the only focus of the website. As for Xiaoxiaoge's charges of self-indulgence, asroma13 acknowledged that not many people took up birding or bird photography out of a conservationist impulse, and yet most people who pursued the hobby did come to favor the protection of nature. Moreover, he wrote:

> If birdwatchers and bird photographers can't indulge in the pleasures of beauty and of finding new species—if we can't sigh with emotion at birds' beauty—then where will we find the reasons and the passion to protect them?

It was asroma13 who, two years earlier, at the age of twenty, had created the Jiangsu Wild Bird Society. In English, he called himself Shrike. I met up with him in Nanjing on a Sunday morning, and while we were riding in a cab to the Botanical Garden, on the city's densely forested Purple Mountain, the car radio happened to air a news report about a flock of migrant swans that the society had observed on a lake south of Nanjing. Shrike had been feeding local editors a steady stream of bird news for the last two years. "If you can get one station or news-paper to run a story, all the others will get interested, too," he said.

Shrike was a tall, high-cheekboned, very young-looking student of biomedical engineering. He said he knew every de-tail of every bird species in Nanjing, and I believed him. On a cold gray day, in two very slow loops around the Botanical Garden—we were there for six hours—he induced an urban park to yield up thirty-five species. (We also encountered three feral cats near a trash dump, the only mammals I saw roaming free in my weeks in China.) Carrying a tripod-mounted camera like a small cross he bore for nature, Shrike led me back and forth through underbrush until we got a good look at a hwamei, one of China's most charismatic and beloved songbirds. The hwamei's plumage was a rich brown except for the crazy white spectacles from which it takes its name (literally, "painted eyebrow"). It was scratching in leaf litter like a towhee, nervously, alert to us. Elsewhere on the Purple Mountain, Shrike said, people set nets to catch hwamei, but the fence around the Botanical Garden kept poachers out.

Shrike had grown up in Nanjing, the only child of an engineering professor and a factory worker. When he was sixteen, he'd bought a pair of binoculars and said to himself, "I should go out and watch some creatures." He wrote "ECOLOGICAL RECORDS" on the cover of a notebook and took it to the Botanical Garden. The first bird he looked at was a great tit (a colorful relative of the chickadee). Six months later, he scratched out the word "ECOLOGICAL" on his notebook and wrote "BIRD." In 2005, via the Internet, he'd found his way to another birder, a police-academy cadet, and teamed up with him to create a forum that became the Jiangsu Wild Bird Society. The group now has about two hundred members, including twenty whom Shrike described as "very active," but, unlike its Shanghai cousin, it doesn't officially exist. "Our joke about ourselves is that we are an underground organization that's been exposed everywhere," Shrike said. "More and more people in the city know about us now, because of all the news coverage. Sometimes, now, when we're out birding, people will go by, and we'll hear them say to each other, 'Oh, they're birding.'"

Besides pollution and habitat loss, the biggest threat to birds in China is the widespread illegal netting and poisoning of them for use as food. In certain ancient cities, including Nanjing, wild birds are also commonly sold as pets or for release at festivals by Buddhists who believe that freeing caged animals brings good karma. (A nun at a monastery outside Nanjing told me that the monks aren't picky about what kind of animals are released; quantity is all that matters.) According to Shrike, the laws against selling wild birds can't be enforced without risking "social instability," and so he and his group were trying to educate the buyers instead. "Our message in our promotions is 'If you love birds, don't trap them—let them fly free in the sky,'" he said. "We also tell people about all the parasites and viruses they can get. We try to persuade them, but we threaten them, too!"

Shrike agreed, rather unhappily, to take me to Nanjing's bird market. There, in a maze of alleys north of the Qinhuai River, we saw freshly caught skylarks beating themselves against the bars of cages. We saw a boy taming a sparrow on a leash by stroking its head. We saw tall cones of bird shit. Least disturbing to me were the cages of budgies and munias that had possibly been bred in captivity. Next-least disturbing were the colorful exotics—fulvettas, leafbirds, yuhinas—that had been extracted from some beleaguered southern forest and spirited to Nanjing. I hated to see them here, but they looked only half real, because I didn't know them in their native habitat. It was like the difference between seeing some outlandish stranger in a porn flick and seeing your best friend: the most upsetting captives were the most familiar—the grosbeaks, the thrushes, the sparrows. I was shocked by how much smaller and altogether more ragged and diminished they looked in cages than they had in the Botanical Garden. It was just as Shrike had told Xiao-xiaoge: what a nature reserve protected was a place. Almost as much as the animal was in the place, the place was in the animal.

The two most popular wild birds in Nanjing, both of them singers, were the tiny, jewel-like Japanese white-eye and the unfortunate hwamei. Newly caught songbirds sold for as little as a dollar-fifty apiece, but after a year of taming and training a single bird might fetch three hundred dollars. The white-eyes were housed in elegant, reasonably spacious cages in which it was possible to imagine, or hope, that incarceration felt something like house arrest. Most of the hwameis I saw, though, were being raised in grim, solid-sided wooden cells, barely big enough for the animal to turn around in. There was a grille of bars in front through which the hwameis peered out in their white spectacles, silently, while their cash value appreciated.

The first thing David Xu did with his new golf clubs was lend them back to me. We were finishing up another long day ("Work first, *then* pleasure") with a visit to the older of Ningbo's two golf courses. Though the air was getting worse by the hour, we were finally in a pretty part of town. Suddenly, the roads were less crowded, the agriculture a little more optional-looking, the detritus of construction discreetly hidden rather than being dumped by the curb, the billboards promising developments with names like Tuscany Lake Valley. China in general, in its headlong pursuit of money, with fabulous millionaires and a vast underclass and a dismantled social safety net, and with a central government obsessed with security and skilled at exploiting nationalism to quiet its critics, and with economic and environmental regulation entrusted to incestuous consortia of businesses and local governments, had already been striking me as the most Republican place I'd ever been. And here, nestled between a strictly protected montane forest and the bright-blue freshwater expanses of Dong Qian Hu—literally, East Money Lake—was Ningbo Delson Green World Golf Club.

The course had been built by a retired businessman who, in 1995, had been flying from city to city in China, looking for something to do with his wealth. On a jet bound for Ningbo, he'd dropped his glasses on the floor; the man who'd picked them up turned out to be Ningbo's mayor. Ningbo had recently decided that it needed a golf course, and it was willing to sell a chunk of forest preserve, at an attractive price, to get one built.

The club's general director, a handsome woman named Grace Peng, showed us around on an electric cart. The fairways were narrow and green and surrounded by a zoysia-like grass that turned almost white in winter. Rippling blond knolls receded into the haze like desert sand dunes; the caddies, most of them female, had white cloths wound over their hats and around their necks, T. E. Lawrence–style. We saw three groups of players on the front nine and none on the back nine. "Golf in China is still for rich people and businessmen—it's very private," Peng said. Life membership cost sixty thousand dollars; for a million more, you could buy a villa in an adjoining gated compound. Peng said that many of the two hundred and fifty life members, including the factory owner who'd given me the golf clubs, played here seldom or never. A few, though, came as often as five times a week and had single-digit handicaps. At the course's highest point, up by the forest preserve, we watched three regulars tee off on a long and unforgiving hole. One of them hooked his drive across the undulating fairway and into gnarly underbrush, and Peng called out to him, "Ha, ha! Not very good!"

I'd intended to take David Xu to the course's driving range and give him a lesson with his new clubs, but as soon as Peng suggested that I play some actual holes myself, I lost all interest in pedagogy. A caddie set about peeling the plastic wrappers off our clubs while a clerk at the rental counter rummaged for golf shoes big enough to fit me. Peng pointed out the new clubhouse that was being built next door to the very comfortable, ten-year-old existing one. "Rich people in Ningbo are quite young," she explained. "It's not like in the U.S., where rich people tend to be older. Things in China change so fast, you have to build quickly. You have to renew your stuff very quickly to catch the new people."

Xu, Miss Wang, and I followed the caddie to the tenth hole. It was a par-five dogleg that required a scary tee shot over water. I surveyed the empty dunelike hillocks and, beyond them, the jagged ridgeline—a faint black cutout. The driver that the caddie handed me was candy-red, gleaming, as light as air. And this, I realized, was golf as it was supposed to be: exotic scenery, brand-new top-of-the-line clubs, and not a soul on the back nine except me and a retinue that consisted of two people being paid by me directly and a third being paid by the government to be nice to me. Xu, Miss Wang, and the caddie stood apart at a respectful distance. I could feel them willing me to excel, and I was overcome with a sense of *responsibility* to excel. To—for once in my life—not overswing. To let the club do the work. To keep my head down and rotate through my hips. I took a couple of practice rips with the virgin red driver. Then I creamed the ball down the center of the distant fairway.

"Nice-uh!" the caddie cried.

"Jonathan, you're really good!" Xu said.

It was my habit, as a golfer, to follow any strong drive with eight or ten atrocious hacks, and I did nearly whiff my next two shots, with a three-wood, at Ningbo Delson Green World Golf Club. My fourth shot, however, rocketed to within eighty yards of the green, and I dropped my pitch right on top of the flag.

"*Nice*-uh!" the caddie said.

The irons I'd been given seemed fantastically well balanced. They felt like fine surgical tools. On the eleventh hole, I three-putted for a double bogey, but not a bad-feeling double bogey. I now deeply regretted having given the clubs to Xu. My tee shot on the par-three twelfth drifted right—"Slice-uh!" the caddie cried—but there was plenty of springy grass to work with, and I carded an easy four. I was looking forward, literally, to the thirteenth tee.

"Jonathan," Xu said gently, "I think we have to go now."

I gave him a stricken look. I knew we had plans for dinner with his boss, but I couldn't believe that the best golf of my life was ending after only three holes. I pressed my putter on Xu and told him to try it, to try putting, to try golf. He placed his hands on the grip experimentally and began to giggle. I dropped a ball ten feet from the flag. He took a few wild, poking swings at it and then pulled the club up to his face and did some more giggling. I suggested that he set up closer to the ball. He took another swipe at it, as if it were a small animal he wanted to scare but not kill. The ball moved a few inches. Xu covered his face and giggled helplessly. Then, gathering himself, he struck the ball harder. It squirted directly at the hole, hit the pin, and stuck there. Xu emitted a thin, high-pitched scream and doubled over, giggling hysterically.

We didn't say much as we drove back into the congested center of Ningbo. I looked out dully at the prolonged predusk, the ground-level objects already twilit, the sun still well up in the sky, apricot-colored, safe to stare at. With construction and traffic and commerce stretching out in all directions—everybody in China still going at it with admirable industry, if not exactly optimism—I was pierced again by the feeling I'd had on my first night in Shanghai. But what I'd wanted to describe then as *advancedness* was, I decided now, more like simple lateness: the sadness of modernity, the period of prolonged unsettling illumination before nightfall.

———

The puffin's maker, Ji, had grown up in Subei, not far from the Yancheng nature reserve. His parents had met as teenagers in Nanjing just before the Cultural Revolution. Like so many young city people of their generation, they'd been sent to the countryside to learn the value of labor from peasants. In Subei, they built a hut out of mud and straw, leaving slits for windows. Ji was born in 1969 and was raised by his grandparents in Nanjing for two years, but his mother missed him and brought him back to Subei. Every year, in early spring, after the family pig had been killed and eaten, the family became too hungry to do anything but lie in bed for weeks at a time, subsisting on congee, waiting for the wheat harvest.

When Ji was fourteen, he applied for one of three hundred openings at the local high school and came in at number 302 on a list of fifteen hundred applicants. Three students ahead of him were disqualified, however, and so he squeaked in. A year later, he squeaked into a better high school in Nanjing, and two years after that he squeaked into the University of Chengdu. There he was swept up in the student reform movement, marching in the street, protesting against corruption, and was fortunate—again—not to be in Beijing in June 1989, for the Tiananmen Square massacre. Like many other talented students of that time, he turned his attention from politics to business and ended up working in the toy division of a provincial import-export corporation. In 2001, he and his wife borrowed money from friends, obtained a letter of credit from Hallmark Cards, and struck out on their own. They now own four factories and employ two thousand people. Their customers include Hallmark, Gund, and Russ Berrie—the top of the market—and Ji was recently named a Model Citizen by his local government, in the category of Labor-Intensive Industry.

"I am the most lucky guy," Ji said. He had agreed to show

me around his headquarters, provided I didn't use his real name. ("Why would I want to advertise?" he said. "Whenever I want to expand, all I have to do is mention that we're the supplier for Hallmark Cards.") His offices were situated beside a pleasant, tree-lined, concrete-bottomed river in an industrial suburb in eastern China. There was a happy bounce in Ji's step as he took me around the small production facilities he maintains there. In the last four years, most of his production has moved inland, to Anhui Province, where, he said, workers will accept substantially lower wages to be closer to their families. Ji obviously benefits financially from lower wages and lower attrition rates, but he believes that society benefits, too—that marriages are strengthened and children better cared for when the parents live close to home, and that bringing factories to rural workers is a more sustainable economic model for China than bringing rural workers to factories.

Ji showed me a robotic machine of his own design which cuts fake fur with lasers. For a small-volume item like the puffin, the fabric is cut by hand. Workers in the design department demonstrated how the pieces are machine-stitched together, with the backing side outermost, how the pointed plastic stems of the animal's eyes are pushed through the fur and cinched with washers, and how the animal is then dramatically turned inside out—dull fabric transformed into furry friend. Polyester fluff is stuffed into its head through a hole in its back, the hole sutured by hand, the seams trimmed, the fur brushed, and a Daphne's tag applied. The whole process takes an average worker about twenty minutes. Ji presented me with three finished puffins, one of them embroidered with my brother's name.

"I imagine that a panda would be a popular head cover in China," I said idly.

"In China?" Ji laughed and shook his head. "The Chinese

want maybe a bald eagle for their head cover. Or the face of George Bush."

I was feeling a certain guilty-liberal disappointment at not having found more industrial horror upstream from my puffin. Its American seller was an animal nut and its Chinese maker a Model Citizen. Even the pollution aspect wasn't obviously terrible. A week earlier, in Nanjing, I'd visited two factories belonging to Nice Gain, an industry leader in fake fur (or, as it's known in the trade, "pile fabric"), and learned of certain advantages that synthetic fibers have over natural fibers. Nice Gain's fake fur begins as big cotton-like bales of acrylic fiber, imported from Japan, which is carded into fluffy rope and fed into computerized Jacquards that knit it into wide, strokable flows of fur. The primary raw material in acrylic fiber is petroleum—no thirsty cotton fields; no overgrazing; and a better use of oil than burning by Jeep SUVs—and the dyeing process is much cleaner with acrylics than with wool or cotton, which are contaminated with miscellaneous proteins. "If the dye coming out is dirty, we can't export the product; it means you never reached it with the dye," Nice Gain's president, Tong Zheng, told me. Because Zheng, like Ji, was at the top of the market and could afford to run a clean operation, he bought his natural fibers precolored and didn't ask his suppliers any questions about the dyeing. ("The one thing I know," he said, "is that if you do it to code, you're the least competitive player in the market. As a good citizen, you soon find yourself out of business.") My puffin's fur was all acrylic, and if the acrylic-fiber plant in Japan was anything like the acrylic-fiber plant I'd seen being managed by teenagers in Cixi, there were no great environmental horrors to be found there, either. The puffin was evidently more of a luxury item than I'd known.

I asked Ji how he felt, personally, about animals, given that his business consisted of making toy images of them. The story he chose to tell was about one of the pigs his family had had when he was a boy. This pig, he said, had been skilled at burrowing holes through the mud and straw of its pen and escaping. Ji's father had finally become angry and pierced the pig's mouth with three or four iron rings; and the pig never escaped again. "Now it's a joke I have with my kids," Ji said. "'You'd better not get a ring in your nose or your belly button, because it will make me remember my pig!'"

Nose rings are a worry because his kids are growing up in North America. Ji and his wife had always wanted to raise them in, as he put it, a "Western environment," and the final push into a new hemisphere came two years ago, shortly after Ji was named a Model Citizen. Because of China's population policy, one thing a Model Citizen really can't do is have more than one child. Ji already had a boy from a previous marriage, and his wife had a daughter from her previous marriage. They were now expecting their first child as a couple, which would be Ji's second. One night, when his wife was six months pregnant, the two of them decided that she should go to Canada to have the baby. Their child was born in Vancouver three months later; and Ji was able to remain a Model Citizen.

There are two competing theories about the connection between economic growth and environmental protection in developing nations. One, which happens to be very convenient to business interests, holds that societies generally start worrying about the environment only after being allowed to pollute their way to middle-class wealth, leisure, and entitlement. The other theory notes that developmental maturity hasn't exactly stopped Western societies from overconsuming resources and laying waste to nature; this theory's proponents, who tend to be apocalyptic worriers, tear their hair at the thought of China, India, and Indonesia following the Western model.

Proponents of the "growth first, then environment" theory may take heart at how closely the explosion of China's GDP was followed by the emergence of Western-style nature lovers. The problem, however, is that China has so little good land and is changing so quickly. A new generation may be learning conservation, but not as fast as habitat is disappearing. Already China's national parks are being loved to death by an increasingly mobile middle class. In North America, you can still take schoolkids to a nature center one busload at a time and let them spend a day or a week watching animals. In Shanghai, where the population will soon hit twenty million, there is only one accessible nature reserve—Chongming Dongtan, on an alluvial island in the Yangtze. The reserve is well managed but heavily stressed by fishermen and upstream pollution. The entire northern third of it is engulfed by a bird-hostile invasive rice grass (according to local legend, the grass was introduced at the behest of Premier Zhou Enlai, who had asked his experts to find him a plant that could increase the size of China), and an enormous wetland park, containing a "vacation villa zone" and "wetland golf," is under construction along the western boundary. Beginning in 2010, a system of bridges and tunnels will link the island directly to the heart of Shanghai. It will be possible to bus every kid in Shanghai to Chongming Dongtan for a day in nature; but the buses would be lined up bumper to bumper across the Yangtze.

Successful Chinese conservation efforts today tend to sidestep the populace altogether and appeal directly to the government's self-interest. In Shanghai, Yifei Zhang, the journalist-turned-WWF-staffer, is trying to get the city government to think about its maximum sustainable population and its future sources of drinking water. The city is currently planning to rely on the Yangtze estuary, but rising sea levels threaten to make it too salty to use, and Yifei is pressing the city to develop an alternative source by cleaning up the tributary Huangpu River and restoring its watershed—which, as a fringe benefit, would create new wildlife habitat. "We never despair, because we don't have high expectations," Yifei said. Upriver from Shanghai, where hundreds of lakes have been permanently severed from the Yangtze, the WWF in 2002 set a goal of persuading the government of Hubei to reconnect just one of them. "Nobody believed it was possible," Yifei said. "It was just a dream—a castle in the air. But we set up a demo site, and after two or three years we got the local government to try opening the sluice gates seasonally, to let the fish fry into the lake. And it worked! We were then able to give small amounts of money to local governments to set up pilot programs. We started with a goal of one lake. As of now, seventeen lakes have been reconnected."

In Beijing I met an exceptionally effective grassroots activist named Hai-xiang Zhou. Zhou had been doing serious amateur bird photography for twenty years—he felt he'd been a national pioneer in this regard—but had come to activism only recently. In the fall of 2005, he'd heard news that avian flu had broken out near his childhood home, in Liaoning Province, and that officials were claiming the flu was spread by wild birds. Fearing an unnecessary slaughter, Zhou had taken a leave from his job and hurried to Liaoning, where he found that waterfowl and migrating cranes were dying from more ordinary causes—hunting, poisoning, starvation.

Zhou wore glasses so big that they seemed to cover half his face. "If an NGO wants to do anything here, it has to be in co-operation with the government," he told me. "Birdwatchers and conservationists can investigate things, but to actually get anything done you have to have an angle. Local people always want more development, while the government officially wants sustainable development and protection for the environment. Since resources are very limited, officials are happy if you can help them to show that they really are doing what they're officially committed to doing. When an environmental project is done well, county leaders get a lot of positive feedback and gain a lot of face."

On a laptop, Zhou showed me photographs of dignitaries smiling on a wildlife observation platform they'd built in his hometown. Zhou is now working on a new project at the Laotie Mountain Nature Reserve on the Liaodong Peninsula. Every fall, the entire migratory-bird population of northeast China funnels through the peninsula on its way south, and there, on public land, local poachers put up thousands of nets to capture and kill them. Most highly prized are the big raptor species, many of them endangered or threatened. A few of the birds are eaten locally, Zhou said, but most are sent to southern provinces, where they're considered a delicacy. Zhou and his daughter, a volunteer at the reserve, are collecting data to present to the central government, so that it can coordinate local policy. His photographs showed wardens chasing poachers by daylight and by headlight. They showed trees that the poachers had chopped down to block the wardens' trucks. They showed confiscated motorcycles. A room neck-deep with balled-up nets of every color—a single morning's haul by the wardens. Cages of small birds left behind as bait for bigger birds. Tree trunks lashed vertically to the tops of other trees, elevating nets to eagle height. Smaller eagle traps hung from high branches and weighted with logs. House-size nets dotted with stricken doves, white-tailed eagles, Saker falcons. Birds still alive with their wings compound-fractured, bones sticking out, the angles gruesome. A confiscated mesh laundry bag stuffed with falcons and owls, many dead, many not, all mashed together like dirty underwear. A poacher in handcuffs, wearing a nice shirt and new sneakers, his face digitally smudged. Sweat beading on the face of a warden extricating a falcon from a net. A pile of forty-seven dead hawks and eagles, each one decapitated by poachers to keep it from biting, all of them confiscated in one morning. A smaller pile of bloody heads found scattered on the ground the same morning.

"The people who do this aren't poor," Zhou said. "It's not subsistence—it's custom. My goal is to educate people and try to change the custom. I want to teach people that birds are their natural wealth, and I want to promote ecotourism as an alternative livelihood."

The migrant birds that make it unscathed past Laotie Mountain are mostly bound, of course, for Southeast Asia: a region well on its way to being clear-cut and strip-mined into one vast muddy pit, since China itself is hopelessly short on natural resources to supply the factories that supply us. The Chinese people may bear the brunt of Chinese pollution, but the trauma to biodiversity is being reexported around the world. And it does seem like rather a lot to ask of the Chinese people that, while working to safeguard Laotie Mountain and achieve breathable air and drinkable water and sustainable development, they also pay close attention to the devastation of Southeast Asia, Siberia, Central Africa, and the Amazon Basin. It's remarkable enough that people like Shrike and Hai-xiang Zhou and Yifei Zhang exist at all.

"To see something being destroyed and not be able to do

anything about it, it's sad sometimes," Shrike said to me. We were standing by a badly polluted river outside Nanjing, surveying a landscape of new factories in what had been wetland two years earlier. But there was still a small area that hadn't been developed, and Shrike wanted me to see it.

ON *THE LAUGHING POLICEMAN*

An actual Swedish person, my college roommate Ekström, introduced me to this book. He gave me a mass-market edition on whose cover was a cheesy photograph of a raincoated man in mod sunglasses pointing a submachine gun into the reader's face. This was in 1979. I was exclusively reading great literature (Kafka, Goethe), and although I could forgive Ekström for not understanding what a serious person I'd become, I had zero interest in opening a book with such a lurid cover. It wasn't until several years later, on a morning when I was sick in bed and too weak to face the likes of Faulkner or Henry James, that I happened to pick up the little paperback again. I was married to another writer by then, and I was devoting a lot of energy to the morbid avoidance of colds, because whenever I got a cold I couldn't write or smoke, and whenever I couldn't write or smoke I couldn't feel smart, and feeling smart was pretty much my only defense against the world. And how perfectly comforting *The Laughing Policeman* turned out to be! Once I'd made the acquaintance of Inspector Martin Beck, I was never again so afraid of colds (and my wife was never again so afraid of how grouchy I would be when I got one), because colds were henceforth associated with the grim, hilarious world of Swedish murder police. There were ten Martin Beck mysteries altogether, each of them readable cover to cover on the worst day of a sore throat. The volume I loved best and reread most often was *The*

Laughing Policeman. Its happily married authors, Maj Sjöwall and Per Wahlöö, had wedded the satisfying simplicities of genre fiction to the tragicomic spirit of great literature. Their books combined beautiful, deft detective work with powerful pure evocations of the kind of misery that people with sore throats so crave the company of.

"The weather was abominable," the authors inform us on the first page of *The Laughing Policeman*; and abominable it remains thereafter. The floors at police headquarters are "dirtied" by men "irritable and clammy with sweat and rain." One chapter is set on a "repulsive Wednesday." Another begins: "Monday. Snow. Wind. Bitter cold." As with the weather, so with society as a whole. Sjöwall and Wahlöö's negativity toward postwar Sweden—a theme in all ten of their books—reaches its delirious apex in *The Laughing Policeman*. Not only does the Swedish winter weather inevitably suck, but the Swedish journalists are inevitably sensationalist and stupid, the Swedish landladies inevitably racist and rapacious, the Swedish police administrators inevitably self-serving, the Swedish upper class inevitably decadent or vicious, the Swedish antiwar demonstrators inevitably persecuted, the Swedish ashtrays inevitably overflowing, the Swedish sex inevitably sordid or unappetizingly blatant, the Swedish streets at Christmastime inevitably nightmarish. When Detective Lennart Kollberg finally gets an evening off and pours himself a nice big glass of akvavit, you can be sure that his phone is about to ring with urgent business. Stockholm in the late sixties probably really did have more than its share of ugliness and frustrations, but the *perfect* ugliness and *perfect* frustration depicted in the novel are clearly comic exaggerations.

Needless to say, the book's exemplary sufferer, Martin Beck, fails to see the humor. Indeed, what makes the novel so comforting to read is precisely its denial of comfort to its main character. When, on Christmas Day, his children play him a recording of "The Laughing Policeman," in which the singer Charles Penrose gives out big belly laughs between the verses, Beck listens to it stone-faced while the children laugh and laugh. Beck blows his nose and sneezes, enduring an apparently incurable cold, smoking his nasty Floridas. He's stoop-shouldered, gray-skinned, bad at chess. He has stomach ulcers, drinks too much coffee ("in order to make his condition a little worse"), and sleeps alone on the living room sofa (in order to avoid his nag of a wife). At no point does he brilliantly help solve the mass murder that's committed in chapter 2 of the book. He does achieve one valuable insight—he guesses which cold case a deceased young colleague has been reworking—but he neglects to mention this insight to anyone else, and by failing to perform a thorough search of his dead colleague's desk he inflicts a month and a half of avoidable misery on his department. His most memorable act in the book is to prevent a crime, by removing bullets from a gun, rather than to solve one.

One striking thing about Sjöwall and Wahlöö, as mystery writers, is how honestly unsmitten they are with their main character. They let Martin Beck be a real policeman, which is to say that they resist the temptation to make him a romantic rebel, a heroic misfit, a brilliant problem-solver, an exciting drinker, a secret do-gooder, or any of the other self-flattering personae that crime writers are wont to project onto their protagonists. Beck is cautious, recessive, phlegmatic, and altogether unwriterly. By nonetheless rendering him with exacting sympathy, Sjöwall and Wahlöö are, in effect, swearing their allegiance to the realities of police work. They do occasionally indulge themselves with their secondary characters, notably Lennart Kollberg, the "sensualist" and gun-hater in whose leftist tirades it's hard not to hear the authors' own voices and opinions. But Kollberg, tellingly, is the one detective who feels ever more estranged from the police department. Later in the series, he finally quits the force altogether, while Martin Beck dutifully persists in rising through the ranks. Although much is made (and rightly so) of Sjöwall and Wahlöö's ambition to create a ten-volume portrait of a corrupt modern society, no less impressive is their openness to discovering, book by book, via the character of Martin Beck, how stubbornly Other the world of police work is.

As long as the mass murder remains unsolved, Beck can be nothing but miserable. He and his colleagues pursue a thousand useless leads, go door to door in freezing winds, endure abuse from fools and sadists, make punishingly long drives on wintery roads, read unimaginable reams of dull reports. To do police work is, in a word, to suffer. We readers, not being Martin Beck, can laugh at how awful the world is and with what cruel efficiency it visits pain on the detectives; we readers are having fun all along. And yet it's the suffering cops who, in the end, produce the beautiful thing: the simultaneous solution of a very old crime and a horrific new one, a solution that turns on a delicious piece of automotive arcana, a solution foreshadowed by the words of witness after witness, "It's funny you should ask . . ." *The Laughing Policeman* is a journey through real-world ugliness toward the self-sufficient beauties of good police work. The book is fueled by the tension between the dystopic vision of its authors and the essential optimism of its genre. When Martin Beck finally does laugh, on the final page, it's in recognition of how unnecessary all the suffering turns out to have been. How unreal.

COMMA-THEN

-------▶

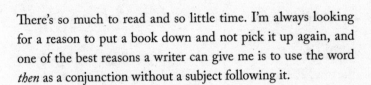

There's so much to read and so little time. I'm always looking for a reason to put a book down and not pick it up again, and one of the best reasons a writer can give me is to use the word *then* as a conjunction without a subject following it.

She lit a Camel Light, then dragged deeply.

He dims the lamp and opens the window, then pulls the body inside.

I walked to the door and opened it, then turned back to her.

If you use comma-then like this frequently in the early pages of your book, I won't read any farther unless I'm forced to, because you've already told me several important things about yourself as a writer, none of them good.

You've told me, first of all, that you're not listening to the English language when you're writing. No native speaker would utter any of the sentences above, except in a creative-writing class. Here's what actual English speakers would say:

She lit a Camel Light and took a deep drag.

He dims the lamp, opens the window, pulls the body inside.

He dims the lamp and opens the window. Then he pulls the body inside.

He dims the lamp and opens the window and pulls the body inside.

When I got to the door, I turned back to her.

I went to the door and opened it. Then I turned back to her.

English speakers really like the word *and*. They also like to put the word *then* at the beginning of independent clauses, but it appears there only as an adverb, never as a conjunction. The sentence "I sang a couple of songs, then Katie got up and sang a few herself" is actually two sentences run together into one, for propulsive effect. Given a similar sentence containing only one subject, rather than two, native speakers will always balk at using *then* without an *and* in front of it. They'll say, "I sang a couple of songs, and then I asked her to sing some of her own."

Obviously, written English employs all sorts of conventions seldom found in spoken English. The reason I'm sure that comma-then is not among these useful conventions—the reason I know that it's an irritating, lazy mannerism, unlike the brave semicolon or the venerable participial phrase—is that it occurs almost exclusively in "literary" writing of the past few decades. Dickens and the Brontës got along fine without comma-then, as do ordinary citizens writing e-mails or term papers or business letters today. Comma-then is a disease specific to modern prose narrative with lots of action verbs. Sentences infected with it are almost always found in the company of other short, declarative sentences with an *and* in the middle of them. When you deploy a comma-then to avoid an *and*, you're telling me either that you think comma-then sounds *better* than *and*, or that you're aware that your sentences are sounding too much alike but you think you can fool me by making a cosmetic change.

You can't fool me. If you have too many similar sentences, the solution is to rewrite them, varying length and structure, and make them more interesting. (If this simply can't be done, the action you're describing is probably itself not very interesting.) The only difference between

She finished her beer and then smiled at me.

and

She finished her beer, then smiled at me.

or, even worse,

She finished her beer then smiled at me.

is that the latter two sound like fiction-workshop English. They sound unthinking; and the one thing that all prose ought to do is make its makers think.

AUTHENTIC BUT HORRIBLE

[on Frank Wedekind's Spring Awakening*]*

- - - - - - - ▶

Frank Wedekind was a lifelong guitar player. If he'd been born a hundred years later, he almost certainly would have been a rock star; the only small reason to doubt it is that he grew up in Switzerland. Whether you consider it a boon or a sorrow that he instead became the author of *Spring Awakening*, the best and most enduring German play of its era, depends a lot on what you value in a work of art. The great strengths of *Spring Awakening*—comedy, character, language—are mostly incidental to good rock. But the play, while lacking in mass appeal, also manages to partake of some of rock's own strengths: its youthful energy, its disruptive power, its feeling of *authenticity*. Indeed, decades after the shocks of Elvis and Jimi Hendrix and the Sex Pistols have ceased to shock anyone, *Spring Awakening* has become, if anything, even more of a disturbance and a reproach than it was a century ago. What the playwright sacrificed in amplification he's making up for in longevity.

Conceived in California and christened Benjamin Franklin, Wedekind was the son of an itinerant young singer/actress and a politically radical physician twice her age. His mother had left Europe at the age of sixteen to follow her sister and brother-in-law to Valparaíso, Chile. The brother-in-law soon ran into financial trouble, which the two sisters alleviated by touring as singers along the coast of South and Central America, and when the sister died, of yellow fever, Frank's mother moved to

San Francisco and supported her brother-in-law's family by working as a performer. She was twenty-two when she married Dr. Friedrich Wedekind, who had emigrated from Germany soon after the suppressed political revolts of 1848. Returning to Germany, where Frank was born in 1864, Friedrich gave up his medical practice and devoted himself to full-time political agitation. The country's mood was becoming increasingly hostile and Bismarckian, however, and by 1872 the family had settled permanently in a small castle in Switzerland.

Though the Wedekind marriage was a stormy one, the family was big and close-knit and intellectually sophisticated. Frank was well liked both at home and at school. By the time he finished high school, he was writing plays and poetry as well as songs that he sang to the accompaniment of his guitar. He'd become a radical atheist and was at once ruggedly well-adjusted and profoundly unfit for conventional employment and a middle-class life. He and his father argued so violently about his career that he finally assaulted the old man and left for Munich to become a professional writer. He wrote *Spring Awakening* in the winter of 1890–91, finishing it on Easter Day. For the next fifteen years he worked to ingratiate himself with the theater world and get his plays produced. His good friends included a shady art dealer and a circus performer, Willy Rudinoff, who was renowned as a fire-eater and birdsong imitator. Wedekind once tried to get a circus to produce his work. He founded and performed in a Munich cabaret called the Eleven Executioners. Over the years, he took to the stage himself more and more, both to forge relationships with theaters and, increasingly, to showcase the antinaturalistic rhythms with which he intended his later plays to be performed. In 1906, as success and fame were finally arriving, he married a very young actress, Tilly Newes, whom he had cultivated for the role of Lulu in his plays *Pandora's Box* and *Earth Spirit* (later the basis for the Alban Berg opera *Lulu*). The couple had two daughters, who would later remember their father treating children with exceptional respect, as if there were no significant difference between them and adults.

Due partly to the rigors of acting, Wedekind sickened during the years of the First World War and died, in 1918, from the complications of abdominal surgery. At his funeral, in Munich, there was a riot worthy of a rock star. Many of Germany's leading literary lights, including the young Bertolt Brecht, were at the cemetery, but so was a mob of the young and the strange and the crazy—members of a cultural and sexual bohemia that had recognized in Wedekind a freak with the courage of his freakdom—and these mourners stormed across the graveyard, rushing for good places beside the open grave. An unstable poet named Heinrich Lautensack, one of the other Eleven Executioners, threw a wreath of roses on the coffin and then jumped down into the grave, crying, "To Frank Wedekind, my teacher, my model, my master, from your least worthy pupil!" while a friend of his, a moviemaker from Berlin, filmed the whole thing for posterity. The exhibitionist mourner and his complicit cameraman: a rock-and-roll world was already in sight.

One useful example of the ongoing danger and vitality of *Spring Awakening* was the insipid rock-musical version of it that opened on Broadway in 2006, a hundred years after the play's world premiere, and was instantly overpraised. The script that Wedekind had finished in 1891 was far too frank sexually to be producible on any late-Victorian stage. When the play finally did begin to appear in theaters, fifteen years later, no local government in Germany or abroad would let it go uncut. And yet even the cruelest bowdlerizations of a century ago were milder than the maiming that a dangerous play now undergoes in becoming a contemporary hit.

The hand-wringing young Moritz Stiefel, whom Wedekind had kill himself over a bad report card, is transformed, in the musical version, into a punk rocker of such talent and charisma that it's unimaginable that a report card could depress him. The casual rape of Wendla Bergmann by the play's central character, Melchior Gabor, becomes a thunderous spectacle of ecstasy and consent. And where Wedekind showed the young sensualist Hansy Rilow *resisting* masturbation—reluctantly destroying a piece of pornography that threatens to "eat away" his brain—we in the twenty-first century are treated to a choreographed orgy of penis-pumping, semen-slinging exultation. Wedekind, without resorting to anything more obscene than a few comically high-flown double-entendres, got Hansy's plight exactly right. He knew that the real fuel of the masturbator's shame is solitude, he nailed the masturbator's weirdly personal tenderness for the virtual object, he understood the corrosive autonomy of sexual images; but this would all be uncomfortably pertinent to our porn-soaked modernity, and so the musical is obliged to sanitize Wedekind and render Hansy's torments as something merely dirty. (The result is "funny" in the same way that bad sitcoms are "funny": viewers emit nervous laughter at every mention of sex and then, hearing themselves laugh, conclude that what they're watching must be hilarious.) As for the working-class girl Martha Bessel, who in the original play is beaten by her father and ardently envied for these beatings by the bourgeois masochist Wendla Bergmann: What else could she become in 2006 but a saintly young emblem of *sexual* abuse? Her supportive, sisterly friends join her in singing "The Dark I Know Well," an anthem to the sorrow of being carnally interesting to grown-ups. Instead of Martha's appalling matter-of-factness about her home life (she says she's beaten "only if there's something special"), there is now a dense modern fog of sentimentality and bad faith. A team of grown-ups creates a musical whose main selling point is teen sex (the first Broadway posters showed the male lead mounting the female lead) and whose female teen characters, shortly after wailing to their largely grown-up audience that they are bad-girl love-junkies, come forward to sing of how terribly, unfairly painful it is to possess a teen sexuality that fascinates grown-ups. If the path from Bratz dolls through Britneywear finally leaves a girl feeling like somebody else's piece of meat, it obviously can't be commercial culture's fault, because commercial culture has such a rockin' great soundtrack and nobody understands teenagers better than commercial culture does, nobody admires them more than it does, nobody works harder to make them feel authentic, nobody insists more strenuously that young consumers are *always right*, whether as moral heroes or as moral victims. So something else must be to blame: maybe the amorphous tyranny that rock and roll still imagines itself to be rebelling against, or maybe those nameless tyrants who make the stultifying rules that commercial culture is forever urging us to break. Maybe them. In the end, the only thing that really matters to teenagers is that they be taken very seriously. And here, among all the ways in which *Spring Awakening* would seem to be unsuitable material for a commercial rock musical, is Frank Wedekind's most grievous offense: he makes fun of teenagers—flat-out laughs at them—to the same degree that he takes them seriously. And so now, more than ever, he must be censored.

The term Wedekind chose as a subtitle for his play, *A Children's Tragedy*, has an odd, unresolvable, almost comic ring to it. It sounds as if tragedy were stooping to get through the door of a playhouse, or as if kids were tripping on the hems of grown-up costumes. Although the eleven-o'clock news may use the word *tragedy* when an adolescent commits suicide, the conventional attributes of a tragic figure—power, importance, self-destructive hubris, a capacity for mature moral self-reckoning—are by definition beyond the reach of children. And what are we to make of a "tragedy" in which the central character, Melchior Gabor, survives intact?

Over the years, many critics and producers have come to terms with Wedekind's subtitle by reading the play as a kind of revolutionary systems tragedy. In these readings, the position of tragic hero is occupied not by an individual but by an entire society which is destroying the children it claims to love. The earliest German productions of *Spring Awakening* highlighted those aspects of the play, suggesting that Wendla and Moritz and Melchior are springlike vital innocents who fall victim to a nineteenth-century bourgeois morality that has outlived itself. For Emma Goldman, writing in 1914, the play was a "powerful indictment" of the "misery and torture" of children growing up in "sex ignorance." For the English playwright and director Edward Bond, writing sixty years later, the play functioned as a denunciation of a "technological society" in which "everything depends on conformity to routine." The problem with these interpretations is not that they're factually untenable—the play does, after all, produce a couple of wrenching deaths—but that they undervalue the play's line-by-line humor. As early as 1911, Wedekind was defending his text against overly earnest political readings, insisting that he'd intended the play to be a "sunny image of life" in which, in all but one of the scenes, he had tried to exploit a "freewheeling humor" for all the laughs that he could get.

The critic and playwright Eric Bentley, the author of one of the less inadequate English translations of *Spring Awakening*, grants Wedekind's point about the laughs but offers the incriminating subtitle as evidence that the playwright was protesting too much. Leaving aside the possibility that the subtitle might simply be ironic, or that it's echoing Goethe's *Faust*, which is also hardly the tragedy that its subtitle promises, Bentley proposes that *Spring Awakening* be read as a "tragicomedy." However sunny or unsunny an image of life it may present, the play is undeniably saturated, from the very first page, with premonitions of death and violence. And the word *tragicomedy* does, in its very awkwardness, like *children's tragedy*, feel true to the doomy absurdities of young love: the laughability of adolescent sorrows, the sorrows of adolescent laughability.

What the word feels less true to is the actual action of the play. Dramatic tragedy, whether Greek or Shakespearean or modern or even half-comic, only makes sense in the context of a morally ordered universe. (*This is what happens to otherwise excellent people, Mr. Hamlet, when they get too self-conscious. This is what happens, Mr. Loman, when you take the big lie of the American Dream home from work with you.*) Tragedy always pays off with the affirmation of some kind of cosmic justice, however cruel, which the audience recognizes from its experience of life. And what's really shocking about *Spring Awakening*—what was shocking in 1906 and, to judge from the vigor of the Broadway musical's suppression of it, no less shocking in 2006—is how casually and thoroughly amoral the play's action is. That both Wendla Bergmann and Moritz Stiefel are initially preoccupied with death may make their later fates seem inevitable; but tragedy requires more than just inevitability. In what morally comprehensible universe does a goofy, vivid, lovable character like Moritz Stiefel *necessarily* meet an untimely end? His death, like so many teen suicides, is random, contingent, meaningless—and thus fully in keeping with the worldview of his atheist friend Melchior, who, by his own account, believes in "nothing in the world at all."

The grown-ups in charge of the play's action are no less helpless than Moritz. You can hate Headmaster Hart-Payne and the other school administrators for their authoritarianism, but they are facing a "suicide epidemic" that they're completely unequipped to make sense of. Their crime is being grown-up and stuffy and unimaginative; they're insecure buffoons, not morally culpable killers. Similarly, you can hate Mr. Gabor for his cold-hearted condemnation of his son, but the fact remains that his son sexually assaulted a girl he didn't love, just for the sensation of it, and can't be trusted not to do it again.

The only intelligible ways to judge the characters in *Spring Awakening* are comic and aesthetic, not moral. And so we're thrown back on Wedekind's insistence that his children's tragedy is, in fact, a comedy. Moritz, on the verge of blowing his brains out, resolves to think of whipped cream when he pulls the trigger ("It's filling and it leaves behind a pleasant aftertaste"). Ilse tells Martha that she knows why Moritz shot himself ("Parallelepiped!") and refuses to give Martha the suicide gun ("I'm saving it as a souvenir"). Wendla, confined to bed by her swelling belly ("our terrible indigestion," in the doctor's words), declares that she is dying of dropsy. "You don't have dropsy," her mother replies, "you have a *baby*." At which point Wedekind, following through on a wonderful joke that he set up ten scenes earlier, when Mrs. Bergmann told Wendla that babies come from marriage, delivers the double punch line:

WENDLA: But that's not possible, Mother. I'm not married . . . !
MRS. BERGMANN: Great God Almighty—, that's just it, you're not married!

Mrs. Bergmann, who is herself so guileless that she lets Mr. Gabor take Melchior's legally incriminating letter away from her, is last seen telling Wendla sugary, protective lies as she ushers an abortionist neighbor into Wendla's sickroom. There are, to be sure, a few genuinely vile adult characters in the play—Moritz's father, Reverend Bleekhead, Dr. Procrustes—but some of the minor male adolescent characters are no less vile, and Wendla's friend Thea shows signs of becoming every bit as conformist and narrow-minded as her parents. The more important adult characters all reveal at least some shred of humanity, if only in the form of fear. Indeed, they not only *do* reveal it, they *must* reveal it; otherwise they couldn't be the subject of real comedy. To laugh well at humanity, both your own humanity and that of others, you have to be as distant and unsparing as if you're writing tragedy. Unlike tragedy, though, comedy doesn't require a grand moral scheme. Comedy is the more rugged genre and the one better suited to godless times. Comedy requires only that you have a heart that can recognize other hearts. Although it's true that Mrs. Bergmann's timidity leads directly to the death of her beloved daughter, this human frailty is also what makes Mrs. Bergmann a full-blooded comic character, rather than just a stock satiric type. You'd have to be a morally absolutist teenager—or a contemporary pop-culture provider pandering to morally absolutist teenagers—not to feel compassion for Mrs. Bergmann in the world of trouble her fear has landed her in.

And just as the adult principals could not be unredeemably bad and still be funny, so the child principals could not be purely good. Moritz's self-pity and his obsession with suicide, Melchior's sadism and amorality, Wendla's masochism and almost vindictively willful ignorance, Hansy's cynical carnality: the cruelest blow that *Spring Awakening* delivers to contemporary pieties, the deep embarrassment that the Broadway musical seeks to camouflage with raunchier shames, is that Wedekind treats his child characters like fascinating little animals—flawed, adorable, dangerous, silly. They fall far to either side of the safe teen middle ground of coolness and righteousness. They're at once unbearably innocent and unbearably corrupt.

Toward the end of his life, Wedekind compiled a list of adjectives to describe himself in contrast to his contemporary and rival dramatist Gerhart Hauptmann. At the bottom of the list of Wedekind's own attributes were the words *authentic but horrible*. The funniness and sadness and resignation of this self-description are the spirit of *Spring Awakening*.

INTERVIEW WITH
NEW YORK STATE

-------▶

This interview took place in December 2007, on the Upper East Side of Manhattan, near the homes of Mayor Mike Bloomberg and then-governor Eliot Spitzer.

NEW YORK STATE'S PUBLICIST: I am so, so sorry! Everything is late this morning, our former *president* dropped in unexpectedly, as he often does, and our dear little state can never seem to say no to Bill! But I *promise* you you'll get your full half hour with her, even if it means rebooking the entire afternoon. You're lovely to be so patient with us.

JF: We said an hour, though.

NEW YORK STATE'S PUBLICIST: Yes. Yes.

JF: Nine o'clock to ten o'clock is what I wrote down here.

NEW YORK STATE'S PUBLICIST: Yes. And this is for a, uh, travel guide?

JF: Anthology. The fifty states. Which I really don't think she wants to end up being the shortest chapter of.

NEW YORK STATE'S PUBLICIST: Right, although, ha ha, she's also the busiest of the fifty, so there may be a certain logic to keeping things brief. If what you're telling me now is that she's just going to be part of some fifty-state cattle call . . . I didn't quite realize . . .

JF: I'm pretty sure I said—

NEW YORK STATE'S PUBLICIST: And it definitely has to be fifty.

There's no way it could be, like, five? A Top Five States of the Union kind of thing? Or even a Top Ten? I'm just thinking, you know, to clear out some of the small fry. Or maybe, if you absolutely have to have all fifty, then maybe do it as an appendix? Like: Here are the Top Ten Most Important States, and then here, at the back, in the appendix, are some other states that, you know, exist. Is that conceivably an option?

JF: Sadly, no. But maybe we should reschedule for some other day. When she's not so busy.

NEW YORK STATE'S PUBLICIST: Frankly, Jon, every day is like this. It just gets worse and worse. And since I am *promising* you your full half hour with her today, I think you'd be well advised to take it. However, I do see your point about length—assuming you really are determined to include the small fry. And what I would therefore love to do is show you some amazing new pictures that she's been having taken of herself. It's a program she set up with one of her foundations. Twenty of the world's top art photographers are creating some of the most intimate glimpses that anybody has ever had of an American state. Really different, really special. I don't want to tell you how to do your job. But if I were you? I'd be thinking about twenty-four pages of unique, world-class photography, followed by an intensely personal little interview in which our nation's greatest state reveals her greatest secret passion. Which is . . . the arts! I mean, *that* is New York State. Because, yes, obviously, she's beautiful, she's rich, she's powerful, she's glamorous, she knows *everybody*, she's had the most amazing life journey. But in her secret innermost soul? It's all about the arts.

JF: Wow. Thank you. That would be—thank you! The only problem is I'm not sure the format and the paper of this book are going to be right for photographs.

NEW YORK STATE'S PUBLICIST: Jon, like I said, I'm not trying to tell you how to do your job. But unless you can think of a way to fit the proverbial thousand words on a single page, there's a lot to be said for pictures.

JF: You're absolutely right. And I will check with Ecco Press and—

NEW YORK STATE'S PUBLICIST: Who, what? Echo what?

JF: Ecco Press. They're publishing the book?

NEW YORK STATE'S PUBLICIST: Oh dear. Your book is being published by a small press?

JF: No, no, they're an imprint of HarperCollins. Which is a big press.

NEW YORK STATE'S PUBLICIST: Oh, so HarperCollins, then.

JF: Yes. Big, big press.

NEW YORK STATE'S PUBLICIST: Because, God, you had me worried for a minute.

JF: No, no, huge press. One of the biggest in the world.

NEW YORK STATE'S PUBLICIST: Then let me just go check and see how things are going. In fact, you might as well have your sitdown with Mr. Van Gander now, if you want to follow me back this way. Just, yes, good, bring your bag. This way . . . Rick? Do you have a minute to talk to our, uh. Our "literary writer"?

NEW YORK STATE'S PERSONAL ATTORNEY: Sure! Super! Come in, come in, come in! Hello! Rick Van Gander! Hello! Great to meet you! Big fan of your work! How's life in Brooklyn treating you? You live out in Brooklyn, don't you?

JF: No, Manhattan. I did live in Queens once, a long time ago.

NEW YORK STATE'S PERSONAL ATTORNEY: Huh! How about that? I thought all you literary types were out in Brooklyn these days. All the really hip ones at any rate. Are you trying to tell me you're not hip? Actually, now that you mention it, you don't look very hip. I beg your pardon! I read something in the *Times* about all the great writers living out in Brooklyn. I just naturally assumed . . .

JF: It's a very beautiful old borough.

NEW YORK STATE'S PERSONAL ATTORNEY: Yes, and wonderful for the arts. My wife and I try to get out to the Brooklyn Academy of Music as often as we can. We saw a play performed entirely in Swedish there not long ago. Bit of a surprise for me, I admit, not being a Swedish speaker. But we enjoyed ourselves very much. Not your typical Manhattan evening, that's for sure! But, now, tell me, what can I do for you today?

JF: I don't actually know. I didn't realize I was going to talk to you. I thought I was supposed to have an interview with the State—

NEW YORK STATE'S PERSONAL ATTORNEY: That's it! There you go! That's why you're talking to me! What I can do for you today is vet your interview questions.

JF: Vet them? Are you kidding?

NEW YORK STATE'S PERSONAL ATTORNEY: Do I look like I'm kidding?

JF: No, it's just, I'm a little stunned. It used to be so easy to see her. And just, you know, hang out, and talk.

NEW YORK STATE'S PERSONAL ATTORNEY: Sure, sure, I hear you. Everything used to be easy. Used to be easy to buy crack on the corner of Hundredth and Columbus, too! Used to be easy to pave the bottom of the Hudson River with PCBs and heavy metals. Easy to clear-cut the Adirondacks and watch the rivers choke on topsoil. Rip the heart out of the Bronx and ram an expressway through there. Run sweatshops on lower Broadway with slave Asian labor. Get a rent-controlled apartment so cheap you didn't have to do anything all day except write abusive letters to your landlord. Everything used to be so easy! But eventually a state grows up, starts taking better care of herself, if you know what I mean. Which is what I am here to help her do.

JF: I guess I don't see how having been open and available and exciting and romantic to a kid from the Midwest is equivalent to having let the Hudson River be polluted.

NEW YORK STATE'S PERSONAL ATTORNEY: You're saying you fell in love with her.

JF: Yes! And I had the feeling she loved me, too. Like she was waiting for people like me to come to her. Like she needed us.

NEW YORK STATE'S PERSONAL ATTORNEY: Hmm. When was this?

JF: Late seventies, early eighties.

NEW YORK STATE'S PERSONAL ATTORNEY: Good Lord. Just as I feared. Those were some wild and crazy years, all right. She was not altogether of sound mind. And you would do her a great kindness—do yourself a big favor, too, incidentally—if you would avoid mentioning that entire period to her.

JF: But those are precisely the years I wanted to talk to her about.

NEW YORK STATE'S PERSONAL ATTORNEY: And that is why I'm here to vet your questions! Believe me, you will not find her friendly on the subject. Even now, every once in a while, somebody gets it in his head to print some more pictures of her from those decades. Usually it's malicious—you're always going to find a couple of disgusting paparazzi outside the rehab clinic, waiting for their shot of somebody infinitely classier than they are, at a single regrettable moment in her otherwise brilliant life. But that's not the worst of it. What's unbelievable are the guys who honestly believe she looked *better* back then, because she was so easy. Think they're doing her some kind of favor by showing her dirty as hell, spilling out every which way, spaced out of her mind, mega hygiene issues, not a dime in her purse. Crime, garbage, crap architecture, shuttered mill towns, bankrupt railroads, Love Canal, Son of Sam, riots at Attica, hippies in a muddy farm field: I can't tell you how many deadbeats and failed artists walk in here all smitten and nostalgic and thinking they know the "real" New York State. And then complaining about how she's not the same anymore. Which—damn right she's not! And a good thing it is! Just imagine, if you will, how *mortified* she feels about her behavior in those unfortunate years, now she's got her life back together.

JF: So, what, I guess this puts me in the company of the deadbeats and failed artists?

NEW YORK STATE'S PERSONAL ATTORNEY: Hey, you were young. Let's leave it at that. Tell me what else you got for questions. Did Janelle mention this great new photography project we've started up?

JF: She did, yes.

NEW YORK STATE'S PERSONAL ATTORNEY: You'll want to leave plenty of time for that. And what else?

JF: Well, honestly, I was hoping she and I could have a more personal conversation. Do some reminiscing. She's meant a lot to me over the years. Symbolized a lot. Catalyzed a lot.

NEW YORK STATE'S PERSONAL ATTORNEY: Sure! Of course! For all of us! And "personal" is great—don't get me wrong about that. Up-close and "personal" is great. She's not just about power and wealth, she's about home and family and romance, too. Definitely go there, with my blessing. Just be sure to avoid certain decades. Let's say roughly from '65 to '85. What sort of stuff do you have from before then?

JF: From before then, hardly anything. A couple of charm-bracelet images, basically. You know—the big New Year's Eve ball at Times Square that came down on TV in the Midwest at eleven o'clock. And Niagara Falls, which I was surprised to learn was turned off every night. And the Statue of Liberty, which we were taught was made out of pennies donated by French schoolkids. And the Empire State Building. Fifteen miles on the Erie Canal. That's about it.

NEW YORK STATE'S PERSONAL ATTORNEY: "About it"? "About it"? You've just named *five* top-notch, bona-fide American mega-icons. Five of 'em! Not so shabby, I'd say! Is there another state that comes even close?

JF: California?

NEW YORK STATE'S PERSONAL ATTORNEY: Another state besides California?

JF: But it was just kitsch. It didn't mean anything to me. For me, the real introduction to New York was *Harriet the Spy* . . . a kids' book. The first time I ever fell in love with a character in literature, it was a girl from Manhattan. And I didn't just love her—I wanted to *be* her. Trade in my whole pleasant suburban life and move to the Upper East Side and *be* Harriet M. Welsch, with her notebook and her flashlight and her hands-off parents. And then, even more intense, a couple of years later, her friend Beth Ellen in the sequel novel. Also from the Upper East Side. Spent her summers in Montauk. Rich, thin, blond. And so deliciously unhappy. I thought I could make Beth Ellen happy. I thought I was the one person in the world who understood her and could make her happy, if I could ever get out of St. Louis.

NEW YORK STATE'S PERSONAL ATTORNEY: Hmm. This is all sounding a tiny bit, ah . . . aberrant. By which I mean the underage aspect. New York, of course, is very proud of her long tradition of diversity and tolerance—come to think of it, give me two seconds here, I've got an idea. (*Dialing*) Jeremy?

Yeah, it's Rick. Listen, do you have a minute for a visitor? Yeah, it's our "literary writer," yeah, yeah, doing some kind of travel guide. We're trying to set him up with some angles, and—Oh. Oh, great, I didn't realize. Tolerance and diversity? Fantastic! I'll bring him right over. (*Hanging up*) The State Historian's got some stuff for you. Made up a whole packet for you. Things have gotten so crazy, the right hand doesn't know what the left is doing.

JF: That's very kind. But I'm not sure I need a packet.

NEW YORK STATE'S PERSONAL ATTORNEY: Trust me, you'll want this one. Jeremy, heh heh, gives excellent packet. And not to burst your bubble, but you might find it comes in handy when you go to write your book. Just in case the interview isn't everything you'd hoped for. Are we clear on the ground rules, by the way? Can you repeat them back to me?

JF: Steer clear of interesting decades?

NEW YORK STATE'S PERSONAL ATTORNEY: Yes. Good. And also your thing for the little girlies.

JF: But I was just a kid myself!

NEW YORK STATE'S PERSONAL ATTORNEY: I am simply warning you she's not going to be receptive to it. Your passion for her and her exciting new projects? Yes! Absolutely! Your passion for some fictional prepubescent Upper East Side chicklet in the brutish 1960s? Not so much. Please follow me back this way.

JF: Do we have some sort of estimate of when I'm finally going to be able to see her?

NEW YORK STATE'S PERSONAL ATTORNEY: Jeremy? I'd like you to meet our "literary writer." A Manhattanite, interestingly.

THE NEW YORK STATE HISTORIAN: Tolerance . . . Diversity . . . And centrality. Are the three watchwords of New York State's preeminence.

NEW YORK STATE'S PERSONAL ATTORNEY: I'll leave the two of you to chat a bit.

THE NEW YORK STATE HISTORIAN: Tolerance . . . Diversity . . . Centrality.

JF: Hi, nice to meet you.

THE NEW YORK STATE HISTORIAN: To the north: Puritan New England. To the south: the great chattel-slavery plantation colonies. In between: a splendid deepwater port and system of highly navigable interior waterways, endowed with a wealth of natural resources and settled by the mercantilist and famously tolerant Dutch. They were among the first nations to make explicit the connection between good business and personal freedom—between enrichment and enlightenment; and New Netherland was their brainchild. The Dutch West India Company expressly forbade religious persecution—a stricture against which the autocratic governor Peter Stuyvesant frequently chafed and inveighed. The first Jews reached New York in 1654, joining Quaker immigrants from England and Puritan renegades from Massachusetts, including Anne Hutchinson and her family. Stuyvesant was reprimanded by his Company for harassing the Jews and Quakers. In his defense, he complained that New Netherland was, quote, "peopled by the scrapings of all sorts of nationalities." Fortunately for all of us, New Netherland's prodigious granddaughter, our dearest Empire State, remains so peopled to this very day. She is the gracious and only conceivable hostess of the United Nations, the ardent champion of equal rights for gays, lesbians, and the transgendered, the ladle of the Melting Pot, the cradle of American feminism. Nearly a hundred and fifty languages are spoken at home by the parents of students in a single school district in Elmhurst, Queens. And yet they all speak the same single universal language of—

JF: Money?

THE NEW YORK STATE HISTORIAN: Of tolerance. But, yes, of money, too, of course. The two go hand in hand. New York's epic wealth is a testament to that proposition.

JF: Right. And this is even somewhat interesting to me, but unfortunately also totally beyond the scope of—

THE NEW YORK STATE HISTORIAN: The Revolutionary War: one long slog of attrition and attenuation. Slippery General Washington forever dodging definitive engagement. In the course of this lengthy never-quite-war, this awkward game of hide-and-seek, of cut-and-run, of bob-and-weave, of peek-and-boo, two battles in particular stand out as crucial turning points. Both of them early in the war. Both of them relatively minor in terms of casualties. And both of them fought where?

JF: This is, wow, this is really—

THE NEW YORK STATE HISTORIAN: Why, in New York, naturally. In centrally located New York. Our first battle of interest: Harlem Heights. Situation dire. Washington and his shaky amateur army perilously bottled up in Manhattan. General William Howe newly arrived in New York Harbor with a veritable armada—upwards of thirty thousand fresh, well-trained troops, including the storied Hessians. Our Continental Army demoralized by heavy losses and available for easy crushing. Critical engagement: Harlem Heights, near present-day Columbia University. Washington's troops fight the British to a draw, allowing the general to escape to New Jersey with his army more or less intact. Terrible lost opportunity for the British, tremendous morale-boosting break for Washington, who lives to fight—or avoid fighting!—another day.

JF: Excuse me—

THE NEW YORK STATE HISTORIAN: Second battle: Bemis Heights, Saratoga. The year: 1777. The British plan for winning the war: simple. Unite Howe's overwhelming southern expeditionary force with eight thousand British troops from Canada, under the leadership of General John Burgoyne— the so-called "Gentleman Johnny." Establish supply lines, control the Hudson and Lake Champlain, sever New England from the southern colonies. Divide and conquer. But it's the boggy northland, the buggy morass. American troops, many of them part-time, dig into Bemis Heights at Saratoga, where, inspired by the heroics of Benedict Arnold, they launch a series of crippling assaults on Gentleman Johnny, who within a week surrenders his entire army. A stirring victory with enormous strategic implications! News of it encourages France to side decisively with the Americans and declare war on England, and through the next six years of war the finest army on the planet proves ever more tentative and ineffectual against the Americans.

JF: Um?

THE NEW YORK STATE GEOLOGIST: Jeremy?

THE NEW YORK STATE HISTORIAN: The lesson? Control New York, control the country. New York is the linchpin. The red-hot center. The crux, if you will.

THE NEW YORK STATE GEOLOGIST: Jeremy, excuse me, I'm just going to take our guest down the hall here for a minute. He's looking a little shell-shocked.

THE NEW YORK STATE HISTORIAN: First capital of the newly formed United States of America, as stipulated by its splendid new Constitution? Site of George Washington's inauguration as our republic's first president? Did someone say . . . New York City? And though our infant state may not have hosted the capital for long, she certainly did have another trick or two up her sleeve! Hemming the young republic in against the Atlantic seaboard: a formidable chain of mountains stretching all the way from Georgia up to Maine. Only three viable ways to get past them and tap the vast economic potential of the mid-continent: far south around Florida through the Gulf of Mexico; far north around Nova Scotia through the inhospitably Canadian waters of the St. Lawrence; or, *centrally, centrally*, through a gap in the mountains cut by the Hudson and Mohawk rivers. All that was needed was to dig a *canal* through some swampy lowlands, and an inexhaustible flood of timber, iron, grain, and meat would funnel down through New York City while a counterflood of manufactured goods went back upriver, enriching its citizens in perpetuity. And lo! Lo!

THE NEW YORK STATE GEOLOGIST: Come on—this way.

THE NEW YORK STATE HISTORIAN: Lo! It came to pass!

JF: Hey, thank you!

THE NEW YORK STATE GEOLOGIST: Who the heck sent you in to Jeremy?

JF: It was Mr. Van Gander.

THE NEW YORK STATE GEOLOGIST: Quite the practical joker, Rick Van Gander. I'm Hal, by the way, I'm the geologist. We can breathe a little better out here. You want a doughnut?

JF: Thanks, I'm fine. I just want to do my interview. At least, I thought that's what I wanted.

THE NEW YORK STATE GEOLOGIST: Sure thing. (*Dialing*) Janelle? The writer? He's asking about his interview? . . . Okay, will do. (*Hanging up*) She's going to come and get you. If she can remember where my office is. Is there something I can help you with in the meantime?

JF: Thanks. I'm feeling somewhat bludgeoned. I had this idea that I could just sit down with New York in a café and tell her how much I've always loved her. Just casually, the two of us. And then I would describe her beauty.

THE NEW YORK STATE GEOLOGIST: Ha, that's not the way it works anymore.

JF: The first time I saw her, I was blown away by how green and lush everything was. The Taconic Parkway, the Palisades Parkway, the Hutchinson River Parkway. It was like a fairy tale, with these beautiful old bridges and mile after mile of forest and parkland on either side. It was so utterly different from the flat asphalt and cornfields out where I came from. The scale of it, the age of it.

THE NEW YORK STATE GEOLOGIST: Sure.

JF: My mom's little sister lived for a long time in Schenectady with my two girl cousins and her husband, who worked for GE. When I was in high school, they moved him away from manufacturing in Schenectady to their corporate headquarters in Stamford, Connecticut. He spent the last years of his career leading the team that designed the new corporate logo. Which turned out to look almost exactly like the old corporate logo.

THE NEW YORK STATE GEOLOGIST: Schenectady ain't doing so well anymore. None of those old manufacturing towns are.

JF: My aunt and uncle escaped to arty Westport. The summer I turned seventeen, my parents and I drove out to see them there. The first thing that happened was I conceived a huge crush on my cousin Martha. She was eighteen and tall and funny and vivacious and had poor eyesight, and I could actually talk to her halfway comfortably, because we were cousins. And somehow it got arranged—somehow my parents signed off on it—that Martha and I would drive into Manhattan and spend a day there by ourselves. It was August 1976. Hot, smelly, polleny, thundery, weedy. Martha was working as the babysitter and driver for three Westport girls whose father had gone to South America for two months with his wife and his mistress. The girls were sixteen, fourteen, and eleven, all of them incredibly tiny and obsessed with body weight. The middle one played the flute and was precocious and constantly bugging Martha to take her to high school parties where she could meet some older boys. The vehicle Martha chauffeured them in was an enormous black Town Car. By August, she'd already smashed one Town Car and had had to call her employer's office to arrange for another. We sailed down the Merritt Parkway in the left lane at high speed, with all the windows open and furnace-hot air blowing through and the three princesses splayed out across the backseat—the older two of them cute enough and close enough to me in age that I could barely say a word to them. Not that they showed the slightest interest in me anyway. We landed on the Upper East Side, by the art museum, where the girls' grandmother had an apartment. The most impressive thing to me was that the middle girl had come to the city for the day without any shoes. I remember her walking up the hot Fifth Avenue sidewalk barefoot, in her sleeveless top and tiny shorts and carrying her flute. I'd never seen entitlement like this, never even imagined it. It was simultaneously beyond my ken and totally intoxicating. My parents were ur-Midwestern and went through life apologizing and feeling the opposite of entitled. You know, and the hazy blue-gray sky with big white clouds drifting over Central Park. And the buildings of stone and the doormen, and Fifth Avenue like a solid column of yellow cabs receding uptown into this bromine-brown pall of smog. The vast urbanity of it all. And to be there with Martha, my exciting New York cousin, and to spend an afternoon wandering the streets with her, and then have dinner like two adults, and go to a free concert in the park: the self I felt myself to be that day was a self I recognized only because I'd longed for it for so long. I met, in myself, on my first day in New York City, the person I wanted to become. We picked up the girls from their grandmother's around eleven and went to get the Town Car out of the art museum garage, and that was when we discovered that the right-rear tire was flat. A puddle of black rubber. So Martha and I worked shoulder to shoulder, sweating, like a couple, and got the car jacked up and the tire changed while the middle girl sat cross-legged on the trunk of somebody else's car, the soles of her feet all black with the city, and played the flute. And then, after midnight, we drove out of there. The girls asleep in back, like they were the kids I'd had with Martha, and the windows down and the air still sultry but cooler now and smelling of the Sound, and the roads potholed and empty, and the streetlights a mysterious sodium orange, unlike the bluish mercury-vapor lights that were still the standard in St. Louis. And over the Whitestone Bridge we went. And that's when I had the clinching vision. That's when I fell irretrievably for New York: when I saw Co-Op City late at night.

THE NEW YORK STATE GEOLOGIST: Get outta here.

JF: Seriously. I'd already spent the day in Manhattan. I'd already seen the biggest and most city-like city in the world. And now we'd been driving away from it for fifteen or twenty minutes, which in St. Louis would have been enough to get you out into pitch-dark river-bottom cornfields, and suddenly, as far as I could see, there were these huge towers of habitation, and every single one of them was as tall as the tallest building in St. Louis, and there were more of them than I could count. The most distant ones were over by the water and otherworldly in the haze. Tens of thousands of city lives all stacked and packed against each other. The sheer number of apartments that you could see out here in the southeast Bronx: it all seemed unknowably and excitingly vast, the way my own future seemed to me at that moment, with Martha sitting next to me doing seventy.

THE NEW YORK STATE GEOLOGIST: And did anything ever come of that? You and her?

JF: I crashed for a night on her sofa four years later. Again the Upper East Side. In some anonymous Co-Op City–like tower. Martha had just finished college at Cornell. She was sharing a two-bedroom with two other girls. I was in the city with my brother Tom. We'd had dinner down in Chinatown with the in-laws of my other brother, who'd married his own Manhattan girl a couple of years earlier. Tom went to stay with one of his art-school girlfriends and I went uptown to Martha's. I remember in the morning, the first thing she did was put Robert Palmer's "Sneakin' Sally Through the Alley" on the living room stereo and crank up the volume. We took an unbelievably crowded 6 train down to SoHo, where she had a job selling ad space for the *SoHo News*. And I thought: Boy, this is the life!

THE NEW YORK STATE GEOLOGIST: Again without irony, presumably.

JF: Totally without irony.

THE NEW YORK STATE GEOLOGIST: "New York is where I'd rather stay! / I get allergic smelling hay!"

JF: What can I tell you? There's a particular connection between the Midwest and New York. Not just that New York created the market for the goods that made the Midwest what it is. And not just that the Midwest, in supplying those goods, made New York what it is. New York's like the beady eye of yang at the center of the Midwest's unentitled, self-effacing plains of yin. And the Midwest is like the dewy, romantic, hopeful eye of yin at the center of New York's brutal, grasping yang. A certain kind of Midwesterner comes east to be completed. Just as a certain kind of New York native goes to the Midwest to be renewed.

THE NEW YORK STATE GEOLOGIST: Huh. Pretty deep stuff there. And, you know, what's genuinely interesting, though, is that there's a connection at the level of geology as well. I mean, think about it: New York is the only state on the East Coast that is also a Great Lakes state. You think it's any accident that the Erie Canal got dug where it did? You ever driven the Thruway west along the Mohawk? Way, way off in the distance on the southern side, miles and miles away, you can see these enormous, sharp river bluffs. Well, you know what? Those bluffs used to be the edge of the river. Back when it was a miles-wide cataclysmic flood of glacial meltwater bursting out of mid-continent and draining down toward the ocean. That's what created your easy route to the Midwest: the last Ice Age.

JF: Which I understand was pretty recent, geologically speaking.

THE NEW YORK STATE GEOLOGIST: Yesterday afternoon, geologically speaking. It's only ten thousand years since you had mastodons and woolly mammoths wandering around Bear Mountain and West Point. All sorts of crazy shit—California condors out Syracuse way, walruses and beluga whales up near the Canadian border. And all recently. Yesterday afternoon, more or less. Twenty thousand years ago, the entire state was under a sheet of ice. As the ice began to recede, all across North America, you got these huge lakes of meltwater with nowhere to go. And it would build up and build up until it found a catastrophic way out. Sometimes it flowed out on the western side, down the Mississippi, but sometimes there were monumental ice dams over there and the water had to find a way out to the east. And when a dam finally broke, it really broke. It was bigger than biblical. It was awe-inspiring. And that's what happened in central New York. There came a time when the way out for all that water was right past present-day Schenectady. It carved the bluffs to the south of the Mohawk, it carved the Hudson Valley, it even carved a canyon in the continental shelf that goes two hundred miles out to sea. Then the ice pulled back farther and farther north until another new exit opened up: over the top of the Adirondacks and around the east side of them and down through what eventually became Lake George and Lake Champlain to the Hudson. So what you see in the Hudson today is in fact a close cousin of the Mississippi. Those two rivers were the two principal southern drainages for a continent's worth of melted ice.

JF: The mind reels.

THE NEW YORK STATE GEOLOGIST: New York City's cosmopolitanism runs pretty deep, too, geologically speaking. We've been entertaining foreign visitors for better than half a billion years. Most notably the continent of Africa, which came over about three hundred million years ago, crashed into America, stuck around long enough to build the Alleghenies, and then headed back east. If you look at a geological map of New York, it looks a lot like a state map of ethnicity. The bedrock geology upstate is fairly white-bread uniform—big deposits of limestone from the time when New York was a shallow subtropical sea. But when you get down toward the lower Hudson and the Manhattan spur, the rock becomes incredibly heterogeneous and folded and fragmented. You've got remnants of every kind of crap that's come crashing into the continent tectonically, plus other crap from various magmatic upwellings due to rifting, plus further crap that got pushed down by the glaciers. Downstate looks like a melting pot that needs a good stir. And why? Because New York truly always was very central. It sits at the far southeastern corner of the original North American shield, and at the very top of the Appalachian fold belt, and on the western margin of all the gnarly New England volcanic-island crappy-crap that got appended to the continent, and in a northwest corner of our ever-widening Atlantic Ocean. The fact that it's a conjunction of all these things helps explain why it ended up as the most open and inviting state in the whole seaboard, with its easy routes up to Canada and over to the Midwest. Because, literally, for hundreds of millions of years, New York is where the action's been.

JF: What's funny, listening to you, is how much less ancient this all seems than my own early twenties. Three hundred million years is nothing compared to how long it's been since I was a senior in college. And even college seems relatively recent compared to the years right after. The years when I was married. If you want to talk about a tortured, deep geology.

THE NEW YORK STATE GEOLOGIST: I don't suppose you married your vivacious cousin?

JF: No, no, no. But definitely a New York girl. Just like I'd always dreamed of. Her people on her dad's side had been living in Orange County since the 1600s. And her mom's name was Harriet. And she had two very petite younger sisters who were a lot like the girls in the backseat of Martha's Town Car. And she was deliciously unhappy.

THE NEW YORK STATE GEOLOGIST: Unhappy was never my idea of delicious.

JF: Well, for some reason, it was mine. Three hundred million years ago. The first thing we did when we got out of school was sublet an apartment on West 110th Street. By the end of that summer, I was so in love with the city, it was almost an afterthought to propose that she and I get married. Which we did, a year later, on a hillside up in Orange County, near the terminus of the Palisades Parkway. Late in the day, we drove off in our Chevy Nova and crossed the Hudson on the Bear Mountain Bridge, heading back toward Boston. I told the toll-taker that we'd just got married, and he waved us on through. It's hardly an exaggeration to say that we were happy then and happy for the next five years, happy being in Boston, happy visiting New York, happy longing for it from a distance. It was only when we decided to actually live here that our troubles started.

NEW YORK STATE'S PUBLICIST: (*Distantly*) Hal? Hello? Hal?

THE NEW YORK STATE GEOLOGIST: Oops—excuse me. Janelle! Wrong way! Over here! Janelle! She can never find me . . . Janelle!

NEW YORK STATE'S PUBLICIST: Oh, this is terrible, terrible! Jon, she's been ready for you for *five minutes* already, and here I'm wandering around and around and around in this *warren*. I know I promised you a half hour, but I'm afraid you may have to content yourself with fifteen minutes. And, I'm sorry, but, *hiding* back here with Hal, you do bear a certain amount of responsibility yourself. Honestly, Hal, you need to install *escape-path lighting* or something.

THE NEW YORK STATE GEOLOGIST: I feel lucky to be funded at all.

JF: It's been nice talking to you.

NEW YORK STATE'S PUBLICIST: Let's *go*, let's *go*. Run with me! I should have sprinkled some bread crumbs behind me . . . A person could lie down and die here, and the world might never know it . . . She hates to be kept waiting even five seconds! And you know who she'll blame, don't you?

JF: Me?

NEW YORK STATE'S PUBLICIST: No! Me! Me! Oh, here we are, here we are, we're coming coming coming coming, here, just go on in, she's waiting for you—go on—and don't forget to ask about the pictures—

JF: Hello!

NEW YORK STATE: Hello. Come in.

JF: I'm really sorry I kept you waiting.

NEW YORK STATE: I'm sorry, too. It cuts into our already very limited time together.

JF: I've been here since eight-thirty this morning, and then, in the last half hour—

NEW YORK STATE: Mm.

JF: Anyway, it's great to see you. You look terrific. Very, ah, put-together.

NEW YORK STATE: Thank you.

JF: It's been so long since we were alone, I don't know where to begin.

NEW YORK STATE: We were alone once?

JF: You don't remember?

NEW YORK STATE: Maybe. Maybe you can remind me. Or not. Some men are more memorable than others. The cheap dates I tend to forget. Would this have been a cheap date?

JF: They were *nice* dates.

NEW YORK STATE: Oh! "Dates," plural. More than one.

JF: I mean, I know I'm not Mort Zuckerman, or Mike Bloomberg, or Donald Trump—

NEW YORK STATE: The Donald! He is cute. (*Giggles*) I think he's cute!

JF: Oh my God.

NEW YORK STATE: Oh, come on, admit it. He really is pretty cute, don't you think? . . . What? You truly don't think so?

JF: I'm sorry, I'm . . . just taking it all in. This whole morning. I mean, I knew things were never going to be the same with us. But, my God. It really is all about money and money only now, isn't it?

NEW YORK STATE: It was always about money. You were just too young to notice.

JF: So you remember me?

NEW YORK STATE: Possibly. Or possibly I'm making an educated guess. The romantic young men never notice. My mother even came to find the Redcoats rather handsome, back in the war years. What else was she supposed to do? Let them burn everything?

JF: I guess it runs in your family, then!

NEW YORK STATE: Oh, please. Grow up. Is this really how you want us to spend our ten minutes?

JF: You know, I was back there last month. The hillside where I got married—her grandparents' house. I was driving up through Orange County and I went back to try to find it. I remembered a green lawn spilling down to a rail fence, and a big overgrown pasture with woods all around it.

NEW YORK STATE: Yes, Orange County. A lovely feature of mine. I hope you took some time to savor the many tracts of spectacular parkland around Bear Mountain and to reflect on what an extraordinary percentage of my total land area is guaranteed public and "forever wild." Of course, a great deal of that land came to me as gifts from very rich men. Perhaps you'd like me to be pure and virtuous and give it all back to them for development?

JF: I wasn't sure I ever actually found it, the land was so altered. It was all hideous sprawl, traffic, Home Depot, Best Buy, Target. Next door to the town's old brick high school there was this brand-new pink aircraft-carrier-size building with signs at the entrance that said PLEASE DRIVE SLOWLY, WE LOVE OUR CHILDREN.

NEW YORK STATE: Our precious freedoms do include the freedom to be tacky and annoying.

JF: The best I could do was narrow it to two hillsides. The same thing was happening on both of them. Building-size pieces of earth-moving equipment were scraping it all bare. Reshaping the very contours of the land—creating these cute little fake dells and fake winkles for hideous houses to be sold to sentimentalists so enraged with the world they had to inform it, in writing, on a road sign, that they love their children. Clouds of diesel exhaust, broken full-grown oak trees piled up like little sticks, birds whizzing around in a panic. I could see the whole gray and lukewarm future. No urban. No rural. The entire country just a wasteland of shittily built neither-nor.

NEW YORK STATE: And yet, in spite of it all, I am still rather beautiful. Isn't it unfair? What money can buy? And trees do have a way of growing back. You think there were oak trees on your hillside in the nineteenth century? There probably weren't a thousand oak trees left standing in the entire county. So let's not talk about the past.

JF: The past was when I loved you.

NEW YORK STATE: All the more reason not to talk about it! Here. Come sit next to me. I have some pictures of myself I want to show you.

LOVE LETTERS

[encomium to James Purdy on the occasion of his receiving the Center for Fiction's Fadiman Award for Eustace Chisholm and the Works*]*

-------▶

I don't know if anyone here remembers last year's college football game between Stanford and the University of California. But just to remind you: Stanford had a much smaller and weaker team with, like, a 2–7 record, but during the first half of the game it looked as if Stanford might actually beat Cal, because its defense was so pumped up that its players had entirely lost their fear of injury. There were young men running at full speed, as hard as they could, with their arms open wide, and flinging themselves against stronger young men who were running just as hard in the opposite direction. There were spectacular, gruesome collisions—it was like seeing people run full tilt into telephone poles—and sickening numbers of Stanford players were getting seriously hurt and carted off the field, and still they just kept flinging themselves at Cal. The experience of watching their doomed effort, these repeated joyous, self-destroying collisions of young people who desperately wanted something, all of this chaos in the context of a larger suspenseful, formally gorgeous game whose outcome was nonetheless pretty well foreordained: I haven't been able to find a better analog for the experience of reading *Eustace Chisholm and the Works*.

Mr. Purdy's novel is so good that almost any novel you read immediately after it will seem at least a little bit posturing, or dishonest, or self-admiring, in comparison. Certainly, for example, *The Catcher in the Rye*, which Mr. Purdy once described as "one of the worst books ever written," will betray its senti-mentality and rhetorical manipulations as it never has before. Richard Yates, whose ferocity sometimes approaches Mr. Purdy's, might do a little better, but you'd have to wipe away every vestige of Yates's self-pity and replace it with headlong love; you'd have to ramp Yates's depression up into a fatalism of such bleakness that it becomes ecstatic. Even Saul Bellow, whose love of language and love of the world can be so infectious, is liable to seem wordy and academic and show-offy if you read him directly after *Eustace Chisholm*. One of the darker chapters in *Augie March* ends with Augie accompanying his friend Mimi to the office of a South Side abortionist. While Bellow draws a curtain over what happens inside this doctor's office, Mr. Purdy in *Eustace Chisholm* delivers—famously, unforgettably—on the horror. (It is an unbelievable scene.) The extreme margins of the stable, familiar world of Saul Bellow (and of most novelists, in-cluding me) are at the extreme normal end of Mr. Purdy's world. He takes up where the rest of us leave off. He follows his queer boys and struggling artists and dissolute millionaires to places like

> This out-of-the-way ice-cream parlor near the state line, a favor-ite stop for truck drivers hauling smuggled merchandise, ladies committing adultery with local building and loan directors, where a preacher was shot to death by a widow who was losing his love, where the local fairies used to come late afternoons . . .

and he instills these locales with a weird kind of *Gemütlichkeit*. You miss having been there yourself the way you miss having ridden on a sleigh with Natasha Rostov. Near the end of *Eustace Chisholm*, two characters walk out onto the rocks piled up along-side Lake Michigan:

They sat down there, remembering how less desperate and much happier, after all, they had used to feel when they sat here the year before, and yet how desperate they had been then too. A few gulls hovered near some refuse floating on the oil-stained water.

What constitutes *in extremis* for most of us is the daily bread of Mr. Purdy's world. He lets you try on desperation, and you find that it fits you better than you expected. His most bizarre freaks don't feel freakish. They feel, peculiarly, like me. I read about the humiliation and incest and self-loathing and self-destruction in *Eustace Chisholm* with the same lively, sympathetic, and morally clear-eyed interest with which I follow the broken engagements and bruised feelings in Jane Austen. You can be sure, when you begin a Purdy novel, that all will most certainly not end well, and it's his great gift to narrate the inexorable progress toward disaster in such a way that it's as satisfying *and somehow life-affirming* as progress toward a happy ending. And when Purdy finally does, as in the last three pages of *Eustace Chisholm*, toss you a tiny scrap of ordinary hope and happiness, you may very well begin to weep out of sheer gratitude. It's as if the book is set up, almost in spite of itself, to make you feel what a miracle it is that love is *ever* requited, that two compatible people *ever* find their way to each other. You've so reconciled yourself to the disaster, you've been so thoroughly sold on his fatalistic vision, that a moment of ordinary peace and kindness feels like an act of divine grace.

Mr. Purdy shouldn't be confused with his late contemporary, William Burroughs, or with Burroughs's many transgressive successors. Transgressive literature is always, secretly or not so secretly, addressing itself to the bourgeois world that it depends on. As a reader of transgressive fiction, you have two choices: either you can be shocked, or you can shock other people with your failure to be shocked. Although Mr. Purdy, in his public utterances, is implacably hostile to American society, in his fiction he directs his attention inward. There isn't one sentence in *Eustace Chisholm* that could care less about whether some reader is shocked by it. The book's eponymous nonhero— a cruel, arrogant, freeloading, bisexual poet who is writing an epic poem of modern America with a charcoal pencil on sheets of old newspapers—is an obsessive reader of the letters and diaries of other people:

> Unlike small towns, cities contain transient persons . . . who carry their letters about with them carelessly, either losing them or throwing them away. Most passers-by would not bother to stoop down and pick up such a letter because they would assume there would be nothing in the contents to interest or detain them. This was not true of Eustace. He pored over found letters whose messages were not meant for him. To him they were like treasures that spoke fully. Paradise to Eustace might have been reading the love-letters of every writer, no matter how inconsequential or even illiterate, who had written a *real* one. What made the pursuit exciting was to come on that rare thing: the authentic, naked, unconcealed voice of love.

Chisholm eventually becomes so addicted to other people's real-life stories that he abandons his own work and devotes his attention entirely to the book's central love: a crazy, unconsummated relationship between a young former coal miner, Daniel Haws, and a beautiful blond country boy named Amos Ratliffe. Purdy is a vastly bigger and tougher and more protean figure than his creation Chisholm—he is the author of forty-six books of fiction, poetry, and drama—but, as an author, he is palpably driven by the same kind of helpless fascination and identification with human suffering. However high Mr. Purdy's authorial opinion of himself may be, however much of a son of a bitch he may appear in his public pronouncements, when he sits down to tell a story he somehow checks all of that ego at the door and becomes *entirely* absorbed in his characters. He has been and continues to be one of the most undervalued and underread writers in America. Among his many excellent works, *Eustace Chisholm* is the fullest-bodied, the best written, the most tautly narrated, and the most beautifully constructed. There are very few better postwar American novels, and I don't know of *any* other novel of similar quality that is more defiantly itself. I love this book, and it's a great honor to be able to select it for the Fadiman Award.

OUR LITTLE PLANET

-------▶

In 1969, the drive from Minneapolis to St. Louis took twelve hours and was mostly on two-lane roads. My parents woke me up for it at dawn. We had just spent an outstandingly fun week with my Minnesota cousins, but as soon as we pulled out of my uncle's driveway these cousins evaporated from my mind like the morning dew from the hood of our car. I was alone in the backseat again. I went to sleep, and my mother took out her magazines, and the weight of the long July drive fell squarely on my father.

To get through the day, he made himself into an algorithm, a number cruncher. Our car was the axe with which he attacked the miles listed on road signs, chopping the nearly unbearable 238 down to a still daunting 179, bludgeoning the 150's and 140's and 130's until they yielded the halfway humane 127, which was roundable down to 120, which he could pretend was just two hours of driving time even though, with so many livestock trucks and thoughtless drivers on the road ahead of him, it would probably take closer to three. Through sheer force of will, he mowed down the last twenty miles between him and double digits, and these digits he then reduced by tens and twelves until, finally, he could glimpse it: "Cedar Rapids   34." Only then, as his sole treat of the day, did he allow himself to remember that 34 was the distance to the *city center*—that we were, in fact, less than thirty miles now from the oak-shaded park where we liked to stop for a picnic lunch.

The three of us ate quietly. My father took the pit of a damson plum out of his mouth and dropped it into a paper bag, fluttering his fingers a little. He was wishing he'd pressed on to Iowa City—Cedar Rapids wasn't even the halfway point—and I was wishing we were back in the air-conditioned car. Cedar Rapids felt like outer space to me. The warm breeze was someone else's breeze, not mine, and the sun overhead was a harsh reminder of the day's relentless waning, and the park's unfamiliar oak trees all spoke to our deep nowhereness. Even my mother didn't have much to say.

But the really interminable drive was through southeastern Iowa. My father remarked on the height of the corn, the blackness of the soil, the need for better roads. My mother lowered the front-seat armrest and played crazy eights with me until I was just as sick of it as she was. Every few miles a pig farm. Another ninety-degree bend in the road. Another truck with fifty cars behind it. Each time my father floored the accelerator and swung out to pass, my mother drew frightened breath:

"Fffff!

"*Fffffff!*

"Ffff—*ffffffff!*—Oh! Earl! Oh! Ffffff!"

There was white sun in the east and white sun in the west. Aluminum domes of silos white against white sky. It seemed as if we'd been driving steadily downhill for hours, careering toward an ever-receding green furriness at the Missouri state line. Terrible that it could still be afternoon. Terrible that we were still in Iowa. We had left behind the convivial planet where my cousins lived, and we were plummeting south toward a quiet, dark, air-conditioned house in which I didn't even recognize loneliness as loneliness, it was so familiar to me.

My father hadn't said a word in fifty miles. He silently accepted another plum from my mother and, a moment later, handed her the pit. She unrolled her window and flung the pit into a wind suddenly heavy with a smell of tornadoes. What looked like diesel exhaust was rapidly filling the southern sky. A darkness gathering at three in the afternoon. The endless downslope steepening, the tasseled corn tossing, and everything suddenly green—sky green, pavement green, parents green.

My father turned on the radio and sorted through crashes of static to find a station. He had remembered—or maybe never forgotten—that another descent was in progress. There was static on static on static, crazy assaults on the signal's integrity, but we could hear men with Texan accents reporting lower and lower elevations, counting the mileage down toward zero. Then a wall of rain hit our windshield with a roar like deep-fry. Lightning everywhere. Static smashing the Texan voices, the rain on our roof louder than the thunder, the car shimmying in lateral gusts.

"Earl, maybe you should pull over," my mother said. "Earl?"

He had just passed milepost 2, and the Texan voices were getting steadier, as if they'd figured out that the static couldn't hurt them: that they were going to make it. And, indeed, the wipers were already starting to squeak, the road drying out, the black clouds shearing off into harmless shreds. "The Eagle has landed," the radio said. We'd crossed the state line. We were back home on the moon.

THE END OF THE BINGE

[on Dostoyevsky's The Gambler*]*

------▶

To be all meat and raw nerve is to exist outside of time and—momentarily—outside of narrative. The crackhead who's been pushing the Pleasure button for sixty hours straight, the salesman who's eaten breakfast, lunch, and dinner while glued to a video-poker terminal, the recreational eater who's halfway through a half gallon of chocolate ice cream, the grad student who's been hunched over his Internet portal, pants down, since eight o'clock last night, and the gay clubber who's spending a long weekend doing cocktails of Viagra and crystal meth will all report to you (if you can manage to get their attention) that nothing besides the brain and its stimulants has any reality. To the person who's compulsively self-stimulating, both the big narratives of salvation and transcendence and the tiny life-storylets of "I hate my neighbor" or "It might be nice to visit Spain sometime" are equally illusory and irrelevant. This deep nihilism of the body is obviously a worry to the crackhead's three young children, to the salesman's employer, to the ice cream eater's husband, to the grad student's girlfriend, and to the clubber's virologist. But the person whose very *identity* is threatened by such abject materialism is the fiction writer, whose life and business it is to believe in narrative.

No novelist ever wrestled with materialism more fiercely and intelligently than Dostoyevsky. In 1866, when his short novel *The Gambler* was first published, the stabilizing old narratives of religion and a divinely ordained social order were undergoing dismantlement by science, technology, and the political aftermath of the Enlightenment; already the way was being paved to the brutal materialism of the Communists (which, in Russia and China and elsewhere, would produce body counts in the tens of millions) and to the morally unchecked pursuit of personal pleasure (which would produce more subtle consumerist corruptions and melancholies in the West). Dostoyevsky's mature novels can be read as campaigns against both kinds of materialism, which he had identified as a threat not only to his vodka-soaked, politically intemperate motherland but to his own well-being. His intemperate youthful idealism, for which he'd done five years of hard time in Siberia, provided the impetus for *Crime and Punishment* and *The Devils*; his sensualism and compulsive nature and caustic rationality were the personally destabilizing forces against which he subsequently erected the fortress of *The Brothers Karamazov* and lesser redoubts like *The Gambler*. Creating narratives strong enough to withstand materialist assault was at once a patriotic duty and a personal necessity.

Traveling in the Rhine Valley in the early 1860s, Dostoyevsky had discovered his proclivity for compulsive gambling, and the experience was still fresh in his mind a few years later, when, famously, he was forced to compose an entire novel in one month. Because of the speed with which *The Gambler* was produced, the book provides a kind of first-draft snapshot of a writer coming to terms with the void he's glimpsed within himself while playing roulette. The action begins in media res; the mode of suspense is one of Crucial Information Withheld; in places, this information seems to be withheld from the author himself. Camping out in a grand hotel, as in a very untidy dreamscape, is a loose family group of desperate Russians and a

few multinational hangers-on. The book's narrator, Alexei Ivanovich, the tutor to the family's younger children, is desperately
if somewhat unconvincingly in love with an older child, Polina,
whose allegiances and motivations remain murky throughout
the book. Alexei Ivanovich's romantic predicament, like the
family's financial difficulties, is basically stock nineteenth-
century storytelling. What's really vivid and clear and urgent in
the book are the scenes in the casino. The stoicism of the gentleman gamblers there, the vileness of the Polish kibitzers, the
attraction that Alexei Ivanovich feels to the "acquisitive sordid-
ness" of his fellow gamblers, the fever in which he loses control
of himself and starts placing bets in a mindless, automatic way,
and the general delirium and timelessness of the casino are all
gleefully described. In *The Gambler*, as in all his later work,
Dostoyevsky makes the case for nihilism almost too well. A
wealthy old Russian lady sits down at the roulette table, and
soon the table has converted her fortune and the enormous narrative potential it represents—it could buy village churches, a
granddaughter's independence, a nephew's obedience—into a pile
of purely abstract, easily squandered counters. The old woman is
described as "not outwardly trembling" but "trembling from
within"; the world has receded; there is only the table. Similarly,
when Alexei Ivanovich stops playing with Polina's money and
goes to the casino to play with his own, he is instantly severed
from the anguished love of Polina that has occupied him day
and night. What drives him to the casino is precisely his devotion to Polina, his wish to rescue her, but once he's in the grip of
his compulsion, there's only one kind of suspense and no story
at all:

> I already scarcely remembered what she had said to me a little
> while ago and why I had gone, and all those sensations that

there had recently been, only an hour and a half before, already seemed to me now something long past, revised, obsolete . . .

And the book itself enacts what it describes. A nineteenth-century novelistic edifice in which it matters whether General Z. will receive his inheritance, and how the French national character differs from the English, and who the beautiful young Polina is secretly in love with, is blown away by a modern story of addiction.

At the end of the novel, Alexei Ivanovich is still in the Rhine Valley; his delirium gives way to remorse and self-loathing, but this is only a prelude to the next round of delirium. Alexei Ivanovich's creator, however, fled Germany and, in short order, sat down and wrote *Notes from Underground* and *Crime and Punishment*. For Dostoyevsky—as for such latter-day literary heirs of his as Denis Johnson, David Foster Wallace, Irvine Welsh, and Michel Houellebecq—the impossibility of pressing the Pleasure bar forever, the inevitable breaking of some bleak and remorse-filled dawn, is the flaw in nihilism through which humane narrative can slip and reassert itself. The end of the binge is the beginning of the story.

WHAT MAKES YOU SO SURE
YOU'RE NOT THE EVIL
ONE YOURSELF?

[on Alice Munro]

-------▶

Alice Munro has a strong claim to being the best fiction writer now working in North America, but outside of Canada, where her books are number-one bestsellers, she has never had a large readership. At the risk of sounding like a pleader on behalf of yet another underappreciated writer—and maybe you've learned to recognize and evade these pleas? The same way you've learned not to open bulk mail from certain charities? Please give generously to Dawn Powell? Your contribution of just fifteen minutes a week can help assure Joseph Roth of his rightful place in the modern canon?—I want to circle around Munro's latest marvel of a book, *Runaway*, by taking some guesses at why her excellence so dismayingly exceeds her fame.

1. Munro's work is all about storytelling pleasure.

The problem here being that many buyers of serious fiction seem rather ardently to prefer lyrical, tremblingly earnest, faux-literary stuff.

2. As long as you're reading Munro, you're failing to multitask by absorbing civics lessons or historical data.

Her subject is people. People people people. If you read fiction about some enriching subject like Renaissance art or an important chapter in our nation's history, you can be assured of feeling productive. But if the story is set in the modern world, and if the characters' concerns are familiar to you, and if you become so involved with a book that you can't put it down at bedtime, there exists a risk that you're merely being entertained.

3. *She doesn't give her books grand titles like* Canadian Pastoral, Canadian Psycho, Purple Canada, In Canada, *or* The Plot Against Canada.

Also, she refuses to render vital dramatic moments in convenient discursive summary. Also, her rhetorical restraint and her excellent ear for dialogue and her almost pathological empathy for her characters have the costly effect of obscuring her authorial ego for many pages at a stretch. Also, her jacket photos show her smiling pleasantly, as if the reader were a friend, rather than wearing the kind of woeful scowl that signifies really serious literary intent.

4. *The Swedish Royal Academy is taking a firm stand.*

Evidently, the feeling in Stockholm is that too many Canadians and too many pure short-story writers have already been given the Nobel in literature. Enough is enough!

5. *Munro writes fiction, and fiction is harder to review than nonfiction.*

Here's Bill Clinton, he's written a book about himself, and how *interesting*. How *interesting*. The author himself is interesting—can there be a better qualification for writing a book about Bill Clinton than actually being Bill Clinton?—and then, too, everybody has an opinion about Bill Clinton and wonders what Bill Clinton says and doesn't say in his new book about himself, and how Bill Clinton spins this and refutes that, and before you know it the review has practically written itself.

But who is Alice Munro? She is the remote provider of in-

tensely pleasurable private experiences. And since I'm not interested in reviewing her new book's marketing campaign or in
being entertainingly snarky at her expense, and since I'm reluctant to talk about the concrete meaning of her new work, because this is difficult to do without revealing too much plot, I'm
probably better off just serving up a nice quote for Alfred A.
Knopf to pull—

> "Munro has a strong claim to being **the best fiction writer**
> now working in North America. *Runaway* is **a marvel**."

—and suggesting to the *Times Book Review*'s editors that they
run the biggest possible photograph of Munro in the most
prominent of places, plus a few smaller photos of mildly pruri-
ent interest (her kitchen? her children?) and maybe a quote from
one of her rare interviews—

> Because there is this kind of exhaustion and bewilderment
> when you look at your work. . . . All you really have left is the
> thing you're working on now. And so you're much more thinly
> clothed. You're like somebody out in a little shirt or some-
> thing, which is just the work you're doing now and the strange
> identification with everything you've done before. And this
> probably is why I don't take any public role as a writer. Because
> I can't see myself doing that except as a gigantic fraud.

—and just leave it at that.

6. *Because, worse yet, Munro is a pure short-story writer.*
And with short stories the challenge to reviewers is even
more extreme. Is there a short story in all of world literature whose
appeal can survive the typical synopsis? (A chance meeting on a

boardwalk in Yalta brings together a bored husband and a lady with a little dog . . . A small town's annual lottery is revealed to serve a rather surprising purpose . . . A middle-aged Dubliner leaves a party and reflects on life and love . . .) Oprah Winfrey will not touch story collections. Discussing them is so challenging, indeed, that one can almost forgive the *Times Book Review*'s former editor, Charles McGrath, for his recent comparison of young short-story writers to "people who learn golf by never venturing onto a golf course but instead practicing at a driving range." The real game being, by this analogy, the novel.

McGrath's prejudice is shared by nearly all commercial publishers, for whom a story collection is, most frequently, the distasteful front-end write-off in a two-book deal whose back end is contractually forbidden to be another story collection. And yet, despite the short story's Cinderella status, or maybe because of it, a high percentage of the most exciting fiction written in the last twenty-five years—the stuff I immediately mention if somebody asks me what's terrific—has been short fiction. There's the Great One herself, naturally. There's also Lydia Davis, David Means, George Saunders, Amy Hempel, and the late Raymond Carver—all of them pure or nearly pure short-story writers— and then a larger group of writers who have achievements in multiple genres (John Updike, Joy Williams, David Foster Wallace, Lorrie Moore, Joyce Carol Oates, Denis Johnson, Ann Beattie, William T. Vollmann, Tobias Wolff, Annie Proulx, Michael Chabon, Tom Drury, the late Andre Dubus) but who seem to me most at home, most undilutedly themselves, in their shorter work. There are also, to be sure, some very fine pure novelists. But when I close my eyes and think about literature in recent decades, I see a twilight landscape in which many of the most inviting lights, the sites that beckon me to return for a visit, are shed by particular short stories I've read.

I like stories because they leave the writer no place to hide. There's no yakking your way out of trouble; I'm going to be reaching the last page in a matter of minutes, and if you've got nothing to say I'm going to know it. I like stories because they're usually set in the present or in living memory; the genre seems to resist the historical impulse that makes so many contemporary novels feel fugitive or cadaverous. I like stories because it takes the best kind of talent to invent fresh characters and situations while telling the same story over and over. All fiction writers suffer from the condition of having nothing new to say, but story writers are the ones most abjectly prone to this condition. There is, again, no hiding. The craftiest old dogs, like Munro and William Trevor, don't even try.

Here's the story that Munro keeps telling: A bright, sexually avid girl grows up in rural Ontario without much money, her mother is sickly or dead, her father is a schoolteacher whose second wife is problematic, and the girl, as soon as she can, escapes from the hinterland by way of a scholarship or some decisive self-interested act. She marries young, moves to British Columbia, raises kids, and is far from blameless in the breakup of her marriage. She may have success as an actress or a writer or a TV personality; she has romantic adventures. When, inevitably, she returns to Ontario, she finds the landscape of her youth unsettlingly altered. Although she was the one who abandoned the place, it's a great blow to her narcissism that she isn't warmly welcomed back—that the world of her youth, with its older-fashioned manners and mores, now sits in judgment on the modern choices she has made. Simply by trying to survive as a whole and independent person, she has incurred painful losses and dislocations; she has caused harm.

And that's pretty much it. That's the little stream that's been feeding Munro's work for better than fifty years. The same elements recur and recur like Clare Quilty. What makes Munro's growth as an artist so crisply and breathtakingly visible—throughout the *Selected Stories* and even more so in her three latest books—is precisely the familiarity of her materials. Look what she can do with nothing but her own small story; the more she returns to it, the more she finds. This is not a golfer on a practice tee. This is a gymnast in a plain black leotard, alone on a bare floor, outperforming all the novelists with their flashy costumes and whips and elephants and tigers.

"The complexity of things—the things within things—just seems to be endless," Munro told her interviewer. "I mean nothing is easy, nothing is simple."

She was stating the fundamental axiom of literature, the core of its appeal. And, for whatever reason—the fragmentation of my reading time, the distractions and atomizations of contemporary life, or, perhaps, a genuine paucity of compelling novels—I find that when I'm in need of a hit of real writing, a good stiff drink of paradox and complexity, I'm likeliest to encounter it in short fiction. Besides *Runaway*, the most compelling contemporary fiction I've read in recent months has been Wallace's stories in *Oblivion* and a stunner of a collection by the British writer Helen Simpson. Simpson's book, a series of comic shrieks on the subject of modern motherhood, was published originally as *Hey Yeah Right Get a Life*—a title you would think needed no improvement. But the book's American packagers set to work improving it, and what did they come up with? *Getting a Life*. Consider this dismal gerund the next time you hear an American publisher insisting that story collections never sell.

7. *Munro's short stories are even harder to review than other people's short stories.*

More than any writer since Chekhov, Munro strives for and

achieves, in each of her stories, a gestalt-like completeness in the representation of a life. She always had a genius for developing and unpacking moments of epiphany. But it's in the three collections since *Selected Stories* (1996) that she's taken the really big, world-class leap and become a master of suspense. The moments she's pursuing now aren't moments of realization; they're moments of fateful, irrevocable, dramatic action. And what this means for the reader is you can't even begin to guess at a story's meaning until you've followed every twist; it's always the last page or two that switches all the lights on.

Meanwhile, as her narrative ambitions have grown, she's become ever less interested in showing off. Her early work was full of big rhetoric, eccentric detail, arresting phrases. (Check out her 1977 story "Royal Beatings.") But as her stories have come to resemble classical tragedies in prose form, it's not only as if she no longer has room for inessentials, it's as if it would be actively jarring, mood-puncturing—an aesthetic and moral betrayal—for her writerly ego to intrude on the pure story.

Reading Munro puts me in that state of quiet reflection in which I think about my own life: about the decisions I've made, the things I've done and haven't done, the kind of person I am, the prospect of death. She is one of the handful of writers, some living, most dead, whom I have in mind when I say that fiction is my religion. For as long as I'm immersed in a Munro story, I am according to an entirely make-believe character the kind of solemn respect and quiet rooting interest that I accord myself in my better moments as a human being.

But suspense and purity, which are a gift to the reader, present problems for the reviewer. Basically, *Runaway* is so good that I don't want to talk about it here. Quotation can't do the book justice, and neither can synopsis. The way to do it justice is to read it.

In fulfillment of my reviewerly duties, I would like to offer, instead, this one-sentence teaser for the last story in Munro's previous collection, *Hateship, Friendship, Courtship, Loveship, Marriage* (2001): A woman with early Alzheimer's enters a care facility, and by the time her husband is allowed to visit her, after a thirty-day adjustment period, she has found a "boyfriend" among the other patients and shows no interest in the husband.

This is not a bad premise for a story. But what begins to make it distinctively Munrovian is that, years ago, back in the sixties and seventies, the husband, Grant, had affair after affair with other women. It's only now, for the first time, that the old betrayer is being betrayed. And does Grant finally come to regret those affairs? Well, no, not at all. Indeed, what he remembers from that phase of his life is "mainly a gigantic increase in well-being." He never felt more alive than when he was cheating on the wife, Fiona. It tears him up, of course, to visit the facility now and to see Fiona and her "boyfriend" so openly tender with each other and so indifferent to him. But he's even more torn up when the boyfriend's wife removes him from the facility and takes him home. Fiona is devastated, and Grant is devastated on her behalf.

And here is the trouble with a capsule summary of a Munro story. The trouble is I want to tell you what happens next. Which is that Grant goes to see the boyfriend's wife to ask if she might take the boyfriend back to visit Fiona at the facility. And that it's here that you realize that what you thought the story was about—all the pregnant stuff about Alzheimer's and infidelity and late-blooming love—was actually just the setup: that the story's great scene is between Grant and the boyfriend's wife. And that the wife, in this scene, refuses to let her husband see Fiona. That her reasons are ostensibly practical but subterraneanly moralistic and spiteful.

And here my attempt at capsule summary breaks down altogether, because I can't begin to suggest the greatness of the scene if you don't have a particular, vivid sense of the two characters and how they speak and think. The wife, Marian, is narrower-minded than Grant. She has a perfect, spotless suburban house that she won't be able to afford if her husband returns to the facility. This house, not romance, is what matters to her. She hasn't had the same advantages, either economic or emotional, that Grant has had, and her obvious lack of privilege occasions a passage of classic Munrovian introspection as Grant drives back to his own house.

> [Their conversation had] reminded him of conversations he'd had with people in his own family. His uncles, his relatives, probably even his mother, had thought the way Marian thought. They had believed that when other people did not think that way it was because they were kidding themselves—they had got too airy-fairy, or stupid, on account of their easy and protected lives or their education. They had lost touch with reality. Educated people, literary people, some rich people like Grant's socialist in-laws had lost touch with reality. Due to an unmerited good fortune or an innate silliness. . . .
>
> What a jerk, she would be thinking now.
>
> Being up against a person like that made him feel hopeless, exasperated, finally almost desolate. Why? Because he couldn't be sure of holding on to himself against that person? Because he was afraid that in the end they'd be right?

I end this quotation unwillingly. I want to keep quoting, and not just little bits but whole passages, because it turns out that what my capsule summary requires, at a minimum, in order to do justice to the story—the "things within things," the interplay of class and morality, of desire and fidelity, of character and fate—is exactly what Munro herself has already written on the page. The only adequate summary of the text is the text itself.

Which leaves me with the simple instruction that I began with: Read Munro! Read Munro!

Except that I must tell you—cannot not tell you, now that I've started—that when Grant arrives home after his unsuccessful appeal to Marian, there's a message from Marian on his answering machine, inviting him to a dance at the Legion hall.

Also: that Grant has already been checking out Marian's breasts and her skin and likening her, in his imagination, to a less than satisfying litchi: "The flesh with its oddly artificial allure, its chemical taste and perfume, shallow over the extensive seed, the stone."

Also: that, some hours later, while Grant is still reassessing Marian's attractions, his telephone rings again and his machine picks up: "Grant. This is Marian. I was down in the basement putting the wash in the dryer and I heard the phone and when I got upstairs whoever it was had hung up. So I just thought I ought to say I was here. If it was you and if you are even home."

And this still isn't the ending. The story is forty-nine pages long—the size of a whole life, in Munro's hands—and another turn is coming. But look how many "things within things" the author already has uncovered: Grant the loving husband, Grant the cheater, Grant the husband so loyal that he's willing, in effect, to pimp for his wife, Grant the despiser of proper housewives, Grant the self-doubter who grants that proper housewives may be right to despise him. It's Marian's second phone call, however, that provides the true measure of Munro's writerly character. To imagine this call, you can't be too enraged with Marian's moral strictures. Nor can you be too ashamed of Grant's laxity. You have to forgive everybody and damn no one.

Otherwise you'll overlook the low probabilities, the odd chances, that crack a life wide open: the possibility, for example, that Marian in her loneliness might be attracted to a silly liberal man.

And this is just one story. There are stories in *Runaway* that are even better than this one—bolder, bloodier, deeper, broader—and that I'll be happy to synopsize as soon as Munro's next book is published.

Or, but, wait, one tiny glimpse into *Runaway*: What if the person offended by Grant's liberality—by his godlessness, his self-indulgence, his vanity, his silliness—weren't some unhappy stranger but Grant's own child? A child whose judgment feels like the judgment of a whole culture, a whole country, that has lately taken to embracing absolutes?

What if the great gift you've given your child is personal freedom, and what if the child, when she turns twenty-one, uses this gift to turn around and say to you: your freedom makes me sick, and so do you?

8. Hatred is entertaining.

The great insight of media-age extremists. How else to explain the election of so many repellent zealots, the disintegration of political civility, the ascendancy of Fox News? First the fundamentalist bin Laden gives George Bush an enormous gift of hatred, then Bush compounds that hatred through his own fanaticism, and now one half of the country believes that Bush is crusading against the Evil One while the other half (and most of the world) believes that Bush *is* the Evil One. There's hardly anybody who doesn't hate somebody now, and nobody at all whom somebody doesn't hate. Whenever I think about politics, my pulse rate jumps as if I'm reading the last chapter of an airport thriller, as if I'm watching Game Seven of a Sox-Yankees series. It's like entertainment-as-nightmare-as-everyday-life.

Can a better kind of fiction save the world? There's always some tiny hope (strange things do happen), but the answer is almost certainly no, it can't. There is some reasonable chance, however, that it could save your soul. If you're unhappy about the hatred that's been unleashed in your heart, you might try imagining what it's like to be the person who hates you; you might consider the possibility that you are, in fact, the Evil One yourself; and, if this is difficult to imagine, then you might try spending a few evenings with the most dubious of Canadians. Who, at the end of her classic story "The Beggar Maid," in which the heroine, Rose, catches sight of her ex-husband in an airport concourse, and the ex-husband makes a childish, hideous face at her, and Rose wonders

> How could anybody hate Rose so much, at the very moment when she was ready to come forward with her good will, her smiling confession of exhaustion, her air of diffident faith in civilized overtures?

is speaking to you and to me right here, right now.

OUR RELATIONS:
A BRIEF HISTORY

-------->

Once there was a mansion in which there lived five brothers. The four oldest brothers, who had played and fought and survived the diseases of childhood together, lived comfortably in the beautifully furnished older wing of the mansion.

The fifth brother, Joseph, was much younger. By the time he came of age, there were no comfortable rooms left for him, and so he was given the raw rooms in the mansion's newer wing. Joseph was a strange, solitary, somewhat frightening child, and although his brothers loved him, they were relieved to have him out of their hair.

Joseph wished to be a gentleman like his brothers, but life was difficult in the raw wing of the mansion. The new wing was a place of Protestant industry, and Joseph went to work.

In time, the old wing grew crowded—too many children, too many mistresses. There came bitter internecine feuds, disastrous debts, terrible drunken brawls. For a while, it appeared that the mansion might fall into ruin and be lost altogether.

But Joseph had been working hard, and his businesses were thriving. The strange little brother turned out to be the person who could rescue the family. Among themselves, the older brothers made fun of Joseph's puritanism and the gaudy style in which he'd decorated the new wing. They were irritated that the little kid was acting like the big brother now. But there was no denying that they'd made a mess of their lives, and they were grateful for Joseph's sacrifices on their behalf.

Joseph, for his part, disapproved of his brothers' lax morals—the mistresses, the too-liberal spending. But he was loyal to his family, and he tried to show his brothers the respect that older relations deserve.

His businesses were doing so well, moreover, that he himself began to relax. He and his new girlfriend, a great beauty from Arkansas, threw lavish parties to which the brothers were usually thoughtful enough to bring a few bottles of wine. Some of them grumbled that the parties were in bad taste, and some of them worried that Joseph was still secretly a prude, but they accepted him as the head of their family, and they adored his new girlfriend.

After eight years of partying, the time came for Joseph to settle down. He assumed that he would marry his good, sensible friend Albertine; but Albertine, alas, was not remotely sexy. One night, in pursuit of a last bit of fun, Joseph flirted with Georgina, a dirty girl from an ambitious family down the street; they ended up fooling around in the backseat of her SUV.

The next morning, Georgina's parents came to the mansion with five lawyers and said that Joseph had to marry her.

"But I don't even like her!" he protested. "She's spoiled and stupid and mean."

Georgina's parents, who had long had designs on the mansion, insisted that marrying her was the only honorable thing to do. And Joseph, who wished to be a gentleman like his brothers, and who felt remorseful about his eight-year party, married her.

How unhappy the mansion was then! Although Georgina was a dirty girl herself, she voiced horror at the loose morals of her brothers-in-law, and she went out of her way to be rude to them. She invited her parents and her parents' lawyers to move in with her. Chiding Joseph for his own liberal spending, she took his money away from him and gave it to her parents.

It looked as if the marriage would be short and unhappy. But then, one night, a bully from a poor neighborhood threw a rock through the window of Joseph's study, scaring Joseph badly. When he went to his brothers, he found that he'd forfeited their sympathy by marrying Georgina. They said they were sorry about the rock, but a broken window was nothing compared with what they'd suffered, over the years, in the old wing of the mansion.

Although Georgina was too stupid and spoiled to think for herself, her parents were shrewd opportunists. They hoped to use Joseph's momentary fright to gain control of the entire mansion. They went to Joseph and said: "This is the logic of war. You're the head of the family, Georgina is your wife now, and only her parents can defend this house. You must learn to hate your useless brothers and trust us."

The brothers were enraged when they heard this. They went to Joseph and said: "This is the logic of peace. Your wife is a bitch and a whore. As long as she's in this house, you're no brother of ours."

And the rich little brother clutched his head and wept.

THE MAN IN THE GRAY
FLANNEL SUIT

-------▶

One of the classic settings in fiction, a little world as reassuring as imperial St. Petersburg or Victorian London, is suburban Connecticut in the 1950s. If you close your eyes, you can picture autumn leaves drifting down on quiet streets, you can see commuters in fedoras streaming off the platforms of the New Haven Line, you can hear the tinkle of the evening's first pitcher of martinis; and hear the ugly fights then, after midnight; and smell the desperate or despairing sex.

Both the comforts and the frustrations of this little world can be found in *The Man in the Gray Flannel Suit*. The novel, Sloan Wilson's first, was published in 1955. It sold extremely well and was quickly made into a movie starring Gregory Peck, but in the decades since then it has fallen out of print. Nowadays the book is remembered mainly for its title, which, along with *The Lonely Crowd* and *The Organization Man*, became a watchword of fifties conformity.

Maybe you enjoy condemning that conformity, or maybe you harbor a secret nostalgia for it; either way, *The Man in the Gray Flannel Suit* will provide you with a pure fifties fix. The main characters, Tom and Betsy Rath, are an attractive WASP couple who divide their labor traditionally, Betsy staying home with three kids, Tom commuting to a fantastically bland job in Manhattan. The Raths conform, but not happily. Betsy rails against the *dullness* of their street; she dreams of escaping from her striving neighbors (who are, themselves, discontented); she's anything but Supermom. When one of her daughters defaces a wall with a bottle of ink, Betsy first slaps her and then goes to bed with her; in the evening Tom finds them "tightly locked in each other's arms," their faces covered with ink.

Like Betsy, Tom is sympathetic in proportion to his failings. "The man in a gray flannel suit" is an object of fear and contempt for him; and yet, because his life of breadwinning and suburban domesticity feels so radically disconnected from his life as a paratrooper in the Second World War, he consciously seeks refuge in gray flannel. Applying for a lucrative new PR job at the United Broadcasting Corporation, he learns that the company's president, Hopkins, plans to form a national committee on mental health. Is Tom interested in mental health?

> "I certainly am!" Tom said heartily. "I've always been interested in mental health!" This sounded a little foolish, but he could think of nothing to rectify it.

Conformity is the drug with which Tom hopes to self-medicate for his own mental-health issues. Although he's honest by nature, he tries hard to be a cynic. "My whole interest in life is working for mental health," he jokes to Betsy one evening. "I care nothing for myself. I'm a dedicated human being." When Betsy chides him for his cynicism and tells him not to work for Hopkins if he doesn't like him, Tom replies: "I love him. I adore him. My heart is his."

At the moral and emotional core of *The Man in the Gray Flannel Suit* are Tom's four-plus years of military service. Whether he was murdering enemy soldiers or falling in love with an orphaned Italian teenager, Tom Rath as a soldier felt intensely alive in the present. His war memories now form a painful contrast to a "tense and frantic" peacetime life in which, as Betsy laments, "nothing seems to be much fun anymore." Maybe Tom is unhappily traumatized by combat, or maybe, to the contrary, he's pining for the sense of excitement and manly engagement that he lost after the war. In either case, he's liable to Betsy's accusation: "Since you've gotten back," she says, "you haven't really wanted much. You've worked hard, but at heart you've never been really trying."

Tom Rath is indeed in a Consumer Age pickle. With three kids to support, he dare not venture down the road of anomie and irony and entropy, the Beat road that Kerouac blazed and Pynchon followed. But the treadmill of consumerism, the comfortable program of desiring the goods that everybody else desires, seems scarcely less dangerous. Tom can see that if he steps onto the hedonic treadmill he really will become a man in a gray flannel suit, mechanically chasing ever higher salaries in order to afford "a bigger house and a better brand of gin." And so, in the first half of the novel, as he squirms between two equally unattractive options, his mood and his tone of voice veer wildly from weariness to rage to bravado, from cynicism to timidity to principled resolve; and Betsy, who is poignantly unaware of why her husband is unhappy, squirms and veers alongside him.

The first half of the book is by far the better half. The Raths are attractive precisely because many of their sentiments are not. And the book's early walk-on characters, as if to mirror the Raths' volatility, are often comic and arresting; there's a personnel manager who reclines horizontally behind his desk, a visiting doctor who hates children, a hired housekeeper who whips the louche little Raths into shape. The first half of the book is *fun*. Immersing yourself in Wilson's old-fashioned social-novel storytelling is like taking a ride in a vintage Olds; you're surprised by its comfort and speed and handling; familiar sights seem fresh when you see them through its little windows.

The latter half of the book belongs to Betsy—Tom's better half. Although their relationship has consisted of three years of puppy love followed by four and a half years of wartime lies and separation, followed by another nine years of making love "without passion" and raising a family "without any real emotion except worry," Betsy stands by her man. She launches a program of family self-improvement. She gets Tom involved in local politics. She sells the hated house and leads the family out of its dull exile and into more exclusive precincts. She volunteers for a life of full-time high-risk entrepreneurship. Most important, Betsy ceaselessly exhorts Tom to *be honest*. The story line, in consequence, gradually drifts away from "Appealingly Flawed Couple Wrestle with Fifties Conformity" toward "Guilt-ridden Man Passively Receives Aid from Excellent Woman." Although people as excellent as Betsy Rath exist in the world, they don't make excellent characters. In a preface to the novel, Sloan Wilson offers such an effusive acknowledgment of his own better half, his first wife, Elise ("Many of the thoughts on which this book is based are hers"), that you may begin to wonder whether the novel is not a kind of love letter from Wilson to Elise, a celebration of his marriage to her, maybe even an attempt to dispel his own doubts about his marriage, to talk himself into love. Certainly something dubious goes down in the distaff half of the book. Certainly, despite the many conflicts chez Rath, Wilson never lets his characters come near the possibility of true unhappiness.

One of the clear implications of *The Man in the Gray Flannel Suit* is that the harmony of society depends on the harmony of each household. The war has sickened the United States by driving a wedge between men and women; the war has sent millions of men overseas to murder and witness death and have sex with local girls while millions of American wives and fiancées waited cheerfully at home, nursed their faith in storybook endings, and shouldered the burden of being ignorant; and now only honesty and openness can repair the bond between men and women and heal an ailing society. As Tom concludes: "I may not be able to do anything about the world, but I can set my life in order."

If you believe in love and loyalty and truth and justice, you may finish reading *The Man in the Gray Flannel Suit* with tears in your eyes. But even as your heart is melting, you may feel annoyed with yourself for succumbing. Like Frank Capra in his goopier films, Wilson asks you to believe that if a man will only show true courage and honesty, he'll be offered a perfect job within walking distance of his home, the local real estate developer won't cheat him, the local judge will dispense perfect justice, the inconvenient villain will be sent packing, the captain of industry will reveal his decency and civic spirit, the local electorate will vote to tax itself more heavily for the sake of school-children, the former lover overseas will know her place and not make any trouble, and the martini-drenched marriage will be saved.

Whether you buy this or not, the novel does succeed in capturing the spirit of the fifties—the uneasy conformity, the flight from conflict, the political quietism, the cult of the nuclear family, the embrace of class privileges. The Raths are a lot more gray-flannel than they ever seem to realize. What distinguishes them from their "dull" neighbors is finally not their sorrows or their eccentricities but their virtues. The Raths toy with irony and resistance in the book's early pages, but by the last pages they're happily getting rich. The smiling Tom Rath of chapter 41 would be an image of complacency, an object of fear and contempt, for the confused Tom Rath of chapter 1. Meanwhile Betsy Rath emphatically rejects the notion that the malaise of the suburbs might have systemic causes. ("People rely too much on explanations these days," she thinks, "and not enough on courage and action.") Tom is confused and unhappy not because war creates moral anarchy or because his employer's business consists of "soap operas, commercials, and yammering studio audiences." Tom's problems are purely personal, just as Betsy's activism is strictly local and domestic. The deeper existential questions that are stirred up by four years of war (or by four weeks in the offices of United Broadcasting, or by four days of motherhood on a dull street in Westport) are abandoned: an unavoidable casualty, perhaps, of the decade itself.

The Man in the Gray Flannel Suit is a book about the fifties. The first half can still be read for fun, the second half for a glimpse of the coming sixties. It was the fifties, after all, that gave the sixties their idealism—and their rage.

NO END TO IT

[rereading Paula Fox's Desperate Characters*]*

------►

On a first reading, it's a novel of suspense. Sophie Bentwood, a forty-year-old Brooklynite, is bitten by a stray cat to which she's given milk, and for the next three days she wonders what the bite is going to bring her: Shots in the belly? Death by rabies? Nothing at all? The engine of the book is Sophie's cold-sweat dread. As in more conventional suspense novels, the stakes are life and death and the fate of the Free World. Sophie and her husband, Otto, are pioneering urban gentry in the late sixties, when the civilization of the Free World's leading city seems to be crumbling under a barrage of garbage, vomit, excrement, vandalism, fraud, and class hatred. Otto's longtime friend and law partner, Charlie Russel, quits the firm and attacks him savagely for his conservatism. "I wish someone would tell me how I can live," Otto says. Sophie herself wavers between dread and a strange disappointment at the possibility that she *hasn't* been infected. She's terrified of a pain she's not sure she doesn't deserve. She clings to a world of privilege even as it suffocates her.

Along the way, page by page, are the pleasures of Paula Fox's prose. Her sentences are small miracles of compression and specificity, tiny novels in themselves. This is the moment of the cat bite:

She smiled, wondering how often, if ever before, the cat had
felt a friendly human touch, and she was still smiling as the

cat reared up on its hind legs, even as it struck at her with extended claws, smiling right up to that second when it sank its teeth into the back of her left hand and hung from her flesh so that she nearly fell forward, stunned and horrified, yet conscious enough of Otto's presence to smother the cry that arose in her throat as she jerked her hand back from that circle of barbed wire.

By imagining a dramatic moment as a series of physical gestures— by simply paying close attention—Fox makes room here for each aspect of Sophie's complexity: her liberality, her self-delusion, her vulnerability, and, above all, her married-person's consciousness. *Desperate Characters* is the rare novel that does justice to both sides of marriage, both hate and love, both her and him. Otto is a man who loves his wife. Sophie is a woman who downs a shot of whiskey at six o'clock on a Monday morning and flushes out the kitchen sink, "making loud childish sounds of disgust." Otto is enough of a jerk to say "Lotsa luck, fella" when Charlie leaves the firm; Sophie is enough of a jerk to ask him, later, why he said it; Otto is mortified when she does; Sophie is mortified for having mortified him.

The first time I read *Desperate Characters*, in 1991, I fell in love with it. It struck me as plainly superior to any novel by Fox's contemporaries John Updike, Philip Roth, or Saul Bellow. It struck me as obviously *great*, and a few months later, although I'm usually in no hurry to do this, I reread it. I'd recognized my own troubled marriage in the Bentwoods', and the novel had appeared to suggest that the fear of pain is more destructive than pain itself, and I wanted very much to believe this. I actually believed that the book, on a second reading, might tell me how to live.

It did no such thing. It became, instead, more mysterious—

became less of a lesson and more of an experience. Previously invisible metaphoric and thematic densities melted into prominence, like images in a random-dot autostereogram. My eye fell, for example, on a sentence describing dawn's arrival in a living room: "Objects, their outlines beginning to harden in the growing light, had a shadowy, totemic menace." In the growing light of my second reading, I saw every object in the book begin to harden like this. Chicken livers, for example, are introduced in the opening paragraph as a delicacy and as the centerpiece of a cultivated dinner—as the essence of Old World civilization. ("You take raw material and you transform it," the leftist Leon remarks, later on. "That *is* civilization.") It's the livers' smell, their *richness*, that first draws the problematic cat to the Bentwoods' back door. A hundred pages later, after the cat has bitten Sophie (the "idiot event"), she and Otto start fighting back. They're in the jungle now, and the leftover chicken livers have become bait for the capture and killing of a wild animal. Cooked meat is still the essence of civilization; but what a much more violent thing civilization now appears to be! Or follow the food in another direction; see Sophie, shaken, on a Saturday morning, trying to shore up her spirits by spending money on a piece of cookware. She goes to the Bazaar Provençal to buy herself an omelet pan, a prop for a "hazy domestic dream" of French ease and cultivation. The scene ends with the eerily bearded saleswoman throwing up her hands "as though to ward off a hex" and Sophie fleeing with a purchase so perfectly wrong, so emblematic of her desperation, that it's almost funny: an hourglass egg timer.

Although Sophie's hand is bleeding in this scene, her impulse is to deny it. The third time I read *Desperate Characters*— I'd assigned it in a fiction-writing class that I was teaching—I began to pay more attention to these denials. Sophie issues them more or less nonstop: *"It's all right," "Oh, it's nothing," "Oh, well, it's nothing," "Don't talk to me about it," "THE CAT WASN'T SICK!" "It's a bite, just a bite!" "I won't go running off to the hospital for something as foolish as this," "It's nothing," "It's much better," "It's of no consequence."* These repeated, desperate-sounding denials reflect the underlying structure of the novel: Sophie flees from one potential haven to another, and each in turn fails to protect her. She goes to a party with Otto, she sneaks out with Charlie for "unlawful excitement," she buys herself a present, she seeks comfort in old friends, she reaches out to Charlie's wife, she tries to phone her old lover, she agrees to go to the hospital, she catches the cat, she makes an "ostrich nest" of pillows, she tries to read a French novel, she flees to her beloved country house, she thinks about moving to another time zone, she thinks about adopting children, she destroys an old friendship: nothing brings relief. Her last hope is to write to her mother about the cat bite, to "strike the exact note calculated to arouse the old woman's scorn and hilarity"—to make her plight into art, in other words. But Otto throws her ink bottle at the wall.

What is Sophie running from? The fourth time I read *Desperate Characters*, I hoped to get an answer. I wanted to figure out, finally, whether it's a happy thing or a terrible thing that the Bentwoods' life breaks open on the last page of the book. I wanted to "get" the final scene. But I still didn't get it, and so I took refuge in the idea that good fiction is "tragic" in its refusal to offer the easy answers of ideology, the cures of a therapeutic culture, or the pleasantly resolving dreams of mass entertainment. I was struck by Sophie's resemblance to Hamlet—himself a morbidly self-conscious character who receives a message that's both extremely disturbing and necessarily ambiguous (it comes from a ghost), goes through agonizing mental contortions trying to decide what the message means, and finally puts himself in the hands of a providential "divinity" and accepts his fate. For Sophie Bentwood, the ambiguous message is not a ghostly admonition but a straightforward cat bite; the ambiguity is entirely inside her: "It was only her hand, she told herself, yet the rest of her body seemed involved in a way she couldn't understand. It was as though she'd been vitally wounded." The mental contortions that follow this insight are not about her uncertainty but about her *unwillingness* to face the truth. Near the end, when she addresses a divinity and says, "*God, if I am rabid, I am equal to what is outside*," it's not a revelation. It's a "relief."

A book that has fallen, however briefly, out of print can put a strain on even the most devoted reader's love. In the way that a man might regret certain shy mannerisms in his wife that cloud her beauty, or a woman might wish that her husband laughed less loudly at his own jokes, though the jokes are very funny, I've suffered for the tiny imperfections that might prejudice potential readers against *Desperate Characters*. I'm thinking of the stiffness and impersonality of the opening paragraph, the austerity of the opening sentence, the creaky word "repast": as a lover of the book, I now appreciate how the formality and stasis of the paragraph set up the short, sharp line of dialogue that follows ("The cat is back"); but what if a reader never makes it past "repast"? I wonder, too, if the name "Otto Bentwood" might be difficult to take on first reading. Fox generally works her characters' names very hard—the name "Russel," for instance, nicely echoes Charlie's restless, furtive energies (Otto suspects him of literally "rustling" clients), and just as something is surely missing in Charlie's character, a second "l" is missing in his surname. I do admire how the old-fashioned and vaguely Teutonic name "Otto" saddles Otto the way his compulsive orderliness saddles him; but "Bentwood," even after many readings, remains for me a little artificial in its bonsai imagery. And then there's the title of the book. It's apt, certainly, and yet it's no *The Day of the Locust*, no *The Great Gatsby*, no *Absalom, Absalom!* It's a title that people may forget or confuse with other titles. Sometimes, wishing it were stronger, I feel lonely in the peculiar way of someone deeply married.

As the years have gone by, I've continued to dip in and out of *Desperate Characters*, seeking comfort or reassurance from passages of familiar beauty. Now, though, as I reread it in its entirety to prepare this introduction, I'm amazed by how much of the book is still fresh and unfamiliar to me. I never paid much attention, for example, to Otto's anecdote, late in the book, about Cynthia Kornfeld and her husband the anarchist artist— how Cynthia Kornfeld's salad of Jell-O and nickels mocks the Bentwood equation of food and privilege and civilization; how the notion of typewriters retrofitted to spew nonsense subtly prefigures the novel's closing image; how the anecdote insists that *Desperate Characters* be read in the context of a contemporary art scene whose aim is the *destruction* of order and meaning. And then there's Charlie Russel—have I ever really *seen* him until now? In my earlier readings he remained a kind of stock villain, a turncoat, an egregious man. Now he seems to me almost as important to the story as the cat is. He's Otto's only friend, his phone call precipitates the final crisis, he produces the Thoreau quotation that gives the book its title, and he delivers a verdict on the Bentwoods—"drearily enslaved by introspection while the foundation of their privilege is being blasted out from under them"—that feels ominously dead-on.

At this late date, however, I'm not sure I even want fresh insights. A serious danger in long marriages is how excruciatingly well you come to know the object of your love. Sophie and

Otto suffer from their knowledge of each other, and I now suffer from my knowledge of *Desperate Characters*. My underlining and marginal annotation of it are getting out of hand. In my latest reading I'm finding and flagging as vital and central an enormous number of previously unflagged images involving order and chaos and childhood and adulthood. And, because the book is not long, and because I've now read it half a dozen times, I'm within sight of the point at which *every sentence* will be highlighted as vital and central. This extraordinary richness is, of course, a testament to Paula Fox's genius. There's hardly an extraneous or arbitrary word to be found in the book. Rigor and thematic density of such magnitude don't happen by accident, and yet it's almost impossible for a writer to achieve them while relaxing enough to allow the characters to come alive and the novel to be written, and yet here the novel is, soaring above all the other American realist fiction since the Second World War.

The irony of the novel's richness, however, is that the better I grasp the import of each individual sentence, the less able I am to articulate what grand, global meaning all these local meanings might be serving. There's finally a kind of horror to an overload of meaning. It's closely akin, as Melville suggests in "The Whiteness of the Whale" in *Moby-Dick*, to a total whiteout *absence* of meaning. It's also, not incidentally, a leading symptom of diseased mental states. Manics and schizophrenics and depressives often suffer from the conviction that absolutely everything in their lives is fraught with significance—so fraught, indeed, that tracking and deciphering and organizing the significance can overwhelm the actual living of life. In the case of Otto and especially of Sophie (who is urged by two different doctors to seek psychiatric treatment), the reader is not the only one who's overwhelmed. The Bentwoods themselves are highly literate, thoroughly modern characters. Their curse is that they're all too well equipped to read themselves as literary texts dense with overlapping meanings. In the course of one late-winter weekend they become oppressed and finally overwhelmed by the way in which the most casual words and tiniest incidents feel like "portents." The enormous suspense the book develops is not just a product of Sophie's dread, then, or of Fox's step-by-step closing of every possible avenue of escape, or of equating a crisis in a marital partnership with a crisis in a business partnership and a crisis in American urban life. More than anything else, I think, it's the slow cresting of a crushingly heavy wave of literary significance. Sophie consciously and explicitly evokes rabidness as a metaphor for her emotional and political plight, while Otto, in his last line, even as he finally breaks down and cries out about how desperate he is, cannot avoid "quoting" (in the postmodern sense) his and Sophie's earlier conversation about Thoreau and thereby invoking all the other themes and dialogues threading through the weekend, in particular Charlie's vexing of the issue of "desperation": how much worse than simply *being* desperate it is to be desperate and also to be aware of the vital questions of public law and order and privilege and Thoreauvian interpretation that are entailed in that private desperation, and to feel that by breaking down you're proving Charlie Russel right, though you know in your heart he's wrong. When Sophie declares her wish to be rabid, as when Otto hurls the ink bottle, both seem to be revolting against an unbearable, almost murderous sense of the *importance* of their words and thoughts. Small wonder that the last actions of the book are wordless—that Sophie and Otto have "ceased to listen" to the words streaming from the telephone, and that the thing written in ink which they turn slowly to read is a violent, wordless blot. No sooner has Fox achieved the most dazzling success at finding order in the nonevents of one late-winter weekend than (with the perfect gesture!) she repudiates that order.

Desperate Characters is a novel in revolt against its own perfection. The questions it raises are radical and unpleasant. What is the point of meaning—especially literary meaning—in a rabid modern world? Why *bother* creating and preserving order if civilization is every bit as killing as the anarchy to which it's opposed? Why not be rabid? Why torment ourselves with books? Rereading the novel for the sixth or seventh time, I feel a cresting rage and frustration with its mysteries and with the paradoxes of civilization and with the insufficiency of my own brain, and then, as if out of nowhere, I *do* get the ending, I feel what Otto Bentwood feels when he smashes the ink bottle against the wall; and suddenly I'm in love all over again.

Special thanks to Francesco Zippel, Sean Wilsey, Wang Juan, Andrea Walker, David Remnick, Jason Pontin, Silvia Pareschi, Antonio Monda, David Kelly, Peter Hodum, Peter Hessler, Jim Harkness, Jeremy Haft, Karen Green, Susan Golomb, Dwight Garner, Jonathan Galassi, Deirdre Foley-Mendelssohn, Henry Finder, and Kathy Chetkovich.